D0683010

A LITTLE KOSHER SEASONING

Also by Michele Guinness

Child of the Covenant
Promised Land

A Little Kosher Seasoning

Michele Guinness

Hodder & Stoughton
LONDON SYDNEY AUCKLAND

Copyright © 1994 Michele Guinness

First published in 1994 by Hodder and Stoughton,
A division of Hodder Headline PLC

The right of Michele Guinness to be identified as the Author of
the Work has been asserted by her in accordance with the
Copyright, Designs and Patents Act 1988.

10 9 8

All rights reserved. No part of this publication may be
reproduced, stored in a retrieval system, or transmitted,
in any form or by any means without the prior written
permission of the publisher, nor be otherwise circulated
in any form of binding or cover other than that in which
it is published and without a similar condition being
imposed on the subsequent purchaser.

British Library Cataloguing in Publication Data
A record for this book is available from the British Library

ISBN 0 340 58600 1

Typeset by Phoenix Typesetting, Ilkley, West Yorkshire
Printed and bound in Great Britain

Hodder and Stoughton
A division of Hodder Headline PLC
338 Euston Road
London NW1 3BH

For my Mama who, like most
Jewish Mamas, is
utterly unique.

Contents

Acknowledgements

Many, many dear friends have fed me with the wealth of their wisdom, and may, or may not, be pleased to see it regurgitated here.

A particular thanks to the churches who have had the dubious pleasure of our ministry, and have given us a great deal more than we could ever have given them. I hope I have done your love and encouragement justice.

Thanks, what else, to my "mishpahah", my mother, step-father, brother and sister-in-law for being such wonderful fall-guys, and for nourishing me with all that's best in Jewish warmth, wisdom and laughter. I wish my father had been alive to read the book. How he would have enjoyed himself.

Thanks to my children whose voracious appetites make writing necessary, and who interrupt the muse at two-minute intervals from the moment they come home from school. But how can I complain about the aggravation, when they also provide such a vital source of inspiration?

And special thanks to that wise critic and partner, my long-suffering husband, who set me on the trail in search of Jewish roots, shared the digging, wrote the short-ened Passover Service at the end of the book and really complains very little about having the intimate details of his private life made public. All things considered.

The Jewish prayers at the end of certain chapters are adap-tations from the Orthodox and Reform Prayer Books.

In the Beginning

In the beginning there was a Mama, a Jewish Mama. There would be of course. There always is, in every Jewish family. A force mightier than wind, fire and water. Not Eve in this case, though she was the first woman to know the sweat, the hassle the Jews call "tsorus", involved in giving birth and rearing a family, and no doubt Cain and Abel felt the repercussions, as well as being the source of most of the tsorus. Not in this case Sarah either, though she was the first truly Jewish Mama, whose wifely manipulations determined the geographical and political destiny of the world, not to mention her husband. No, this was my Mama, whose influence over the people in her orbit has been equal in formidability to Eve, Sarah, Rebecca and every other Jewish Mama since.

There she sat, my Mama, on her twenty-first birthday, in a nursing-home bed, enveloped in cards and flowers, a tiny, dark, curly-headed baby on her lap and a heavy infection within, lamenting, in a fevered haze, the golden days of her vanished youth. The lament lasted only as long as the fever, and her willingness to put up with the food and regimented existence of a nursing home. Few Jewish Mamas have the stomach for anyone else's cuisine, especially the institutionalised, stewed variety. Fewer still can cope with being told what to do. The infection was the final straw. She wasn't paying for that! She could have picked up a germ in one of the larger, public hospitals – free. So she swept up her belongings, including the tiny, chuckle-headed bundle, and took them to the place where a Jewish Mama reigns supreme: home.

Home was a rambling, nineteenth-century, stone house, built on a hill overlooking a rabbit warren of smoking, higgledy-piggledy miners' cottages, dominated in its turn by the vast wheel of the local pit shaft, looming large in every window at the back of the house. My father was the local doctor, and he loved every bent and bronchial figure waiting at the surgery door, coughing as if his ribcage was about to split. The women came in slippers, pushing prams and bearing gifts of tinned salmon, gold at a time of post-war rationing, to say thank you. He delivered their babies at home by the open fire, and they called their baby girls Michele.

"That's a pretty name you've called your little girl, Doctor. Where does it come from?"

"Michele Morgan, the Hollywood film star," he told them.

Pointless to explain the Jewish tradition of calling a new baby after a deceased relative, to keep the name alive in the family, or to say that it was French for Michael, the name of his beloved father, who had died an over-worked tailor, paying off debts to a son-in-law, incurred as part of a dowry. There had been a family business. Michael, who changed his name from the Germanic-sounding Lipman, when he abandoned his native, Jew-despising Latvia and finally took root in England, had owned the first charabancs in Middlesbrough. Until a partner absconded with all the profits. His was not the stereotypical Jewish success story.

But my Pop turned the tide, became a doctor, and fulfilled his parents' dearest wish: to give something back to a country which had granted them sanctuary from the pogroms of Eastern Europe. Then came the practice house, and a Mama to keep it tidy.

It is said that psychotics build castles in the air and neurotics live in them. My mother cleans them! It appears to be a racial hazard, handed on from mother to daughter, or mother-in-law to daughter-in-law. There might just as well be some ceremony for Jewish baby girls, a ritual on the eighth day, when, just as the baby boys lose part of their anatomy, the girls are presented with an addendum: a feather duster.

My Mama's commitment to the environment is total – as long as it begins and ends at her front door. Within that environment all is perfection, no speck or spot or blemish, no picture off-true, no curtain fold a centimetre wider than the next, no book or magazine left out, unless it lies on the coffee table – in a symmetrically pleasing manner – no armchair or settee out of the official indents made by the castors on the carpet, lest the place look "a mess". A fly on the wall would not have had the gall to defy her. Nor did we.

There was, unfortunately, in my childhood home, a small hatch between the centre of command, the kitchen, and the sitting-room, where members of the family would try, to their folly, to read a book or watch the television. At periodic intervals the hatch doors would fly open with the familiar pinging sound of plywood being jerked off a plastic catch, a head would appear firing orders, volleying complaints, barking out quasi-unrecognisable comments, with a final reminder to sit up straight, tidy away our legs and keep our feet off the upholstery. A second ping and the assault was over, the head gone, and a kind of peace restored as we sat in the dazed silence, which denoted an assimilation of the information in order to follow its instructions. Even the dog groaned in his sleep and tucked away his paws. Many a time my quiet, gentle father, hiding in his armchair behind a medical journal, feigning deafness, would turn over the pages and sigh, as he ruminated no doubt on the appositeness of the proverb which said that they that sow the wind, reap the whirlwind. As a young soldier, back from the Second World War, he had been enchanted by my mother's teenage vivacity and chatter. Both he enjoyed, if that is the right word, in full measure, to the end of his days. But little did he guess that surviving a hurricane would have been a more tranquil proposition than living with Mama.

Her fear of God has always rested in his possible intervention in her life at the least convenient moment, at ten in the morning for example, before she has had a chance to start on the bathroom. Husbands and children, managed properly, are as amenable as furnishings to being tidied and organised. God is another matter. He can, and regularly does, defy her. He refuses to observe the daily routine, disrupting it with dozens of happy little festivals, requiring endless cooking, preparation, people and mess. Sometimes he brings nachus, blessings, sometimes tsorus, but you never know which in advance. And have a sneaky suspicion, since he's so unpredictable, that it may be the latter. So you worry, about what little game he may have up his sleeve, especially when things seem to be running too smoothly. Aunt Sophie, who's as fit as an ox, may this Passover get a cold and take to her bed, and if she does, her family will have to stay and look after her, and there'll be nobody to read the service and the food will be wasted, and all that expense will be for nothing. So why look forward in anticipation, when we're all going to have a miserable time anyway? Worse still, what if, one day, God forbid, there's nothing to worry about?

My Mama bites off life in great chunks and spits out the bits she doesn't like. I have experienced both her biting and her spitting in full measure in the course of my chequered history. When I was very small, when the pull of the pleasures of lost youth overcame her and she felt the urge to party and dance, or when there were guests for a dinner party and the children were to be seen briefly, scrubbed and polished little trophies that we were, I only needed spitting as far as the nanny. We actually had a nanny, because doctors weren't just well off in those long-forgotten, olden days. They were very, what is euphemistically referred to in Jewish parlance as, not wanting to tempt a somewhat capricious Providence, "comfortable". We could afford "a staff", as opposed to today, when Mama's only little treasure around the house is called, proprietorially, "my woman".

In my adolescent years, the spitting became a little more pronounced than the biting, and I found myself catapulted on a damp and icy blast as far from the maternal nest as one almighty puff would carry me. That was the time when I tried to explain to her that having read the forbidden bit at the back of the Bible, usually known as the New Testament, I was now convinced that Jesus was the Messiah. Yet more offensive was the radical step I took of being baptised. And then there was the day I told her I wanted to marry a young man, who, though he had what might well pass for a Jewish nose, had little else that would pass for Jewish. Every Mama's favourite fantasy died for her in that instant. She would never see me married under the chuppah, the canopy of flowers in the synagogue. All the little plans formed that day so long ago when she sacrificed her youth for a bite of the chunk of life called "having babies", tumbled to the ground and lay there like a pile of rotting fruit. The Mama in her had failed and that hurt.

But she agreed to meet him. Not in her home. She wouldn't compromise her principles, wouldn't give the faintest hint of encouragement to her other children, by having her eldest daughter's non-Jewish intended over the doorstep. But we found neutral territory, and I proudly waved my engagement ring under her nose, as daughters must. She took hold of my hand, squinted at the third index finger as if she had suddenly developed a problem with her ability to focus, and said, "You call that a diamond?"

He was only a schoolteacher, my intended, with barely enough savings for the honeymoon. But the teacher didn't stay a teacher. And if in the beginning there was Mama, forging and forming what there was of the Jewish part of me, then later there was a clergyman. And being married to a minister of the Church has certainly shaped the Christian side of my entity. And given my mother the opportunity for many a happy lament at Jewish dinner parties.

"What does your son-in-law do for a living?"

It's the question which follows, "You have children?" for what else should a Mama want but that her daughters should be "comfortable"?

"Oy, don't ask," she usually replies, shaking her head, the sufferings of Job negligible compared to hers. "You'll never guess."

And then, with just a little prompting, they force it out of her, because she can't resist seeing the expression on their faces. Sometimes, she says loudly, "I won't be around for bridge next week. I'm staying with my daughter – at the manse!"

"Never mind," say the fellow guests, patting her hand, "my son-in-law has an alcohol problem. We all have our crosses to bear."

"And who knows, I may be mother-in-law to the Archbishop of Canterbury one day," she says hopefully. "Though I doubt it. They don't seem to have any ambition, these Christians."

If ambition had been an influential factor in my husband's life there would have been a job for him in the family brewery, rather than the Church. He is after all the youngest great-great-grandson of the Arthur Guinness of Dublin whose signature is scribbled across the famous bottles and cans of stout. His degree in engineering would have opened the door, even if his line of the family, being missionaries and ministers for the most part, had opted for another kind of spiritual inheritance and foresworn the last of the shares.

"But, Dad," I said to my father, trying to lessen the blow of my marrying out, "he is one of the Guinnesses. Your name will be in the family tree, where it says, 'Michele, daughter of . . .' It's just like marrying into the Kennedys in the States."

He looked up momentarily from his inevitable medical journal and said, "And did you have to pick one of the poor relations?"

We married in a Free Church. With no chuppah, no

stamping on the glass, no dancing. With minimal ceremonial and none of the traditions which had been the fabric of my childhood. My family came to the reception, but not to the service. I couldn't see how to make the two separate cultural and religious parts of my identity fit together, so I let the Jewish in me die a little, and buried it in the deepest recesses of my soul. Occasionally it kicked. Often at Communion Services, which seemed such a rigid formalisation of the warm, happy, homely Sabbath and Passover services I remembered. My indigestible past, I told myself. With constant doses of ecclesiastical antacid it would settle down one day. In a Church which laid little obvious store by it, neither would I. Educated at a Christian school, I was, my father told me proudly, totally assimilated. We were not like the ultra-Orthodox, Hasidic community, who walked around in long frock coats like Eastern Europeans of the last century. We did not make an exhibition of ourselves, incurring the deserved hostility of our neighbours. We blended, like chameleons, into our environment. And we gave of our best to those who bestowed upon us the generosity of their acceptance.

I wanted to belong. I was not, then, mature or secure enough to take the risk of being who and what I was. If it would have helped, I would have died my hair blonde and had plastic surgery on my nose. But I couldn't sustain the former, or afford the latter.

But, ironically, nor did I realise how Jewish I was, until I found myself in totally non-Jewish surroundings. Yet here was an institution, revolving around the life and sayings of a Jew, based on a book written by Jews for Jews, which should, in theory, have been more, not less, Jewish than any other. Sitting in my pew, a dangerous thought began to form in my mind. Supposing Jesus came back now. Supposing he walked into this building. Radically different from a synagogue, would he know what it was? Would he feel any more at home than I did? Or would he wonder, equally unable to get his mind around such a quantum leap, how the Church, from its

Jewish beginnings, could have ended up like this?

Over the centuries, the Jewish rites and rituals Jesus knew have been buried beneath a vast historical mound of Christian adaptations and addenda, so that like the Communion Service, they are no longer recognisably Jewish. Jewish practice can be eradicated. Jewish roots cannot. They are still there, embedded so deep that the Christian people of the world have long since forgotten how Jewish they are.

"Well that was very nice, thank you," one man said to us as he left the church hall after a Passover service we had led. "It's good to know that the Jews use our psalms as well."

It was only my husband's firm grip on my arm which saved the poor innocent from a throttling.

When did a Jewish Church cease to be kosher? I studied Church history for the answers and then, at last, understood why so much of Christianity was all Greek to me, in a manner of speaking. For though born in an entirely Jewish context, the Church grew up in a Gentile environment, a Roman Empire, dominated for centuries by Greek culture and thought, since Alexander the Great had conquered the world. In AD 70 the Romans responded to a Jewish revolution by rasing Jerusalem to the ground, and driving out all the Jews, including the Church, which, at the time, was an unpopular Jewish sect. Ironically, the first Jewish Christians had refused to become involved in the revolt, which in Jewish eyes made them national enemies. The gulf between Orthodox Judaism and the Church widened beyond repair in AD 135, when Jewish Christians again refused to become enmeshed in political sedition. From that point on Christianity became a Gentile, not a Jewish, movement. Sickened by constant Jewish hostility, the Church began to distance itself from its source. Two centuries later, when the Emperor Constantine was converted and Christianity became the official religion of the Roman Empire, observing a Jewish festival, such as the Sabbath or the Passover, was an offence punishable with excommunication.

And it was through the Gentiles that the philosophy of thinkers like Plato the Greek, exalting the spirit, debasing the body, began to extend its influence, and still weaves its web around the Church today. Just as well he lived so long ago. Plato and I would never have got on. It seems illogical to me that this bag of skin and bones we carry around with us hinders rather than helps our spiritual progress. If God had thought so, we would all have been disembodied ghosts, floating through the stratosphere. Love them or loathe them, we are stuck with physical kitbags, which demand food and water and sleep, which walk and run, sing and dance, touch and hold, expand and contract, sneeze and rid themselves of waste matter, usually at maximum inconvenience. A child fully grasps the wonder of the incarnation at that moment when it asks, as they all do, "Did Jesus have to go to the toilet?"

Our bodily needs and functions do have a maddening, unfortunate way of interfering with any attempt at conforming to self-invented notions of piety. So we cover up the "unholy", human bits, like someone caught in the nude. The spiritual side of our lives is hacked off from the rest, deposited in a separate compartment where it cannot be tainted, a strong box, safe from the ravages of home, the factory or the office, only taken out and given an airing on Sundays and special occasions. Going to church, reading, praying, meditating are holy things to do. Washing, eating, laughing, watching the television, emptying the dustbin, feeding the cat, all the countless, repeated, routine little rituals which make up human existence are not.

Judaism, at its best, does not divide the sacred and secular in this way. Human beings are an indivisible unity of mind, body and spirit. All of life, its public and its private bits, the hum-drum and the special, how you work and play, how you eat and how you pray, whether you laugh or cry, joke or hurt, can, potentially, be infused with a sense of the presence of God. There are blessings for everything – food, new clothes, good news, bad news, smelling a fragrant plant, or the opposite, hearing thunder, seeing a rainbow, brushing your teeth – prayers which bless God, not the item or activity, which, since God made it, is already holy. The Halakah, the rabbinic application of the law, is intended to help every Jew experience the divine in the prosaic acts of every day. That's why there is such a long blessing to say when you've been to the toilet. It's the one thing we all have to do many times a day. It might as well be a religious event!

Judaism at its worst is a series of regulations so complex that remembering what to do and how to do it, leaves no time for meditating on anything vaguely divine. Splitting hairs is a favourite Jewish pastime. Ten people in a room will guarantee at least eleven opinions. For centuries interpreting the Torah, the law given to Moses on Sinai, has been a constant source of exercise for the rabbinic brain. For example, "Keep the Sabbath holy" is all very well, but what does that mean? Do no work? But what exactly constitutes work? Lifting a load? A stick? Lighting a match? A fire? A candle? So work was defined in 39 categories, then redefined into a further 39 subdivisions, creating a grand total of 1,521 Sabbath laws. This morass of legislation, handed down orally, was finally collected in a vast tome called the Talmud, which, as well as containing many fascinating legends and stories, also dispenses such life-changing insights as, "If fasting from cabbages, remember also to fast from young cabbage shoots." There are rules covering every aspect of life, from personal hygiene and sexual intimacy, to the dimensions of a booth in the garden for the Feast of Tabernacles. Rules which were then developed further with the advent of electricity, television, computers and other technology unknown to Moses. Rules the ultra-Orthodox Hasids struggle to keep, and the not-so-Orthodox love to break.

But in the end, except for the fundamentalists, playing the game has never meant abiding by all the rules.

Observance from the Orthodox to the Reform and Liberal wing varies enormously. But religious practice, all the colourful traditions and celebrations, is the same the world over, and has preserved the unique, separate identity of the Jewish people.

These were the special qualities I mourned and missed: the warmth, the vivid colour, the storytelling by candlelight, the sense of history, the taste of the food, the drama of a festival, the wonderful, motley patchwork which made up the Jewish way of life. Not the hypocrisy of keeping whatever laws you pleased and imposing the rest on everyone else. The sort of hypocrisy Jesus decried, which first drew me to him. But then he was free to criticise. He was a Pharisee. A Pharisee who embraced the best of Pharisaism, living out its great potential for finding God in the ordinary, rejecting the legal nit-picking, which destroyed the divine spark.

And that was what I wanted. I knew, as the years passed, that limiting God to certain compartments in my life was dishonest, inadequate, unreal. I wanted to feel as well as trust, use my body as well as my brain, every second of my existence, so that believing was like breathing. And that is the essence of Jewishness, the ideal. Shalom, the wholeness of body, mind and spirit I believed to be my birthright as a Christian, would elude me until I acknowledged and embraced the Jewish in me. Integrating a Jewish and Christian spirituality became a great adventure, spanning the years of childbearing and raising a family, discovering a career, the mid-life crisis and the beginnings of bodily disintegration. There have been dizzying, dazzling heights and endless, flat plains, craggy, skin-tearing climbs and gentle, lush valleys. I have been at odds with the Jews and at odds with the Church. Keeping to the path has been more like walking a tightrope. But what is faith without risk? Life in a deck chair watching the world go by. Not the life in all its vibrant, technicolour abundance I had been promised.

*

We were flying down the fast lane of the motorway in her plush, maroon Jaguar sports car, my boss and I, returning to the office after the funeral of one of our much-loved little six-year-olds.

"Do you believe in all that?" she suddenly asked me.

"In what?"

"In God."

After several years as a journalist, working as press officer for a children's hospice confronted me with issues of life and death in a way no other job could ever do.

"Yes, I do," I said with a gulp, watching the speedometer needle rise, and wondering whether that belief was about to be put to the test. "Do you?"

I admired the chairman of the charity's trustees enormously. From small beginnings she had become one of the wealthiest businesswomen in the area, but despite her achievements, despite her power, her femininity, integrity and honesty had remained intact. She enjoyed every minute of her success. She enjoyed life.

"I'd like to think there was a heaven, that God was there waiting for little Becky, but I don't know."

A thought occurred to me.

"It seemed real for you in the church, didn't it?"

"It always does. I enjoy going to church. Singing the hymns makes me feel good. But it all seems . . . remote . . . irrelevant somehow on a Monday morning with the nitty-gritty of a business to run and a full diary."

"You're saying that faith isn't real if it's confined to a building, it must affect the rest of the week?"

"Oh yes, otherwise it seems a bit of a sham."

I found myself telling her about my own struggle to live Christianity the Jewish way, finding God in the mundane events of every day, at home, in food, festivals, symbols. And it occurred to me that this might be an important dimension for a Church which in recent years has been exploring new ways of communicating with God, rediscovering meditation and the medieval, mystical, and even Celtic, tradition. What if, in its search for spirituality, it was to go further back, to its roots? Human beings who don't know their roots have a sense of disorientation. Christians without a feel for Judaism flounder a little in the entirely Jewish world of the New Testament.

This book is an attempt to discover a Jewish spirituality which, in bringing out the best in Christianity, fully integrates the two. There is no one way to do that, any more than there is one way to practise any faith. People are always asking me how they can celebrate the Jewish festivals. But we also need to celebrate the great Christian festivals more. There seems to be a certain ambivalence about many of them, because of their apparent pagan connections. I have friends who stoutly refuse to celebrate Christmas. And what they miss! I hope that putting the festivals back in their Jewish context will restore that missing confidence, and enable Christians to rediscover their long-lost, rightful inheritance. As to how that might be practically possible, this is a very rough guide. All suggestions should be adapted to suit dozens of individual and corporate needs.

I have followed the seasons in an attempt to convey the Jewish sense of the rhythm of life. Sabbath lasts from sundown to sundown. Holy days may move, but always occur roughly at the same time of the year, heralding the arrival of autumn, or the imminence of spring. There are times for eating, and times for fasting, a time to light candles and a time for darkness, a time for singing and a time for silence, a time for kissing and a time for having a good cry. For Grandma and Grandpa life goes on just as it did when they were the grandchildren at the family table. The festivals come round again, as they do every year, one much like another, same food, same stories, same jokes, except that time has moved on and another loved one is missing, another child old enough to join in the family arguments and answer back. Repetition is not a problem. Their familiarity is their charm. It adds a sense of suspense, a sense of slow, inexorable movement towards the climax of history.

For the Christian West the journey from childhood to grey hairs can appear downhill all the way, though relatively cheerfully, to Armageddon, the final curtain, with only the thought of eternity to cushion the bump at the end. Perhaps that's why the Church seems to make so little of life's punctuation marks. Birth and death may be accompanied by certain, modest rituals – on request. Everything else in between, apart from weddings, from puberty to the grave, can so easily seem a shapeless blur. We have a stab at Christmas – for the sake of the children – with a nativity and an awful lot of cards and carols. Easter raises a little, controlled enthusiasm. Harvest, outside the rural communities, is rather an embarrassment. Pentecost receives a mention, in passing. No one seems to make a really good attempt at a Sabbath any more. Perhaps this is the penalty of restricting festivals to a church building, rather than celebrating them in our homes as well. If the Church is no longer the focal point of the community, all that is left is a token nod in the direction of something vaguely resembling a Christian calendar. If the minister happens to remember what day it is.

So now, forget the pressure of work, the need to achieve and the frenetic pace of existence. Just be for a while. Rediscover the simple, seasonal pleasures, and the leisure to celebrate them at home. And as you read and explore this wonderful new world, let this Mama leave you with the ultimate in Jewish wisdom. "Enjoy, enjoy!"

AUTUMN

The Jewish New Year begins in the seventh month of the Jewish calendar. Contrary as ever, do I hear you say? Jews are always late for everything, except their own funerals, which have to take place as quickly as possible, and are arranged almost as they draw their last breath. "If he goes in the next hour or so, we can just fit him in tomorrow." They're late for parties and late for meetings. They even walk into the synagogue anything up to two hours after the service has begun, sometimes just in time for the final prayer. "Jewish time" is officially half an hour later than the stated time. But who in their right mind would celebrate a new year in its seventh month?

In fact, it isn't as illogical as it sounds. Although the Jewish year officially starts with the Passover, the birth of the nation, its deliverance from captivity, its receiving of the Law and the beginning of its special relationship with God, Rosh Hashanah is supposed to mark the anniversary of creation, when time began and human beings first became subject to the ticking of a vast universal clock. And even if God didn't bring the world into being some time in the Jewish equivalent of September, not to worry. Why shouldn't the world, like the Queen, have an official birthday? And since seven is a holy number, why not celebrate it in the seventh month?

Christians of course are not superstitious about numbers. No such nonsense. A new year is a new year, and begins where it should begin, in the first month. The only problem with that is that very little begins in January. That's because it has already started – in September.

One early September morning, with only the slightest nip in the air to suggest that the long halcyon days of summer are almost over, thousands of bleary-eyed children, lugged out of bed before their time, awkward in ill-fitting uniform, satchels bulging with first-day paraphernalia, make their sluggish way to the great portals of education, to start afresh. A new academic year has begun. And the only fresh-faced, bright-eyed little bundles amongst this heaving mass of juvenility are those who

cling to Mother or Father's hand, not yet aware that
school is work and work is for ever.

I remember it so well, that strange mixture of regret
and anticipation churning in the pit of the stomach, the
excitement and the fear: a new classroom, a new desk,
a new timetable, a new form teacher. How would she
react when I told her I would need time off at the end of
the week for the Jewish New Year? I would be back for a
week, then off for the Day of Atonement. Back for a few
days then off for the beginning of Tabernacles. Back for a
week, then off for the end of Tabernacles. Being a Jew in
the autumn is a bit like being a human boomerang. It's
surprising how exhausting having fun can be. Especially
for the cook in the family. And a little bit scary if you're
the only Jewish child in your class in a Church school.
I would watch every new teacher's eyes, looking for
the faintest glimmer of irritation, of disapproval, feeling
shame and rejection if I found it, relief if she smiled with
understanding. I didn't want to be different. Didn't want
to be the class Jack-in-a-box, popping up occasionally to
grace with my presence this august centre of learning. But
I did enjoy the New Year festivals.

And missed them terribly, when, later, I joined in
the mass displacement of tousled-haired youngsters in
regulation denim and oversized jerseys, heading back to
academia. It is September and all over the world, trunks
and bicycles are on the move. "The students are back,"
the cities declare and groan under the weight of it.

Then later, married to it, I watched that invincible
army, the teaching profession, wistfully collect its books
and bags from the dusty shelves and corners where they
have lain, close its front doors, head for its car, ruminating
sadly on Bognor and Betws-y-Coed, Mull and Majorca,
Brittany and Brighton, wondering whether the last weeks
were a mere hallucination. Real life begins again.

And some people love the autumn. Not I. As the
luscious green of tree and field degenerates into cop-
per and rust, as hill and dale dissolve into a mass of

molten bronze and burgundy, I lament the long, lazy, golden days of summer, swallowed up in misty mornings and dim, dank evenings.

Autumn, a time of fresh beginnings, of hunting out the long-abandoned thermals, and putting on the blessed tights again. A time for enduring, like a monk, hair shirt and itchy legs. Hello again to antifreeze and gas bills, cracked lips, hot water bottles and chilblains. No, I can't say that autumn is one of my favourite seasons. It's a beginning with too many endings. Sweeping up the leaves, we gather what has not blown away already, the remnants of another lost year. The dead wood is hacked from tree and rose bush and burned on a massive bonfire. And our only excuse for adding to the fog and smog is a failed attempt, long ago, at anarchy and terrorism. Not that I'm opposed to celebration. In fact, the very opposite. But it seems extraordinary to celebrate a nearly successful plot to annihilate the government when so much of our hard-earned tax is deployed in preventing it happening today.

Hard on the heels of Guy Fawkes' Day comes my birthday. Is that a cause for celebration? As far as my children are concerned it is. Like cardinals choosing a new pope they closet themselves in the kitchen to concoct a grand surprise. All is well until my husband joins them, throwing the weight of his opinion into the melting pot. Then the sound of raised voices reverberates around the house and reaches me in my attic haven. I don't emerge until the long-awaited smoke signal tells me the whole process is over and I can come down. Then, with all the grace I can muster, I force myself to blow out my candles and swallow my cake. With every succeeding year it seems to stick more firmly to the throat and gullet. And that is no reflection on the efforts of the cooks. I simply resent the ageing process, the reminder that my season of "mellow fruitfulness" draws ever nearer. Life is good, very very good, and I'm greedy for more than my three score years and ten. They are but a drop in the ocean of eternity, so why do I live life fighting its flow? Birthdays simply mark the stage of the tide. Another beginning, another year of opportunity, and not a farewell to those that were long-since engulfed in the passage of time.

What we need in autumn, to lift our sinking spirits out of the death and decay of the natural world, is a really good festival, a "spiritual" New Year, the chance to say goodbye to the past and open our arms wide to the future. Which is exactly what the Jewish New Year is.

One October night some years ago, we chanced, as a family, as so often happens at that time of the year, to find ourselves in impenetrable fog on the motorway. Visibility was almost nil. We might have stopped at a service station, except that a vague, yellowish tinge to the left of us as we passed them, was the only indication we had that they were there. It was impossible to have advance warning of any junction. How on earth would we know where to turn off? Would we stand a greater chance of finding the cross-country route, or should we opt to stay on the motorway, and simply hope that we would find our way off the M1 on to the M62 when the time came? For the sake of the children in the back of the car I forced my voice to stay as calm and unworried as if we were out for the day looking for a place to picnic.

Into my mind flashed the old, familiar story of the children of Israel in the wilderness, familiar because it is recounted year in, year out at the Passover and is part of the fabric of any Jewish child's existence. My ancestors had been caught in a forty-year fog, called the desert. But they were given a pillar of cloud by day, and a pillar of fire by night to guide them. Was similar assistance now too much to ask? So I asked the One who had led my however-many great-grandparents to the land of promise, to lead us safely home.

I'm not a great believer in miracles, not for myself at any rate. They tend to happen to other people. So when a vast Asda lorry suddenly rose up in front of us, its four extra-powerful fog-lamps forging a way through the gloom, only the children's triumphant whooping in the back of the car convinced me it wasn't a mirage. "I asked for a pillar of fire," I said to my husband, who was staring tensely at the windscreen, the skin stretched tautly over his knuckles on the steering wheel.

"Then you have one, courtesy of Asda," he said, "if I can just keep it in view, yet stay well behind."

There was a large Asda depot half a mile from our house. But since we were still well over an hour away, and with supermarkets all over the country waiting for deliveries, it was hardly possible that the lorry would take us all the way home. But it did. The quicker, cross-country route. There's efficiency for you. The driver must have wondered what one poor old Ford was doing following it so closely into the back of beyond. And when at last it turned into the industrial estate at the bottom of our little town we tooted and clapped and cheered.

That lorry has become for me a symbol of God's presence on our journey, hidden when the way ahead is clear, almost visible when fog obscures the view. Once a year at least we need the chance to look back and look forward, realigning our sights, allowing the light of God to penetrate any darkness and bring the road ahead into clearer focus. This is exactly how the Jews see their autumn festivals, a time for confession and cleansing, for laying the past to rest, and for looking forward in expectation. And what better time than in this season of endings and so many new beginnings?

I

Sound the Trumpet

There was never a proper goodbye, nor a proper hello, as I moved between worlds when I was a student. No official departure from one community. No recognition that I had arrived back in another. I was a displaced person, part of a faceless, disembodied mass, at the most crucial and difficult time in my developing maturity. Academic years came and went in a rather baggy, formless shape.

As a child the new academic year was marked out by having to stop work as soon as you started, by Rosh Hashanah, festival of new winter clothes, sweet and stodgy autumnal food, and the Rabbi blowing on the ram's horn, until the veins in his temples swelled to such a size, that my vivid, childish imagination conjured up a nightmare scenario of bits of brain splattered across the synagogue. A loud blast on the shofar was supposed to rouse a snoozing congregation to the opportunity for reflection on past failure and future potential. Instead, there was often no more than a cracked, shrill little bleat. Our parents sang, "Tekiha, teruah," roughly translated, "Wakey, wakey," a little bit too lustily, but the Rabbi was, after all, doing his best, and deserved the moral support of his congregation. And we children, unaware of the capriciousness of wind instruments, giggled uncontrollably. The child without the wit to stifle his vocal cords was frozen mid-chortle by a deadly and terrible stare from the maestro at the front.

"The Lord has gone up with a shout and the sound of the shofar," says Psalm 47, repeated in its entirety seven times. No wonder the service seemed a little repetitive. But if the shofar was supposed to waken the dead, why was Uncle Moshe still snoring downstairs in the corner? He had passed into unconsciousness some time during the fifth rendering, and the rest of the men were too engrossed in their own chatter to poke him in the ribs when the Rabbi rose to his feet. Auntie Sadie, on the other side of the gallery, waved frantically, the feathers of her New Year hat fluttering with the effort, and pointed at the sleeping figure of her husband, slumped in his seat below.

"What? What's she trying to say?" her sons and nephews mouthed at the women upstairs. By which time most of the congregation understood, even if they didn't.

But when the shofar is played properly, and far be it from me to suggest that this is an easy feat, no one sleeps. It sounds a little like the bellowing of a rhinoceros, trying to attract a mate from a herd more than twenty miles away. The aim is to make the congregation, not to mention the entire neighbourhood, tremble, as they remember that God is an absolute monarch in the universe he made. It is also supposed to drive Satan away. The Apostle Paul must have heard some virtuoso performances on the shofar. He knew it had the power to raise all the dead. "When the final shofar sounds," he said to the Church in Corinth, "the dead will rise up, never to die again, and we shall all be changed." To the Thessalonians he described the day an archangel would sound a blast on the shofar, heralding the triumphant reappearance of Christ. In fact, the shofar seems to have inspired some of his happiest visions.

It always has had happy associations. In the early days of the Jewish people, it was used as a kind of bush telegraph sending messages across the miles, such as "Down tools, lads, the Sabbath's almost here." In fact it was probably the Hebrew equivalent of the shop floor manager's whistle. Except of course, like everything else in Judaism, it has its own symbolic significance, derived from the story of Abraham and Isaac. God tested his servant to the limit when he asked him to sacrifice his only child. In Isaac the old man had invested every dream he had ever dreamed, his future and the future of his people. But he was prepared to trust the King of the Universe, and give him what he loved most in the world. So God provided a ram, caught in a thicket, as a substitute. The ram's horn has been used on important occasions ever after, and Jewish sheep have been giving hedges a wide berth.

Just as the shofar curves, say the Jewish people, we, like Abraham, must bend to God's will. And he, the "All-Merciful", must remember how vulnerable we are. A lamb is shorn at the end of summer, and throughout the autumn, until the new wool grows, is at the mercy of the climate. With no natural protection, an early cold snap could kill it. So its horn symbolises the way at the beginning of every new year our future hangs in the balance. As we move out into uncharted waters, we have only one guide and protector.

The old Hasidic sage, Levi Isaac of Berdichev, once told the story of a king who was lost in a forest. Eventually a wise old peasant found him and escorted him safely home. The king was so grateful that he gave the peasant a key government job. Several years later the official fell from favour, as they are wont, and was summoned to appear before his majesty. He arrived, wearing the ragged old clothes he had worn the first time they met. And the king, remembering that meeting, forgave him. So, said Rabbi Levi Isaac, does the shofar remind God of his people's good beginning, the sacrifice of Abraham, their commitment at Sinai to accept his kingship and his law. So he will remember the noble intentions we had when we first met him, forgive our failure to live up to them, and help us fulfil them in the year ahead.

From the eve of Rosh Hashanah there are ten days of "awe", the Yomim Noraim, as they are called. Ten days for dealing with all the unfinished business of the past year, for quiet reflection on lessons which could be learned, for sorting out broken relationships, for giving charity, for tying up any remaining loose ends.

Some Jews will even perform a ceremony, which began in the Middle Ages, known as Tashlich. I used to watch, bemused, the annual pilgrimage of the ultra-Orthodox Gateshead community down to the seafront at Whitley Bay. Their black frock coats and hats looked somehow out of place in this gaudy world of candy floss, edible rock and amusement arcades. I wondered whether they were ever tempted to have a paddle, but they never did. Instead they sang and swayed and emptied pocketfuls of pebbles into the water.

Now that I understand what they were doing, it strikes me as quite a useful little ceremony. "Tashlich" means "cast away", as in, "You will cast their sins into the depths of the sea," from the prophet Micah. The idea is to take a handful of pebbles, allow each one to represent a sin, or any event whose memory has the power to cast a shadow over our future, hurl it into water, whether a stream or a pond or the sea, and watch it sink, without trace.

My daughter, Abby, when she was little, used to fill her pockets with stones, shells and any other debris she found, buttons, crab legs, rusty metal, whenever we went to the beach. Then, before we left, she would chuck away the rubbish, but always hang on to the more attractive-looking pieces in her collection. A contemporary parable of the way many of us handle the darker side of our lives!

A friend of mine who is a minister has increasingly found, over the last years, that he is being involved in a great deal of what my husband refers to as "shit-shovelling", helping people offload all kinds of human mess dredged up from the past, which has to be carted away before they can progress into the future. He now encourages the person to write it all down, then together, they tear up the paper confession, place it in an ashtray and symbolically burn it. It worked very well until he once nearly set a retirement home alight. Presumably, the more aged we are, the more paper there is to burn. Happily it's never too late to be free. But I think I'll stick with casting my personal debris into the North Sea.

Despite the need for quiet reflection, Rosh Hashanah is a festival, a chance to look forward with excitement and expectation, a time to let your hair down and romp, not sit in a miserable heap on the carpet. At home, Jews everywhere light their candles, drink wine and eat bread, as they do on the Sabbath. The loaf is round, not plaited as it is at Shabbat, wishing everyone a full, well-rounded new year. The family eats pieces of apple dipped in honey, remembers the promised land, and prays for a sweet new year.

We ate carrots, lots of them, in a stew called Tzimmis, because they're sweet, and because the Hebrew word for carrot means "to increase", so eating them in abundance is like praying for abundant blessing. Why we couldn't simply stick to a prayer, I never understood. They were not my favourite vegetable. Perhaps that's where my curly hair comes from. But even the lowly carrot is preferable to swallowing as many pomegranate seeds as you can, eaten in some families as a prayer to God to multiply our good deeds. Definitely preferable to eating a fish head, as some Jews do, in the hope that we may be "the head and not the tail" of God's handiwork.

My mother never quite entered the spirit of the occasion.

"Please God, may next year not be like the last," Mama's Rosh Hashanah refrain. "Well at least it can't get any worse."

"You said that last year, and it did," we remind her.

That cheers her up for a while, then she says mournfully, "This year it definitely can't get any worse."

She is in good company. Ezra, the priest, had the same problem with all the Jews after they came out of captivity in Babylon. When, for the first time in years, they observed Rosh Hashanah, so Nehemiah says in the

Old Testament, they were so overwhelmed by the words of the service that they all broke down. Ezra had to say to them, "This is not the time for weeping and wailing. Go home and have a really good party. Have plenty of food and wine. Share it out with anyone who hasn't enough. And the joy of the Lord will make you strong."

If ever there was a phrase Christians tend to quote to one another out of context, it must be those last few words. But joy, as Ezra understood it, was not an abstract emotion, plucked from the blue, or cranked up in our souls like the engine of an old motor car. It was the natural result of having a really good time with friends and family. Cheering the body does wonders for the soul.

The Church isn't exactly famous for partying. Though Jesus himself doesn't seem to have been averse to enjoying himself. On the whole we feel much happier with the quietly reflective side of life. But our spirits need tranquillity and euphoria, each in contrast to the other, and when more so than at a new year, a time to look back with quiet thankfulness and look forward in exuberant anticipation. In an extraordinary way, and this is their secret, the Jews manage to combine solemnity and laughter, reverence and joy, times of awe with times of feasting. Which is why the festivals, working their special magic on body, emotion and spirit, celebrated at home and in the community, are the key to Jewish survival.

IDEAS FOR CELEBRATING A NEW YEAR

It is possible to mark the arrival of a new year, a significant "rite of passage", with reflection and celebration, either at the beginning of a new academic year in September, with the return of children to school, and students to their colleges. Or at the traditional time in January. Here are some recipes, and a meditation, which may help.

Any suggestions made at the end of chapters can be used as part of a celebration at home. Or they can be adapted and used in church, either as part of a service, as a celebration after the service, or in the Sunday School.

Rosh Hashanah marks the birthday of creation, and may also provide a chance to think about how we treat the environment.

RECIPES

NEW YEAR BREAD

The traditional Sabbath loaf or chollah (recipe on page 154) is round instead of plaited, to signify the promise of a rich and full new year. Raisins or sultanas can be added for extra sweetness.

TZIMMIS

An easy sweet, cheap and cheerful stew. Serves 6.

1kg carrots
700g potatoes
a beef brisket joint (about 1kg in weight)
4 tbsp. golden (corn) syrup
1 tbsp. cornflour
2 tsp. salt
pepper

Trim the fat off the meat and cut into cubes. Peel and chop the carrots. Put the meat and carrots, with 2 tablespoons of the syrup, salt and pepper into a large casserole. Barely cover with hot water, bring to the boil and simmer, or slow cook for two hours. Allow to chill and when cold skim off any fat. Meanwhile peel and cut the potatoes into large cubes. Dissolve the cornflour in a little of the stock, then add to the stock in the casserole. Arrange the potatoes in the casserole too, and add a little water until they are just submerged. Add the remaining syrup and a little more salt. Cover and cook very slowly for as long as possible – at least another four hours! Your stew should be a deep golden colour. If not, uncover and cook for a further half hour.

Optional: do add your favourite dumplings too, about an hour before serving.

This may be served with a selection of cold meats if desired.

LEKACH (HONEY CAKE)

This traditional New Year cake needs to mature for a week, wrapped in foil, in an airtight tin.

200g plain flour
150g caster sugar
250g clear honey
100ml cooking oil
2 eggs
1 tsp. bicarbonate of soda dissolved in 100ml of orange juice or strong coffee
1 tsp. mixed spice
1 tsp. cinnamon
½ tsp. salt
optional: 50g chopped nuts

Mix together all the dry ingredients, then add the honey, oil and eggs and beat well until smooth. Dissolve the bicarbonate of soda in the orange juice or coffee, and add to the mixture. Pour into a parchment-lined loaf tin and bake for about 1 hour 15 minutes, until firm.

This cake improves with keeping, and can be iced with coffee or orange icing just prior to serving.

APPLES

Serve in slices with a bowl of honey to dip them in.
Alternatives: apple strudel or toffee apples.

Then say: "Blessed are you O Lord our God, King of

the Universe, who creates the fruit of the tree. May it be your will, O Lord our God, God of our fathers, to grant us a happy, pleasant and sweet new year."

MEDITATION FOR A NEW YEAR

At the beginning of a new year, O God, I want to open my innermost self to those deeper thoughts and feelings which I often shut off from my mind and heart in my preoccupation with worldly pursuits and pleasures.

Grant me real responsiveness to your spirit, so that I may consecrate my mood of the moment by influences and sentiments which will outlast the moment.

Now, let me learn lessons from the past, before the old
     year is gone.
Help me to put past experiences in their true perspective.
Let me see how much more numerous were my blessings
     than my privations,
how my losses, trials and sorrows contained the seeds of
     higher good,
how needlessly I fretted over things which at the
     time seemed all-important, and now seem small and
     insignificant.
Let no self-deception hide my sins and shortcomings from
     me,
the neglected opportunities,
misspent time,
gifts and abilities perverted to lower purposes against my
     own better judgement.
Grant, that like Jacob, wrestling with an adversary in
     the dark, I may not let the departing year go, until
     I have wrested a blessing from its trials and mistakes.

And now, by your grace, may I turn into blessings the
     endless possibilities of the new year which stretches
     out before me in solemn mystery.

tti

Let its message of time and eternity remind me of the
    uncertainty of human life and the passing of all
    earthly things.
But let me not live in fear of death.
My times are in your hands.
You will be with me wherever I go.
Relying on your wisdom and loving generosity, let me
    face the unknown with courage and hope.

We are strangers to the year ahead.
We do not know which way to go.
We need your light to lead us.
Guide us in the safe way.
Bless our home, and our relationships,
keep and protect our affections,
strengthen our loyalties,
and increase our powers of helpfulness.
Inscribe me, I pray, in the Book of Life,
help me to understand that life is measured more in terms
    of character, ideals and service, than in length of
    days.

May the beauty of the Lord rest upon us. Establish the
    work of our hands – the work of our hands, establish
    it, Lord. Amen.

2

Of Bumps, Bulges and Babies

Jewish tradition has it that it was at Rosh Hashanah that God heard and answered Hannah's prayer for a child. Which is why her story is always read in the synagogue on the first day of the festival, to emphasise the power of prayer in determining destiny.

Experience tells me that that is a daring, if not fool-hardy, interpretation of the story. The whole area of fertility is a potential minefield, when placed in the context of faith and prayer and destiny. The Bible is full of stories of childless women, who usually manage, in altogether exceptional circumstances, to produce, over and against the odds. And I've often thought how galling that must be for the countless couples today who find themselves unable to do what all their contemporaries are doing, prospective grandparents are willing them to do, and society expects them to do: namely, reproduce like a pair of rabbits.

My concern was confirmed when we lived in Coventry, though goodness knows what geography had to do with it, and I found myself surrounded by couples with fertility problems. One couple couldn't stop producing, and had five babies in as many years (it would have been six if a twin had not sadly miscarried), refuting in the process all the claims of the medical profession of major technological and scientific advances in the field of contraception. The others, and why the imbalance only God knows, would have willingly given not only their right arms, but any relevant part of their anatomy, to be smitten with such adversity. In fact, such was their pain, surfacing often at those morning services called "Family Services", a misnomer for "Children's Services" where any childless adult can feel surplus to requirements, that I could quite understand why in Bible times, Eli the priest thought Hannah was just another wino, drunk by lunchtime. She hurt so deeply she couldn't speak, crushed not only by the shame of her wayward reproductive system, but also by the endless pregnant bulges of her arch-rival and fellow-wife. Lying prostrate in the temple she tried to move her mouth, but no intelligible words emerged. Just an occasional moan or a whimper. In one sense she was beyond praying, in a traditional way at any rate. And I've seen how childlessness and other experiences of profound loss can produce that kind of pain. I've held and rocked women who were too numb to pray any more.

And yet there was one occasion when I was given the tiniest insight into how Eli might have felt when he heard that Hannah was pregnant. On my doorstep one evening stood a close friend, who had been waiting seven years for a child. Some days she coped with the feelings of desperation. On other days despair threatened to overwhelm her. Today was one of those days. Would I pray again with her that God would give her a child?

My heart sank. I really couldn't manage to muster the tiniest twinkle of anything even vaguely resembling faith. But to say no would have compounded her feelings of inadequacy. So I smiled with all the grace I could paint on my face, and invited her in. And nine months later became the godmother of a beautiful baby girl.

Some years later I told the story in *Prayer for the Day* on Radio 4, in an attempt to explain how God shows us that we can, sometimes, be involved with him in determining destiny. I said that he occasionally gives us miraculous answers to our prayers, without our having a scrap of faith, in order to encourage us gently out of the shallow end of the swimming pool, where our feet touch bottom, to the deep end, where we have to swim.

In the post came one of the saddest letters I have ever seen, full of pain and bitterness. After seventeen years of childlessness, said the writer, she was glad that I was able to do what no fertility clinic could, and solve her problem in an instant. Her lack of faith had obviously closed her womb.

I said I was very sorry if I had hurt her. I never intended to suggest that all infertility was cured by prayer. I had no idea why one friend was given the gift of a child, while others were left to struggle on with their emptiness. It was all part of the eternal mystery. And if there was no Mystery, there would be no God.

She reminded me very much of an aunt, whom I loved dearly, and who had been childless, a great stigma in the Jewish community, where children carry on the family name and are a tangible sign of God's blessing. As I now regularly remind myself! In my fancy-free, single days, at a Jewish wedding in a posh hotel, I once accompanied my aunt to the Ladies'. Next to me, as I combed my hair at the mirror, sat a woman, creating a work of art out of powder and lipstick.

"We never wanted children," she said nonchalantly, compressing her lips between a paper tissue, and surveying the result of her effort. "Too much like hard work. We preferred our independence."

My aunt, drying her hands and not actually party to the conversation, froze. Her eyes, always warm and alive in my memory, hardened over into two dark, icy ponds.

"You selfish woman," she hissed at the astonished face in the mirror, "I would have given anything, anything to have a child. How could you be so selfish?"

A momentary, stunned silence followed, then the icy ponds began to melt, and I got up quickly, took her arm and guided her gently towards the door. I paused for a second to look back at the woman, and her stricken, ghostly face in the mirror made my stomach lurch, because I knew instinctively, as she sat, lipstick poised in mid-air, that her words had been a form of protection, a means of hiding her own anguish. And now, instead of reaching out to each other in mutual comfort and consolation, because of their unresolved pain, two women had unwittingly poured themselves a double dose of suffering.

Mercifully I've never had to plumb those depths myself. I know, but only in miniature, something of the distress the whole reproductive process can cause. And I fully agree with Jenny Cooke, who wrote an indispensable little booklet on childbirth, that producing babies is not the pre-ordained pleasure it was supposed to be, but subject instead to the sullying influences of the fall of woman from her paradise estate. Well may we have a little taste of the pleasure at the starting post, after that it seems to be downhill all the way to the menopause as far as the female organs are concerned.

Joel, our now giant-sized teenager, obligingly appeared on cue, right between summer holidays abroad. That he almost hit Christmas, a fact which has been the bane of my life ever since, was somehow overlooked. Strange how we mortals now feel ourselves in control of birth, even if death still defies us. We go beyond the lesson of Hannah and Rosh Hashanah and rather than having a part to play in destiny, take it firmly into our own hands. Naturally I assumed, having taken charge the first time round, that the second time would be just as straight-forward. It wasn't. And after several barren, increasingly unnerving months I took myself to the doctor's for the examination which every woman dreads.

"There's no way you'll conceive through that lot," he concluded, which wasn't very enlightening, since I wasn't privy to the same view of the situation.

"Through what?" I asked, unsure of how detailed an answer I wanted. He explained, in the verging-on-the-incomprehensible way that doctors sometimes do, that damage had been done when Joel was born, that I would need a little minor surgery, and that he would refer me to a gynaecologist.

The "little, minor surgery" grew by the month. It began with an attempt to burn away the problem. No one had warned me not to turn up for my appointment on a bicycle! When fire failed to work they tried the deep freeze treatment. I defrosted on the way home. When that failed too, I was admitted to hospital for surgery under general anaesthetic. It turned out to be one of the most negative experiences of my medical life, for I was wretchedly bullied and browbeaten, as were all the other patients on the ward, by a harridan of a nursing sister who couldn't have been more at home in a concentration camp.

"What do you think you're doing? Where do you think you're going? Stay on your bed. Put your shoes in your locker. Lay your dressing gown straight. Go to the toilet when I say so."

And that was the day before the operation.

Only now, many confidence-building and assertiveness-training years later, do I realise that no one has the right to abuse their authority, and that it is not necessary to submit to that kind of manipulation or humiliation. Christ himself, though subjugated physically at the end, was never subjugated mentally and remained, in an extraordinary way, in complete control of every situation.

I went home a wreck. And though the world swam before my eyes as the anaesthetic still swirled its way round my system, Peter was unable to take time off from his teaching job, and I was left with a hyperactive toddler who rampaged his way around the house. What does a poor Jewish girl do caught in such an extremity? She calls for Mama, what else! And Mama cooked and cleaned, made chopped liver and minded the baby, while Pop, as doctors do, lambasted "that horse of an anaesthetist" (it was a lady doctor of course), who in removing the tube from my throat had also removed most of the skin from my bottom lip.

I survived. And, several months later, we moved to Nottingham so that Peter could study for the ordained ministry. Convinced that all was not as it should be, I went to see my new GP, happily a woman doctor at last, and was told that far from disappearing the old problem was worse than ever. There would be no baby, not for the foreseeable future. A course of tablets and iodine pessaries was prescribed. Extraordinary, the nasty tricks the doctors find to play inside our bodies. I was to return in two weeks to be referred to a gynaecologist, again.

I remember so well the feeling of utter dejection as I trudged around the square where we had rented a house, to see another couple from the college, the only people we really knew at that stage. John and Ros Harding, with their three boisterous children, struck me as an approachable, caring family. Instinct proved right. I needed someone to listen, and they listened with sensitivity and concern. I didn't think I wanted them to pray. I had had a close friend in Manchester with secondary infertility. I convinced myself and her that she would have a second child. I became more convinced as the chances grew slimmer. That was optimism, not faith. She never did conceive. I suspected that the false hope had hurt her more than the childlessness and didn't want to make any more mistakes. The Hardings prayed anyway, and I trudged back home to the tablets and the pessaries, comforted a little, but very weak in faith.

Two weeks later I went back to my doctor, clutching a sample in the empty tablet bottle, demanding a pregnancy test. And that was just the beginning of the little miracle which was to be Abby, "Father's delight".

Apart from severe nausea for the entire duration of the pregnancy, Joel's entry into the arena of life, rather than slow but deadly, had been fast but uneventful. I told Peter when we married that I was rarely ill, and never sick. And spent eight horrendous months disproving it, carrying a bowl around with me for good measure. I took the now-banned drug Debendox throughout, and it helped me survive, which is why I have such a deep concern about our increasingly litigious society, apportioning blame and hunting compensation for every possible mishap in life. My father prescribed the drug for thirty years, and never once had the slightest cause for fearing it might have impaired a foetus. It was the last available drug to control vomiting in pregnancy. Now women have to survive alone, without any help. The writer Charlotte Brontë died of pregnancy sickness. That fact was a comfort to me. I always knew, in whichever loo, behind whichever tree I was, that it must be possible to die of it.

Along with constant *mal de mer*, Abby's development was one worry after another. I had taken two courses of antibiotics in the first four weeks of her conception. The uterus was too high, the doctor said. She never filled it properly, but seemed to sit halfway up with the crown of her head pushing into my lungs and ribcage. I couldn't breathe. All the signs of what was to come were there, from the very beginning. Fortunately I wasn't medically minded enough to know I had just cause to panic. But Jane Grayshon, whose husband was studying at the college, and who was already struggling herself with the intense, physical pain she was to describe so graphically in her books, was then a midwife at the maternity hospital. She told me in no uncertain terms that the moment labour started I was to get myself to the hospital.

Eventually, weakened by nausea and the stress of acclimatising to a new life, scarlet fever struck and I was ill for weeks.

"I thought coming to a theological college would be an exciting, stimulating, stretching adventure," I wailed at my poor husband, who took himself off into another bedroom at night, while I paced the floor, alternately itching and daubing my poor weeping skin with phenol oil, "and the only thing to stretch is my stomach. And that means there's more of me to itch!"

I visited the doctor daily so that she could monitor the baby's heartbeat, which thankfully remained loud and strong, but even that did little to eradicate my neurotic fantasies of a poor, puzzled little creature, floating *in utero* with flaking, itchy skin.

The Hardings observed my increasing anxiety and prayed again. The baby, John felt sure, had been called "Faithful", for its hand would never let go of the hand of the Almighty, nor would his hand cease to protect it, all its life long. How I held on to those words the long and frightening night of her birth. I was admitted after what had started as a routine ante-natal visit. An X-ray, taken the previous week, had revealed what was known already, that the foetus was sitting head up, not down, but also that being barely five foot, I was unable to deliver a breach baby.

"Why doesn't this X-ray show me where the placenta is?" demanded the consultant, the formidable, wonderful Miss Baker. I felt safe in her hands.

Her registrar shrugged. "I'll turn the baby," he said. "She delivered normally the last time. There's no reason why she shouldn't this time."

I managed a grateful smile. Joel's delivery had been a disappointingly mechanical affair. I had been wired up like a battery hen, allowed no control over my own body, and ultimately had been unable to breastfeed. It had left me feeling cheated and inadequate. This time I intended being in control of the birth.

"And do you know what you're doing?" Miss Baker barked.

My gratitude evaporated.

"Yes," said the registrar uncertainly, and proceeded.

He pushed until my entire insides seem to give way and revolve. And almost at once a young nurse, trying to curb the alarm in her voice, said, "The heartbeat's gone!"

We watched the machine in silence, and slowly it revived, "Beep, beep, beep . . . beep . . . beep," an irregular, half-hearted affair. I breathed again.

They left me attached to the monitor for some hours, popping in and out to listen to the feeble little beep, shaking their heads and tutting as it faded and revived.

"I wish they'd just get on with a caesarian," Jane Grayshon said, and unknown to me, went back to the Thursday night college communion service and told them to pray and pray hard if the Guinness baby was to live.

In the early evening they decided to induce by breaking the waters, my last chance of a normal delivery. As the registrar stood over me with a blade, ready to lunge, I remember thinking what a gruesome business the whole thing was and hoped that it wasn't too disturbing for Peter, at his end of the spectrum. The waters broke in a gush, and down with them came the umbilical cord. I felt it against my skin, warm and damp and slimy, as the doctor barked tersely into an intercom, "Emergency section." I was turned on to my knees and ordered to keep my head down, as low as possible so that the baby would slip back into the uterus. No one spelt it out to me but I was vaguely aware that the cord ceased to function after a certain length of time, starving the baby of oxygen. How long I couldn't remember.

Within seconds we were hurtling along the corridors, I, on my knees, face pressed against the trolley, and the Sister who wheeled us along with one hand and held the cord up inside me with the other. A young nurse stopped us and asked "for a quick word, Sister".

"Can't you see I'm busy?" the Sister hissed.

And all the time I concentrated on how to avoid having my knees jammed in the groove where the two parts of the trolley joined.

"Sign this."

A slip of paper slid beneath my face. I raised my head to read it, but the Sister pushed it back down. So I took aim and signed, hoping it was my consent to the operation I was giving. It could have been anything.

I was calm, wonderfully, totally at peace. There was never any question in my mind but that this baby would be protected and cherished by a Father to whom she was dearer than any father on earth. Even when I came round some time later feeling as if I'd been run over by a double-decker bus, with Peter shouting excitedly in my ear, "It's a girl, it's a girl, she's all right, she's alive, look at her," all I could manage was a feeble, "Get me the morphine."

It was some days later that the wonder, and the trauma, really caught up with us. Delayed shock struck with a ferocity which took our breath away. We were suddenly two quivering heaps of jelly. We simply needed a little time together as a family. But Peter, by some strange irony, was in the midst of a training placement with the hospital chaplain which required long hours of work experience on the wards – in another hospital. His day started at seven, and ended long after any possibility of visiting me. He asked the chaplain for compassionate leave, and was refused. Joel, only a little chap, was shipped from bed to bed and house to house, until he broke down and howled under the stress. With no husband to visit me and no parents nearby to coo over their new grandchild, I howled too. We were all at breaking point.

Jane Grayshon took stock of the situation, reported back to Peter's college tutor and the placement was cancelled at once. But I've long since wondered how a hospital chaplain, finely tuned to the slightest needs and intimations of the patient, could fail to apply the same criteria to a trainee. But then isn't there a danger for all caring professionals, even, and perhaps especially, those in the Church, reared on the Protestant work ethic, to be so overpowered by the magnitude of human need, so committed to the job, that they walk all over those nearest to them? Which is why the Jews observe so strictly their seasons of rest and festival, their time to work and time to stop. After an experience like ours, time to take stock was what we most needed.

A new life needs time to establish its own rhythm and explore its world. For all we know those first few days may be the most important in our whole existence. I knew all there was to know about "bonding", that special relationship the psychologists tell us must develop between mother and child, and had been determined to foster it by breastfeeding from the moment of birth. A caesarian section had robbed me of that. In those vital first hours my baby was left alone in a cot, while I lay in a heavy drug-induced stupor. What if this little life had been scarred already by emotional deprivation and neglect?

Now that truly was faithless. The first day I held her, balanced on top of the pillow which protected my raw and tender stomach, I fell madly in love with the sloe-eyed, dark-lashed little bundle. A daughter. That thought tapped into immense reserves of ferocity and protectiveness I never consciously knew were inside me. I was barely aware of the fight to secure a better world for women. But as I held my daughter, and wonder of all wonders, she snuggled up and fed from me, on and on and on, I knew in my heart that I wanted this girl-child to inherit a world where she was equal to any man, where she could stand side by side with her brother.

At least we didn't have to face the dilemma of whether or not to go ahead with circumcision, or how to do so, as we did with Joel. In the end we chose to have him circumcised, because we wanted him to grow up identifying with the Jewish community. But through a daughter the racial and cultural heritage of our family, handed on through the women, would continue anyway.

"The Lord has filled my heart with joy;
How happy I am because of what he has done!"

Hannah's hymn, echoed years later by a young Jewish girl, about to give birth to the Messiah, was mine. For we knew, all three, from our experience of the reproductive process, what every Jew hears at Rosh Hashanah; that God in some mysterious, inexplicable way, for reasons known only to himself, involves human beings in the destiny of his world.

But sometimes that involvement can be too heavy a burden to bear. In this whole area of the sanctity of life, couples can be called upon to make decisions which may make them feel as if they're being forced to do God's job for him. I have felt so, as I have wrestled with friends over the rightness or otherwise of in-vitro fertilisation, and then, more especially, when dear friends of ours decided to terminate a severely Down's syndrome baby. Our hearts ached for them, and we learned then that our own personal views, drawn up in the cold, clinical school of ethics, untouched by personal dilemma and tragedy, were largely irrelevant. Their agonising decision was made thoughtfully and carefully, for many reasons, and all we could do, all we wanted to do, was to stay with them and try to comfort them in their bewilderment and pain.

My old Pop used to say when I was a child, "It's vital to have principles," and he was one of the most highly principled men I ever knew, "but principles must always bend for people. When they don't, a fanatic is born." And how his words echo still in my mind whenever I am faced with the wealth of imponderable ethical dilemmas the fertility process can spawn. There are no easy answers. The Pharisees, with their meticulous code of practice, tried to provide them, by tying up all the loose ends. Jesus, raised within that system, challenged their rigidity by submitting everyone he met to sensitive, individual treatment, not an unbendable rule-book.

And had I known, as I sat, spellbound and awe-struck, gazing at the beautiful baby in my arms, that my grand excursion into the reproductive realm was but the start of my gynaecological pilgrimage, I might have asked the consultant to insert a zip.

3

And of Endings

I was delivering parish magazines in the little mining town where Peter was serving his curacy.

"Thank you, love," said one elderly lady, opening her door and snatching it out of my hand, before I had time to push it through the letter box. She must have seen me coming up the path.

I expressed some pleasure at her anticipation. We had been working hard to produce a creative, interesting read.

"Oh, I only get it for the deaths," she said.

At that time, as we and our friends were all very much into giving birth, the idea seemed a little morbid. But my mother-in-law explained that once you reach seventy your circle of friends appears to shrink by the month. Outliving them all becomes rather a challenge.

From birth to death is not such a quantum leap for the Jewish people, for death is an integral part of life. It is also a kind of a birth, the passage into a new, unknown existence, which is why someone will always sit with a body, candles burning on the coffin, all through the night, or nights, until the funeral, to make sure that this important last journey isn't undertaken alone.

The "High Holy Days", Rosh Hashanah, Yom Kippur and Sukkot or Tabernacles, are a time to visit the relatives' graves, to show honour and respect, to ensure that their memory lives on in those who loved them. And in those whose emotions were not quite so positive! I have heard Mama mutter less than complimentary remarks at a certain grave, something about a miserable old codger, and thank God it was the Almighty who had to cope with his grumbling now, and not us. And then, as she passed the graves of an aunt and uncle, renowned for their incompatibility in life, she would muse on their probable incompatibility in death.

"Can you hear anything? She's probably giving him hell, just as she always did. I don't know how he manages to lie there so quietly."

My husband, in the course of his ministerial duty, was once asked at a funeral visit by the grieving wife whether he thought she would be reunited with her husband one day. He took immense care with his answer. He didn't want to compound her pain. He said he believed that there would be no such thing as marriage in heaven, Christ seemed to make that clear, but we must trust God that heaven would be heaven, and therefore we would recognise those we had loved.

"Thank God," the woman sighed with relief, "he led me such a dog's life down here, I wouldn't want more of it up there."

It now seems entirely sensible to me that if the new year festivals are a time for a general sort-out, so that we can proceed, unencumbered, into a new era in our lives, then we should all have an annual occasion for dealing with the feelings, memories and regrets the dead leave behind them.

When we were children I dreaded the annual pilgrimage to the Jewish cemetery, probably because of the memory of a certain trauma, produced when my brother and I were left waiting in the car outside together for what seemed an eternity. On one occasion the dear little lad found, on the back window-ledge, the leather walking-stick my father had confiscated from a Nazi officer during the war, which converted at frightening speed into a lethal sword. With enormous enjoyment he unsheathed it and

brandished it round and round the car, almost decapi-
tating his sister in the process.

We could never understand what our parents found to
do for so long out there in the chill autumnal weather.
Now, I really appreciate the opportunity to go to my
father's grave, to speak to him directly in the words of
the familiar and lovely prayers, to tell him how much his
life was an inspiration to me, and how much I still miss
him. There are no flowers on Jewish graves, nothing that
will wilt and fade. I pick up instead a pebble, smooth and
polished, which will survive the elements and the passage
of time far better than human beings, and lay that beside
him, a symbol of the way he will live forever, in my heart,
and in the tales I tell of him to my children.

I find myself talking to them about him often, but particularly when I have "Jahrzeit", the annual anniversary
of his death, when I light a memorial candle and leave
it burning in the centre of the table for a whole evening
and all the following day. That's my Pop's special day, a
time to think of him and find him again, tucking me into
bed, still dressed in his white doctor's coat, singing George
Formby songs and accompanying himself on the ukulele,
jangling coins in his pocket as we stopped at the candy
shop on the way home from school, buying the teachers
cream cakes on school sports days, playing cricket in
the street, dancing the twist when it was the latest rage,
savouring good red wine, admiring a fine pair of female
legs. "What a man he was, your grandpa, my Pop."

And as I take stock I realise that he is with me in
the words I speak, in the attitudes I adopt, in the goals
I have, in the dreams he dreamed for me, so many
of which have come true. Most important of all, he is
responsible for the way in which I see God. Unknown
to him, that was his greatest gift to me.

He actually died at the end of October, on Shemini
Azeret, the eighth and final day of Tabernacles, and of
all the high holy days, a special day of rejoicing. The
Bible only allows for seven days of Tabernacles, so no

one knows how the tradition of the extra day arose, except that since Shemini means eighth, and Azeret, "waiting" or "holding back", the accumulated wisdom of the ancients was that God was like a king who had invited all his people to a feast and was having such a good time that he didn't want it to end. So he says to them, "Don't go yet. I can't bear it. Let's have fun for just one more day." So the Jews have made that day an opportunity to celebrate the giving of the torah, the law, which is why it is also known as "Simchat Torah", the Joy of the Law.

Only those very close to the heart of God are supposed to die on Shemini Azeret, the deeply religious and Orthodox. My father was neither. But I think it is quite in keeping with the divine sense of humour to aggravate the holier members of the community by giving my bacon-loving, lawbreaking, yet God-fearing Pop a special invitation to a party normally reserved for the pious.

Prayers in remembrance of the dead are said not only on the anniversary of the death and at Shemini Azeret, but also on Yom Kippur, Pentecost, Passover, the Sabbath, in fact at any and every opportunity. My step-father, who had lost both his parents by the time he first married, tells the story of how the shammus, the verger of the synagogue, sidled up to him after the wedding service and whispered in his ear, "I've said chay v'rachmin, prayers for your dead."

"Thank you," said Boris.

The shammus nodded and winked and Boris handed him a ten shilling note.

He still didn't move.

"That was for your father," he said, waving the note. "But you are an orphan."

Boris dug into his pocket, temporarily aggravated with a mother who been inconsiderate enough to join her husband, leaving her child so unprotected in the world, and was about to hand over another note, when his new wife intercepted it with a deft snatch of the hand.

"Enough," she said.

"Phew," muttered the shammus, "the ink's not dry in the register and look who's the boss."

Jewish tradition maintains that charity should be dispensed whenever you remember your departed loved ones, for God may be more disposed to forgive them their sins. Whether tips count as charity is another matter.

Constantly recalling the dead, investing their memory with special honour, does give every Jew a profound sense of history and continuity. I know that I was called after my very pious great-great-grandmother, Malchah Golda, who was so devout that after her death her body was laid in the synagogue for twenty-four hours, a rare token of respect, especially for a woman. In many ways, though she would not have understood in her lifetime the path I have taken, I like to think that she does now, and that I walk in her footsteps, after a lapse of several more secular generations! The Christian Church tends to have little real appreciation of the immense richness of its history and heritage. Yet there have been so many great examples, so many martyrs. My own children are ignorant of Augustine, Ambrose, Thomas Aquinas, Teresa of Avila, Wycliffe, or Josephine Butler, to name but a few, who suffered so much to hand down the faith that we follow. And I have often wondered whether, instead of trying to call a halt to the relatively new tradition of Halloween, with its sinister implications, we should not be organising great All Saints Day celebrations, with candles, fireworks, and dramatised versions of the lives of the saints. What an opportunity to recall, with thankfulness, the achievements of those who have influenced us the most.

Not many people find their own death the most absorbing of topics, I have to say, but it seems to have a certain charm for some Jews, including my mother. One of her greatest pleasures in life is working out who will inherit what after she's gone. The greatest threat for any misdemeanour, from answering back to not phoning weekly with all the news ("So you don't have a mother any more?"), has always been, "You'll get cut out of the will!"

And now of course there's not only a will. There's a letter to be read "after I'm gone", so that I can still tell you what to do from beyond the grave! It contains a detailed list of her every trinket, with instructions about who should own it first, second, third in the event of any inconvenient early demise, which might ruin the chain. It took her days to work out the minutiae, and she did it, with relish, consulting her children, and smacking her lips.

"You've always wanted Aunty Sadie's sapphire ring?" she said to my sister, "You're not getting it. You can have the emerald brooch instead."

"You want great Grandma's white gold and diamond earrings?" she said to me, "The ones she carried across Lithuania at the end of the last century, hidden in a pair of stockings, when she fled, as a girl, without a penny in her pocket, from the Cossack soldiers, who were plundering, pillaging and murdering our people?"

Oh yes, I wanted the earrings with the romance and adventure and history attached to them.

"You married out. You married a man of the cloth. What do you want with diamonds? You can have them until Susie's old enough to wear them, her eighteenth birthday. Then you hand them over."

Susie is my niece, aged thirteen, raised in a "proper" Jewish family. Which means I have custody of the earrings for a few more years.

I have to confess that Mother's way of disposing of her worldly goods provided me with a very salutary exercise in not getting too attached to possessions, however strong their sentimental value.

She, for her part, found immense enjoyment in ordering her own departure into the next life, even though she was still in her sixties, with potentially many years of nachus (pleasures) to come. She struggled for several weeks with a gold initial on a chain, the first letter of her own name, until she remembered that I have a son whose name begins with the same initial. Then, with everything accounted for, she slept well in her bed, certain, like many Jews, that should she not awaken in the morning, her memory would live on in the next generations.

Jews in fact have very little interest in their own ultimate destination. This life is much more important than the next. As an inquisitive child at Cheder, my Hebrew classes, I was always asking the rabbi what happened to us when we died.

"Forget this little obsession with the hereafter, Malchah, and concentrate instead on your irregular verbs."

"But . . ."

"No buts, this life is what matters." Tugging at his beard. "Do you want a diploma in Hebrew, or not?"

I didn't. But hadn't the heart to tell him. He thought it such an achievement – for a girl. I would much rather have discussed the theological intricacies of immortality. Which was why, when I read them for the first time, the words of Jesus, "In my Father's house are many mansions. I'm going to prepare one for you," hit me with such devastating effect. No rabbi had ever spoken to me confidently about an after-life before. And what a relief it was to have my instincts confirmed. More than that, unlike my Hebrew teachers, Jesus told me how to ensure a place, and it was extraordinarily, almost foolishly simple. My teachers spoke to me of the mitzvot I needed to perform, the good deeds which would go into the scales to balance out my debits, hopefully swinging them in my favour. I knew what I was like inside, and wasn't so sure that the scales wouldn't condemn me to an eternity in some black and boiling cauldron, stoked by demons over an open fire, as in a medieval painting. Jesus said, "Trust me and follow me." That seemed pretty straightforward by comparison. With hindsight, I'm not so sure that following him is the easy option, but at least I can trust him to take responsibility for the debits.

In fact many Jews criticise Christians for what they see as their unhealthy absorption with the next life. Westerners do tend to define spirituality, in the old Greek, philosophical tradition, as a kind of rarefied, other-worldly, piety.

But why be miserable now, says Jewish thinking, waiting for the fun to come? And it is possible for Christians to so concentrate on the pain, the suffering, and the sacrifice of being a disciple, that they miss the richness of the here and now. Many saints have shown me how to live. Few have shown me how to die. And it does seem as if those who have enjoyed life the most, die the best.

That struck me forcibly when Frank Lake, the founder of Clinical Theology, a form of Christian psychotherapy, came to deliver his farewell lecture at the college where Peter was a student of theology. Everyone wonders how they will feel as they confront the final enemy. What is it like to be terminally ill? This man did more than any I have ever met to allay my fears. He said that he had come to terms with having cancer and, with the pain under control, was not afraid of dying. On the contrary, how could he, who had spent his life delivering others from their feelings of guilt, have anything but joyous anticipation, when he was about to meet the God he loved so dearly face to face. He went home, put all his affairs in order, finished the book he was writing and laid down his pen, summoned his family and friends, so that he could say goodbye, and died peacefully.

"It's a lovely road you'll travel home on," he said to one of his favourite colleagues as she was leaving.

Thinking he was making some profound theological observation on the Christian life, she made the appropriate spiritual-sounding noises in response.

"No, I mean the road back to Nottingham," he chortled. "Wonderful countryside."

"Trust him to make me laugh," she said, "even at the end. I laughed all the way home, and it certainly eased the pain of parting."

It took me a long time to realise that another reason why Jews spend so little time thinking about the next life is that they have little concept of hell. Theoretically, the soul can still be punished for sins committed in this life, and the living, by prayer and charity, can atone for the dead, but there is no such thing as eternal damnation, so graphically etched on the visual memory of the Christian West by the terrifying medieval paintings in art and history books, galleries and churches. The body will rise, and will eventually enjoy a rather glorified extension of what we have now, in a land flowing with smoked salmon and chicken soup. Which is why wealthy Jews like Robert Maxwell are buried at the foot of the Mount of Olives, so that they can be first to meet the Messiah when he comes, of course.

I remember being very impressed with Catherine Marshall's account of how, after her husband's death, in her immense grief, she had asked God to show her where he was. And she saw him in a dream, in a garden, tending the roses he had always loved so much. I told my mother about it. I thought it would comfort her after Pop died to know that in heaven we would do what we had always enjoyed in life.

"So when I arrive the Almighty will put a duster in my hand," she said.

The point seemed to have been lost somewhere.

The Jewish community in fact copes well with bereavement. Not only do they have a sense of continuity when the name of the deceased is given to a new baby, and that baby, if a male, grows up to read his deceased ancestor's portion of the law in the synagogue; not only do they recall the deeds of the dead, for good and ill, at every available opportunity; they also have a code of practice surrounding mourning so complicated that there's barely time to grieve.

"What do we do now?" we all asked my brother repeatedly after my father died. "Can we eat this? Wear that? Watch the television? Speak now?"

"Don't ask me," he said. "Look it up."

So we did, in a weighty tome called *Rules for Mourners*. It made wonderfully soporific bedtime reading.

We discovered that between the death and the funeral we were not allowed to eat meat or drink wine. We also found old pullovers to wear so that we could make a cut, about four inches long, in them, on the right for a spouse, on the left for a parent. Suddenly, all the stories I had read in the Old Testament about rending clothes in grief came alive. It was a distinctly odd sensation to walk around for a week with part of my jumper hanging in shreds. It marks you out. It makes you feel conspicuous. It is a powerful external symbol of the tearing sensation inside, which bereavement undoubtedly is. The world sees your pain. You don't need to explain your tears. And that is an immense relief.

For seven days, known as shiva (the Hebrew word for seven), we were to stay at home, while the community came to us, to mourn with us, and, twice a day, to pray with us. An official prayer meeting requires a minyan, ten men. That was no problem in the evening when the house was packed with people. But in the morning, when the men were at work, my poor brother despaired, and rang round the community, begging and borrowing spare men, to ensure that prayers could be said. It puts a new perspective on Jesus' words, "Where two or three are gathered together, there am I in the midst."

"Forget the ten men," he said, in effect. "Simply do it."

But it was a strangely comforting experience to hear the sound of those hauntingly sad, yet beautiful, words, which begin the prayer of remembrance, rising softly up the stairs to my room, as I got up each morning. *"Yiskedal v'yiskadosh shemay rabah."* May the great name of the Lord be blessed. Amen and amen. It is a wonderful song of praise and trust, transcending all pain and sorrow, one of the most familiar prayers of the Jewish people, and one which always has the power to bring a lump to my throat, because of its many wistful associations. Singing it at every shiva provides the opportunity to let down the barriers which normally hold human beings apart, enabling them to weep together and identify with each other in the common experience of loss and bewilderment.

It has an almost reflex action. It is a necessary trigger, which says, "Permission granted to cry now – even to the men."

Throughout the day we sat on low stools and received our visitors, who arrived, laden with food. The bereaved must not shop or cook. The community takes care of them. Our fridge bulged with every imaginable delicacy from fresh salmon and gefüllte fish, to strudel and chocolate cake. One could feast on the fat of the land, if only one had an appetite. It amused me to see my mother's non-Jewish friends arriving with flowers, while her Jewish friends humped in vast tureens of chicken soup. It seemed to symbolise a major difference between the two cultures.

Because, in fact, sitting there on our low stools, waiting to be served, we were reduced to a kind of childish dependency on others, and bereavement is the one time in our lives when that is not only acceptable, but necessary. When a loved one dies the body seems to produce its own instant anaesthetic. The faster the numbness wears off, the sooner the real grieving process can begin, and all the Jewish rituals are designed to create the kind of environment in which that can happen. Helplessness means resting in the loving support of others. It means having time and space to attend to the inner life, without the usual physical distractions. Small children are taken off for the day to play, so that their parents have a little calm and quiet. Much as I loved my children, much as I needed the sound of their laughter and play, a wonderful symbol of new life in death, yet I also needed a chance to mourn, and valued the tranquillity I was given.

But I also valued company. The visitors who sat came and sat quietly, holding my mother's hand. Those who reminisced about my father, what a character he had been, made us laugh, telling tales of him we had never heard before. Even those who rattled on about their own problems, distracted us for a few, brief moments. For life goes on.

But we in the Christianised West, with all our apparent belief in the after-life, do not, on the whole, cope with death well. My sister-in-law was horrified when a non-Jewish colleague of hers, a fellow teacher, returned to work the day after her mother's death.

"I must take my mind off things," she said by way of explanation.

"Must you?" asked my sister-in-law. "Don't you need time to grieve?"

"Oh no, keep busy, that's by far the best way."

"It strikes me as a very dangerous way," my sister-in-law said to me afterwards. "Her grief is bound to catch up with her one day. That's where, I suppose, the rules and regulations work for us."

The problem is that unlike the Jews who go into automatic pilot, we don't know how to handle bereavement. We don't know what to do or say, so we stay away from the bereaved, and justify it by telling ourselves that they need to be left in peace, when perhaps what they really need is friendship, someone to sit with them or hold them. They might, heaven forbid, want to chat about their memories of the loved one. They might, even worse, begin to cry. And then what would we do? We are embarrassed about what are seen as negative emotions, so instead of facilitating them, press them down or button them up. And end up colluding in spinning a web of silence around those who so badly need to talk. We force them, and ourselves, into a kind of stoical, dry-eyed acceptance, which may not in fact be the healthiest way of dealing with the situation.

We have formalisation, not ritual, undertakers who take over and insist that a coffin must be carried by total strangers, not the family, for they alone know how to shoulder it properly. So four po-faced professionals in black, expressions fixed by habit and expectation to fit the sobriety of the occasion, though what they have to mourn about nobody knows, process down the aisle with precious Aunty Gladys. The family walk behind, exposed, conspicuous, on show. Will they or won't they lose control? We all hope they won't.

Who said a coffin had to be shouldered? In a rather disorderly, but comforting mob, we rolled Dad up to the grave on a trolley, lowered him down, then relatives took it in turns to take up the spade and shovel the earth over him. It was all very normal and natural. Until one of my great-uncles tried to drag the shovel out of my husband's hands – because he wasn't Jewish. Bigotry has a way of disrupting the most sacred circumstances.

Occasionally, a solitary individual finds the courage to break through the straitjacket of formality. We heard, when Peter was at theological college, of one minister who took the funeral of a young man who had died in a car crash. His distraught young widow came out from her pew during the service, and crawled beneath the coffin, where she sat, alone, sobbing. No one moved. No one knew what to do. With great courage, the minister went and sat next to her, and conducted the entire service, holding her hand, from beneath the coffin. I have always thought, in the same circumstances, that is exactly what Jesus would have done. After all he halted a funeral procession so that he could comfort a woman who had lost her only child. He more than anyone knew what it meant to follow his instinct, reject convention, risk his reputation, so that compassion could dictate the norm.

KADDISH

(The most famous of all Jewish prayers, recited on every Sabbath and festival, and when a memorial candle is lit. The words have brought me immense comfort in times of bereavement. The bereaved lead the prayers when they are said communally.)

Leader: May the great name of the Lord be magnified
and hallowed
throughout the world which He made
according to His will.

the world which He will one day make anew,
where the dead will be revived and raised to
eternal life.
May He establish His kingdom soon and
reign in glory,
even during our lifetime, and the lifetime of the
House of Israel.

Response: Amen. May His great name be praised for
ever, and to all eternity.

Leader: Glorified, praised, exalted, honoured and
magnified be the Name of the Holy One,
blessed be He,
though He is far above all the hymns and
praises human beings can offer.

Response: Amen. May the name of the Lord be blessed
from this time forth and for evermore.

Leader: May He grant us heavenly peace and
abundant life.

Response: Amen. My help is from the Lord who made
heaven and earth.

Leader: May the great Name of the Lord be
magnified and hallowed
throughout the world which he made
according to His will.
May He establish His kingdom soon,
and reign in glory, even during our
lifetime.

Response: Amen. May the name of the Lord be blessed
for ever and ever.

Leader: May comfort, healing, sustenance and
deliverance be granted to all of us, and to
Israel.

Response: Amen. May He who ordains peace in heaven, grant us His peace.

PRAYER AT A GRAVESIDE

(You may also like to leave an arrangement of small, polished stones or pebbles, depicting your grief.)

In the peace and tranquillity of this sacred place I think of the one I loved so dearly, and remember with thankfulness how his/her life enriched me, what blessings he/she brought me. How precious the thought of him/her is. And I miss him/her as much as ever as the days go by.

Help me, O God, to be worthy of my cherished memories, to live this short life of mine, numbering my days, to be better, nobler, more caring, sensitive, purer in my motives.

Teach me the real meaning of life. Help me to realise daily that goodness is not in vain, and that death is not the end. So will I, like my dear one, one day rest in your everlasting love.

As the heavens are high above the earth, so are your ways beyond human understanding. So also does your immense love extend as a protective canopy over all your children. In your presence is my light, my comfort and my peace. Amen.

4

Oy Veh, it's Yom Kippur

There is nothing many Jewish people enjoy more than a really good moan. Weeping, wailing and gnashing the teeth is a way of life. My Mama's a professional. She gets upset when there's nothing to moan about. She knows just how therapeutic it is. Which is why, of course, the All-Merciful inspired someone to invent the telephone. But when groaning is compulsory, as it is on Yom Kippur, the Day of Atonement, that's another matter. "Happy New Year," say the Rosh Hashanah greeting cards. "And well over the Fast," they add ominously, as if Yom Kippur was a two-week, not a twenty-four-hour, fast, as if it was a feat of endurance risking life and limb, rather than a temporary inconvenience for the stomach.

For every adult over the age of thirteen Yom Kippur is a total fast, not only from food (watch out for the interesting orchestration of gut and wind instruments), from washing and bathing (have your air freshener handy throughout the day), shaving (the men in the synagogue look like a gathering of escaped convicts in bowler hats), sex (no one can check up on you), and wearing leather (thank heavens for plastic). In the time of Jesus, people used to rub themselves with olive oil after their bath, a slightly greasier and smellier version of the moisturiser. Presumably, most of the time, everyone knew who had, or had not had, a bath each day by the distinctive smell and shine. No odour, no shine and they were fasting.

Jesus told the Pharisees to counter tradition and have their usual aromatherapy when they were fasting, even without the bath. That way, no one could guess that's what they were doing. Displays of piety get up the nose far more than the smell of body lotion.

Today it is still the men who make the biggest meal of the occasion. By about three o'clock in the afternoon, having spent the entire day in the synagogue, my maternal grandmother, a tiny bird of a woman, and then in her seventies, used to whisper that she was gasping for a cuppa, or better still, a ciggy or a whisky, but she stood stalwartly in her pew in the gallery, prayer book in hand, watching with undisguised disdain as some six-foot giant below, overcome by hunger pangs and the heat, crumpled in a heap and was manhandled out into the fresh air.

Despite these interesting little distractions the occasion never lost its sense of solemnity for me. The most important annual event in the whole of Judaism, it is the culmination of the "Days of Awe" and self-examination, an opportunity for the entire community to come together to confess its sins, to ask God for his mercy and forgiveness, and to resolve to do better in future. The reading of the story of Jonah, who, when he repented and faced up to his responsibilities, became the vehicle for an entire nation to give up its corruption and injustice, underlines individual collusion in national culpability. My failures taint everyone else, my family, community, nation. On Kol Nidrei, the Eve of Yom Kippur, if I have hurt someone, I must obtain their forgiveness, and make reparation before the service begins, or I cannot expect God to forgive me. When Jesus taught his disciples to pray, "Forgive us as we forgive those who sin against us," it was not a radically new notion, except that releasing others from our bitterness now became an ongoing, not an annual, necessity.

Anyone who has ever been in the synagogue on Kol Nidrei finds it an unforgettable experience. Max Bruch, the composer, and there is some doubt that he was actually Jewish, was inspired by its haunting, wistful chants to write one of his most beautiful pieces of music. The minister stands on the platform, his hands held high by two leading members of the congregation, like Moses, whose arms were supported by Aaron and Hur, when he prayed for the children of Israel in their battle against the Amalekites, like the High Priest of old in the Temple, interceding for the people. Quietly and reverently he begins to sing.

He reminds the congregation that tonight, everyone is equal. It is futile to take a surreptitious glance at your neighbour and think that he or she is a greater sinner than you. Your own pride and gloating needs attention. When the High Priest brought incense into the Holy of Holies, mixed with the sweet spices was a foul-smelling herb called galbanum. It symbolised the presence of certain well-known sinners in the congregation. They were to be welcomed, for the greater the sinner, the greater the potential repentance. A vivid picture, and was it there in Jesus' mind the night that Mary Magdalene poured perfume over his feet, and he had to remind his host that "He who is forgiven little, only has a little love to give"? And what of certain parables, of wheat and tares, sheep and goats?

Kol Nidrei means "the annulment of vows". Now everyone is released from those unwise promises so rashly and easily made, and the minister's voice, barely a whisper, as if in awe of the presence of the King, gradually rises to a crescendo. The congregation join in as the realisation grows that the King of the universe is also a merciful and forgiving father, granting release from all the mess and damage of human stupidity. Suddenly the chanting stops. For once there is silence in the synagogue. What is there left to say? Everyone goes home to bed, ready and prepared for the marathon to follow.

The Yom Kippur service takes all day so there is no time to eat anyway. Many of the prayers of confession are exactly as they were when the Temple was standing. My favourite moment came late in the afternoon, when all the men covered their heads with their prayer shawls and began to chant and sway, so that all I could see beneath me was a shimmering sea of white and silver. This is the moment when the minister utters the tetragrammaton, JHWH, the mystical name of God, who alone has the power to forgive sins. In the days of the Temple only the priest was initiated into the secret pronunciation. Which is why Jesus' contemporaries were so shocked to hear him use it so freely. How did he know how to pronounce it, let alone have the nerve to say it? Some whispered that this was the secret of his magical powers, his ability to perform miracles. That he took for himself the same rights and privileges as a High Priest, there is no doubt.

"Yom Kippur" means "Day of Covering", from the Hebrew verb "kapper", "to cover". The same word is used for a skull cap. Gruesome though it may seem to our refined sensibilities today, the Bible says that human failure to live up to God's laws is covered only by the blood of sacrifice. The Talmud repeats, "There is no atonement without blood." In the time of the Temple two goats were sacrificed. One, the "Azazel" or scapegoat, carrying the sins of the people, was taken out into the desert and pushed backwards over a cliff. The other was killed in the Temple. The High Priest then sprinkled its blood before the Ark in the Holy of Holies, as he interceded for the people.

On the whole there are no longer blood sacrifices in Judaism. There is a hint of it, however, in a ceremony known as Kapparoth, or "atoning sacrifices", which some Orthodox Jews perform at home. First, the celebrant must lay his or her hands on a rooster for a male, a hen for a female. This is easier said than done, as anyone who has ever had cause to chase a chicken will know. Once, when we were on holiday on a farm in France, my son was asked to put the chickens to bed in their shed. All he had to do, said the owner, was do as he did, shout, "Here chicks", shake a bucketful of grain, and they would all run after him. Joel followed the instructions, and they all ran in fifty different directions, squawking. It took the whole family more than an hour, chasing them in ever-dizzying circles, shouting, "Stupid chickens", to round them all up.

Once you have the aforementioned fowl firmly by the legs, the aim of the exercise is to wave it round and round your head, shouting, "This is my substitute. The bird will die. And I will live a long and happy life," always hoping of course that there are no Animal Rights supporters leaning over the garden fence.

Most Jews would find the idea a little barbaric. They believe that the day itself is enough to ensure complete forgiveness. The letter to the Hebrew Christians in the New Testament, however, says that the temple rituals would never become obsolete. They were simply superseded. When Christ, the High Priest, interceding for the people, also laid down his life he became the Azalel, the once-and-for-all, everlasting scapegoat.

One might be tempted to imagine that because the Jews now have no Azalel, that they are more troubled by guilt than the average Christian. This is not always the case. There can be immense stress in being a Christian. "Be perfect as your heavenly father is perfect." "Love your neighbour as yourself." "Do good to all men." And haven't I, like so many others, tried to be a holy, loving, self-negating Christian? And ended up a miserable failure, a crumpled heap of despair? Many Roman Catholics have recorded their struggle to be free from the burden of childhood guilt. Evangelicals, similarly, often find it hard to reject the temptation to follow a set of rules and regulations as rigid as the Talmud. We have to grab by the throat the freedom our Azalel bought us. For the joy of absolute forgiveness is so easily snatched from us by our oh-so-human need to submit to our own little systems and ideologies.

While Christians are living up to their own aspirations, Jews have to live up to the expectations of their relatives. Hard to know which is the greater affliction. But on the whole relatives are kinder – if only marginally. Judaism is more humanistic than Christianity. And this is where, more than in any other aspect, the two part company. Christianity says that humanity is flawed and doomed inevitably to fail. Jews believe that human beings are essentially good, made in the image of God, but being frail, are prone to fail. They commit "sins", not "sin". Life is a kind of a ladder. A "mitzvah", a good deed, sends a person up a rung or two, an evil deed back down again. But there are no snakes to interfere with the game. This may well be why the Jewish people have produced so many Nobel prize winners, out of all proportion with their numbers. Success is a natural expectation, not a snare to be avoided. Judaism is basically optimistic. I had an aunt who used to take hold of me by the chin every time she saw me, and submitting my face to close scrutiny, say, "Greatly improved." The greatest back-handed compliment of all time.

But if human beings are essentially good, Jesus is only a few rungs up the ladder of perfection. At Yom Kippur, even they who stand on the bottom rung can get a fresh foothold, higher up. So he is only what we could all potentially be. This somewhat destroys the Christian doctrine of the Incarnation. And gets round the lack of animal sacrifice. But it does make explaining a Hitler rather difficult.

My brother felt some years ago that his knowledge of his faith was shamefully scant. He decided to take part in a teaching programme set up by the more Orthodox Jews of Gateshead, seriously concerned for their more worldly, law-breaking brethren on the other side of the River Tyne.

"What sort of things are they teaching you?" I asked him.

"I'm learning about mitzvot, good deeds," he said, "which make me a better Jew."

I said that since my good deeds were somewhat erratic, I thought it was an altogether happier arrangement to receive the forgiveness Christ had bought for us on the cross. Belief versus behave, but belief was simpler, surely?

"What a cop-out," he replied. "Trust Christians to want the soft option. Keeping the law requires effort."

"And do you keep it?" I asked him. "I can't say I've noticed a radical change."

"Ah," he said, thoughtfully, "ah. Well. Not exactly. But my teacher says that for me, it's a mitzvah just to know what I should do . . ."

"Even if you don't do it?"

He nodded, a little sheepishly, and I thought I could almost see the cogs turning in that great computer in the brain, registering, "Really must try harder in future."

"Now that," I said to him, "sounds to me like the ultimate cop-out."

Getting round the legal requirements of Judaism is a favourite Jewish game.

"They're a funny lot," said one cleaner to another, when she was describing the joys of working in a Jewish household. "They have one festival when they eat in the dining-room and smoke in the bathroom. And another when they smoke in the dining-room and eat in the bathroom. And then they have this especially holy one when they eat and smoke in the bathroom."

The latter, of course, is Yom Kippur.

A friend told me how she was staying in a Jewish home in New York one Yom Kippur.

"Please excuse me but I won't be eating with you," said her host, "but the refrigerator is full. Help yourself to whatever you want."

So she went to make herself a meal, and could hardly believe her eyes when she found the fridge full of pork, and other strictly non-kosher delicacies.

"Excuse my asking," she said, "but I don't understand why the fridge is full of pork."

"Listen," her host replied, "what do you want of me? I'm a good Jew once a year. Isn't that enough?"

Potentially it is a wonderfully liberating, purging experience to have a grand, communal, public confession every now and again. We in the West no longer live simply with the weight of our own failures on our shoulders. The media has ensured that we are sated every day with the injustices of our world. Poverty, war, exploitation, rape, pillage and plunder assault our minds almost before we have had the time to digest our first cup of coffee in the morning. My husband is a real saint. He not only brings me coffee in bed. He then reheats it in the microwave, when the Sleeping Beauty who shares his bed has failed to respond to his first efforts to awaken her. And by the time he has made two trips to the kitchen the radio has alerted him to all the worst news of the day. In fact, we have a "no discuss" and "no moan" policy operating until after breakfast, or the chances are I wouldn't get up at all.

What do we do with our outrage, our anger, our profound sense of indignation, sadness and helplessness at the sort of world in which we live, and will, one day, bequeath to our children? What do we do with our own collusion in creating it? I can of course absolve myself from all responsibility, pass the blame off elsewhere, and sue! That is one aspect of our increasingly litigious society, and the principle of passing the buck seems to start quite young.

My little Abby, at eight, in the way children do, sometimes had the insights of an eighty-year-old. She greeted me in a state of high excitement one day when I came in from work. Had I heard about the accident at school?

I hadn't.

"Well," she said and launched into her story with relish.

I half listened, while the other half of me planned the tea.

Apparently her friend Sarah had been propelling herself around the playground like a miniature torpedo, when along came Mark Higginbotham playing at torpedoes in the opposite direction. Their heads met and Helena, who had witnessed the disaster, had rushed across the playground to tell Abby and her friend Samantha that

Sarah was pouring blood from an enormous gash across one eyebrow.

"Hmmph," Samantha had said, "don't bother telling me, she's not my friend any more."

Abby was shocked at her friend's callousness, until Samantha's face crumpled and the little girl broke into an enormous howl.

"Whatever's the matter?" Abby asked.

"It's all my fault for breaking friends with Sarah. If she'd been my friend she'd have been playing here with me."

At that point Helena burst into tears too. "No, it's my fault. I persuaded her to play torpedoes."

They were quickly joined by several other little girls who all began to cry as well, saying it was their fault. No it wasn't, it was Samantha's fault. No, it was Helena's fault. Then they all agreed it was Mark Higginbotham's fault, since he was a boy, and felt much better.

Abby rattled on. "I didn't cry," she said, proudly, "I said, 'What a nonsense!'"

It was that point that she suddenly had my full attention.

"What did you say?" I asked her.

She repeated confidently, "I said, 'What a nonsense!' Well, it was no one's fault, was it? Except theirs. It's silly to blame other people all the time."

Abby was right. We begin with a massive sense of guilt, which becomes too uncomfortable to carry, then look for somewhere suitable to dump it. Usually on someone else's unsuspecting shoulders. And it is a nonsense. Human beings make grossly inadequate scapegoats. We simply crush each other.

Acknowledging our own failures is so much easier when we all do it together. Which is why I often long for a Christian equivalent of Yom Kippur, a chance to clear the air. For without ritual what do we do with our guilt and self-doubt, our creaking relationships and our profound disappointment with government and nation?

Most churches have a weekly "General Confession". But it doesn't always seem to be enough. The words roll over us before we can capture and absorb them.

There is a Christian tradition of times of penitence, largely in the more Catholic wing of the Church, but far from exclusively so, at Lent, and to a certain extent, in Advent. But while the Jews, in their Days of Awe, look for what they can positively do, some Christians look for what they can give up. And this highlights one essential difference between the two. Putting relationships right benefits the community. Mortifying the poor old body benefits the individual. The Jewish attitude to penitence, and in fact to religion in general, is corporate and communal, the Christian attitude tends to be private and personal. There's nothing wrong with giving up sweets for Lent, as long as it isn't a substitute for treating the family with consideration. Real fasting, said the prophet Isaiah, is about actively fighting injustice, caring for the poor, behaving with integrity.

Though not as popular among Christians as it used to be, fasting from food can be a useful tool. It says, "I'm so sorry that I don't even want to eat." The Jews believe that as the body is purged of its poisons, the spirit is symbolically cleansed of waste matter. Also, our spiritual life, often pushed into second place by the clamouring of eyes, mouth and stomach, can now receive our full attention. No planning, shopping, cooking or washing up. There is so much free time in the day when we don't have to worry about what to eat.

As a teenager I faced the opportunity with the same dread and stoicism as the rest of the community. No one ever explained why we did it. I felt cold and shivery and listless. I couldn't wait for that heavenly moment, when the Rabbi gave one long blast on the shofar, to say that God had forgiven his people, and the Great Book, opened at Rosh Hashanah, was finally sealed. We all rushed home, downed a glass of milk and soda water to settle our insides, and subjected our stomachs to a massive assault.

Strange, but now that I have experienced the usefulness of fasting, the strange way it seems to sharpen and clarify so many spiritual perceptions and sensations, I wish I had the guts to do it more often. Perhaps it should, at the very least, become an annual discipline.

Richard Foster in his classic book on spirituality, *Celebration of Discipline,* calls fasting a great "Christian tradition", and lists the "Christians" who fasted. In fact his "Christians" were all Jews. Fasting is a great Jewish tradition, and it does seem appropriate that a people who so exalt the joys of eating, introducing cheesecake, blintzes, poppy-seed bread and pastrami to the nation, should also know the value of abstention.

5

So, Who's Doing the Catering?

You don't really miss it, until you have to do without it. Then suddenly you would even be thankful for the bits you normally cut off and leave on the side of your plate. For me, cauliflower stalks and turnip. Why is it always the humble vegetable which suffers from a lack of appreciation? Not when food is scarce. "Oh the leeks, the onions and the garlic we enjoyed when we were back in Egypt," wailed my ancestors in the wilderness. They must have smelled wonderful in what they now looked back to, in their deprived state, as the good old days! Imagine wanting to give up your freedom for a bowl of vichyssoise and a garlic dip? But I suppose manna stew, mannaburgers and mannapudding become rather limited in their appeal after a while. Even manna fries, and manna lasagne soon lost their charm for a nation sated with the luxury of variety of flavour and taste, who had forgotten that most people survived, as they do now in the Third World, with one basic commodity as their staple diet.

Every night they hallucinated, not only about the onions and garlic, but about a land which flowed with milk and honey. No doubt the milk and honey would have given the manna porridge a more authentic Highland taste. It also fed and watered the dream which kept them going. And ever since those forty wilderness years, when manna sustained the body, and milk and honey sustained the soul, food has had great symbolic significance for the Jewish people.

Whereas most of us eat to live, occasionally stopping to savour what we're shoving down our long-suffering gullets, when we have the time, Jews live to eat. Food is a thrice-daily cause for celebration. And there is no celebration without food.

"You want meat?" the long-suffering Almighty asked his people, when they moaned about manna. "I'll give you meat!"

And it rained poultry from heaven. Which is how, presumably, the traditional Jewish love for chicken first began. My mother will swear to her dying day that no non-Jew can ever cook a chicken how it should be cooked.

"First, they don't kill it right. Then they don't clean it right. Then they don't stuff it right."

One of the greatest evils of the present age, she claims, is packet stuffing mix, "They call it stuffing? That minced-up cardboard has destroyed its reputation and ruined the traditional roast chicken dinner."

She could be right. Many of my friends tell me they don't like stuffing, until they eat my home-made variety, made the Jewish way.

Ultimately, says Mama, in a conspiratorial whisper, with great smacking of lips, "They don't cook it right. What the Goyim don't realise is that the skin is the best bit – and it must be dry and crispy, not greasy and slimy, so that it tastes as if the poor animal's spent its last days swimming like a fish in the sea, not trotting happily round a farmyard.

One of my earliest memories is of the crackling and spitting of the pan on the cooker as Mother rendered down chicken fat. Into the pan she placed not only the chopped-up fat, removed from the bird's entrance hole, but also any extraneous skin, cut into small pieces. They were fried in the liquefying substance, removed when cooked, drained on brown paper and served up as a special weekly delicacy called grebens. We fought over them, my brother and sister and I. They were much tastier, much crunchier, much more succulent than potato crisps.

Mama strained the liquid fat into a large jam jar and kept it in the fridge. Stuffing, boiled in a piece of the chicken's intestine, known as helzel, chopped liver pâté, kneidlach dumplings, every favourite Jewish delicacy was made with chicken fat or "schmaltz", which not only gave Jewish cuisine its distinctive flavour, but also lent a colourful new Yiddish word to the English (or rather American) language. It also, no doubt, warmed our arteries, providing them with the kind of cosy, furry lining which helped many a Jewish man on his premature way into the next life.

No tiniest bit of the chicken was ever wasted. My father's favourite Sabbath *hors d'oeuvre* was the boiled heart, stomach and neck. How he slurped and squelched his way through this particular delicacy, reserved only for him. And this was their second starring part. For they had already contributed towards the production of that indispensable feature of Jewish life: chicken soup.

Jews of the world were delighted to read a few years ago that scientists had discovered what they had known for centuries: that Jewish chicken soup is the best and only cure for the common cold. And virtually every other affliction which ails humankind! It released, said medical research, and this piece of information was not for the delicate or squeamish, any infected mucus which blocked the higher nasal passages. It drained the sinuses, cleared the head, allowed for a tasty, speedy recovery.

There's an old Jewish tale that a man collapses and dies at a large function. "Functions" and "affairs" incidentally are favourite Jewish words to describe those almost weekly, palatal orgies, celebrating births, barmitzvahs, graduations, wedding anniversaries, any event which merits a large, communal nosh-in and sharp elbows, to get anywhere near the table, let alone the smoked salmon.

"I hear Mrs Greenberg is having an affair," says one woman to another upstairs in the synagogue.

"Who's doing the catering?" asks the other.

You have to get your priorities right. Food, not sex, is always uppermost in the Jewish Mama's mind.

At this particular function where the man collapses and dies is a little old Jewish lady.

"Give 'im some chicken soup," she shouts from the back of the throng.

"Madam," says the young doctor who has been attempting resuscitation, "chicken soup won't help." To which the reply, "But it won't hurt either."

As a little girl I learned very quickly, to the detriment of my ever-expanding waistline, that food, as well as being the cure for all that ailed me, was the very *raison d'être* of those who prepared it. To refuse it was an insult of mammoth proportions, a personal rejection.

"What do you mean you're full?" my grandmother would ask of me, in a voice I had learned to dread. Being full was never a remote possibility. The word "full" did not exist in Gran's vocabulary, though she herself was a wiry little woman and anything but the conventional, well-rounded Jewish granny.

"I've stood here all day making this strudel for you. It's your favourite."

And I would smile a weak assent and endeavour to swallow another unwanted mouthful, while my mother, sitting opposite, would wail and lament my loss of a waistline.

"Can you never say no? You'll be lucky to get a man at all, with your figure."

I was caught, painfully, between two contradictory forces. And it was Gran, Mama's Mama, who always won, as we all knew she must. It was the way of things in our matriarchal society. My poor father, who had given up any attempt at protest about anything within minutes of his engagement to my mother, usually ended the evening in the bathroom, swallowing half a bottle of antacid.

Fortunately Gran was a wonderful cook and baker. No one else's Rosh Hashanah tzimmis could live up to hers.

Her Passover meringues and coconut pyramids melted their way down into the stomach. No supermarket doughnuts compared with those she served at Hanukkah, the Feast of Lights, when fried food commemorated the miracle of the holy oil which lasted eight days. Her spicy lokschen or noodle puddings, filling her entire bungalow with the enticing smell of cinnamon, honey and apples, the fat of the land of promise, filled our bellies and sent Grandpa soundly asleep on every other major festival. Each occasion had its own special food, reflecting the message it wanted to convey, and because we knew what to expect, my brother, sister and I looked forward to it with mouth-watering anticipation.

Gran's wish was our command, and so we ate until we could hardly get up from the table. But whenever we suggested that she tried eating some of the food she had so lovingly prepared she always declined.

"I'm packed," she said, and went on waiting on us. She was never just "full". And it was years later, after she died, weighing a mere thirty-five kilos, that the staff in the nursing home asked us when we had first realised that she was anorexic. It had never occurred to us that she was. We were shocked. But apparently she had lived on little other than Woodbines and double whiskies for years. Which explained why it was that in later life she so often wobbled her way around the bungalow and complained about her legs not being what they once were. She, as a girl, had succumbed to the same pressure that I faced, and dealt with it by gaining pleasure from feeding others, rather than herself.

"I was the most beautiful girl in the north-east," she used to say to us, "I had a wonderful figure."

"She was the most modest too," my brother used to whisper to me.

I was in my twenties before I sorted out my attitude to food and realised that I no longer needed it as a source of comfort or to supplement any affection I felt I lacked. That was part of the healing process of finding faith.

But I never quite overcame the notion that there was one way to a man's heart – through his stomach. That was far too deeply ingrained. And, of course, contained more than just an element of truth.

"We have no dowry for you," my mother lamented daily, when I reached my teens, surveying my cosy, dumpling shape with a sad shake of her head, "so you'll have to get by on your cooking."

So, like many Jewish daughters before me, I learnt the culinary secrets which are passed on from one generation to the next, the traditional fare which is centuries old and has travelled the world, absorbed from, and passed on wherever Jewish people have settled. At Passover they still make a sweetmeat of chopped dried apricots, a recipe acquired when they were slaves in Egypt. With the Jews no experience is ever wasted.

Legend has it that the art of Jewish cuisine began on the day that our great Mama, Rebecca, with a clever use of herbs and spices, managed to convince her husband that the insipid flesh of a young goat was really wild venison. If you can hoodwink a man that easily, said her descendants, you can get away with anything. "Taste with economy", says Evelyn Rose, the great doyenne of the kosher kitchen, and this has been the Jewish culinary motto ever since. Rebecca must have been quite a cook if one of her sons was prepared to sell his inheritance for a bowl of lentil soup!

Many of the more familiar dishes, like gefüllte fish, migrated from Eastern Europe with the masses who fled poverty and persecution at the end of the last century. Fish, on the Baltic coast, was plentiful and cheap. Mixing it with onions and breadcrumbs made it go further. Presumably chicken was the only meat and a luxury, which is how the tradition to squeeze as much out of the poor bird as its poor carcass will allow, first arose.

The Friday night soup ritual filled me with fascination. Mother would bind a leek, a parsnip and a carrot into a bundle and put them into the pressure cooker with the fowl, which was already immersed head-first in a grossly indecent pose – its last act of defiance. After a few moments the mixture would begin to bubble and brew and my job was to skim off the filthy scum which rose to the surface. How I ever managed to eat it later will remain for ever one of life's little mysteries. But we all did, chasing round our soup bowls the dozens of tiny matza-meal dumplings which bobbed up and down in it like unexploded sea missiles. It was followed by the traditional dish of cold fried fish and salad. The actual chicken reappeared at Sabbath lunch on Saturday, cold and in pieces, lacking a little *je ne sais quoi*, which was presumably in the soup. It was irrelevant that by the affluent sixties we no longer needed to live so frugally. The tradition of the soup which looked like dirty dish water and tasted better than fine old whisky had been far too long established.

More than tradition, I learned how to keep a kosher kitchen, to soak the meat in salt water to ensure that no blood was left in it, to make cheese sauces with water if they were accompanying meat. It is true that though they may seem strange to us now, the dietary laws imposed on the Jewish people so many centuries ago have a sound medical basis, and reveal an insight into hygiene unusual for its time. The pig is renowned for internal abscesses, worms, and other nutritional delights. Seafood, another taboo, for the humble prawn and lobster have no gills, is a major food-poisoning risk. Mixing milk and meat together, forbidden for it contravenes the command not to boil a kid in its mother's milk, may apparently cause digestive problems. God, it would appear, was as concerned about salmonella then as any government health department official today. And though now, in these hygienically enlightened days, I contravene most of the dietary laws, I cannot bring myself to eat animal blood for its own sake. But then, the dietary regulations were not simply imposed for hygienic reasons. They were intended to make human beings think before they eat, so that they partake thoughtfully and appreciatively, not simply to satisfy a basic need, like an animal. Though some would no doubt argue that I obviously haven't met their cat, or dog. But food was given a moral dimension, and blood was prohibited because of its symbolic value, rather than any nutritional hazard. It is a symbol of life. And life, for the Jew, is infinitely precious. It is all you have. Which is why the death of one Israeli soldier in the Middle East can cause a national outcry. So I give blood sausage a wide berth. But perhaps that is because I am so used to the way food acts as a symbol for me, releasing all kinds of unbidden associations and memories.

Only a few months ago I found myself in a restaurant automatically picking up the piece of parsley which so daintily decorated my plate. I played with it a while, swinging it to and fro between my thumb and index finger, and it was only when I popped it into my mouth and experienced that strange, almost bitter taste that I realised what I was doing, and the memory of so many Passovers, and the lambs' blood, daubed on the doorposts of the homes of the children of Israel, so that the Angel of Death would pass them by, suddenly came flooding back. For the parsley, dipped in salt water and passed from person to person, represents the sprigs of hyssop which were used as a paintbrush. And so I am transported back through the years of my own existence, and beyond, into the history of my ancestors and their experience of redemption.

The famous twentieth-century French novelist, Marcel Proust, who wrote a series of novels entitled *Remembrance of Things Past*, based his entire philosophy of life on just such an experience. As a younger man the swift passage of time, the inability to capture and hold on to any lovely moment, left him with feelings of desperation and hopelessness. Then one day, as he was drinking his tea, he took a sponge finger and dunked it in his mug. As the soggy biscuit touched his palate, his life was transformed. The smell, the taste, the feel of that sponge finger on his tongue, recalled one particularly precious event and enabled him to relive it as fully as he had the first time around.

I suspect that if eating could help us fully recapture our lost youth, we would drive the needle off the scales altogether. I would not base my *raison d'etre* upon it, but I can identify with Proust's sense of wistfulness and joy at inadvertently rediscovering moments which had long since vanished into the past. And food can provide a hinge. I often wonder whether, in the age of the freezer, mass-production and storage, when every food is plentiful all year round, and no food reserved for any one season or occasion, I haven't robbed my children of some important, and rather magical, sensations: the first raspberries of summer, autumn red cabbage cooked in brown sugar and wine vinegar, spicy winter sweet mince, stuffed into pies, spring new potatoes, dripping in butter, food with seasonal associations, recalling every previous autumn, winter, summer and spring, giving a sense of anticipation, the rhythm of life, and the faithfulness of God. Since we eat everything all year round, there are few special treats, reserved for certain festivals, reminding us of the stories and legends of our people, enhancing the occasion with their particular taste and smell. While the Jews reserve eating apples dipped in honey for Rosh Hashanah, deep-fried doughnuts for the Feast of Lights, the sweet, plaited loaf for Friday evenings when it becomes a reminder of the sweetness and the unity of Sabbath rest, few non-Jews appreciate the history and significance of the traditional food they eat, let alone value it as a spiritual aid.

But taste, touch and smell can stimulate God-consciousness, can stir up the warm, thankful feelings and associations which constitute a genuine thanksgiving, rather than the forced, ritualised "Grace" many of us feel constrained to say at every meal. We are all terribly conscious at last that what we put into our bodies affects the quality of our physical lives. In Jewish thought there is no distinction between the physical and the spiritual, so food feeds the spiritual life too. When I was a student, Mother was concerned that I should take "home" with me into a new term, so I was the only member of the campus to arrive back after the vacation with a potful of chopped liver and chopped herring. There were no fridges in our rooms, so I hung my precious trophies on ropes from my window, and prayed for cold weather. That first week back I was always inundated with visitors, especially from the Christian Union, who had never seen herring in that disguise before and regarded it as one of the wonders of the world. Whenever the hordes called, the pots were towed into the room on their pulley systems, and placed in the centre of the floor, with two knives and a box of cracker biscuits. Everyone dug in together and those first gatherings of a new term were turned into a special occasion. Who knew what lay ahead in the weeks to come? What joys or trauma were reflected in the sweet and sour of the herring, the differing ingredients chopped up together with the chicken liver? But whatever befell, we faced it together.

Any food, no matter how despised, from the humble burger to a boiled egg, can become a symbol, as the Apostle Peter discovered the day he thought his hunger pangs were causing him to hallucinate. He stood on the roof of a house near Joppa, just before lunch, the smell of food wafting up towards him, and as his taste buds started to ooze, he watched a sheet being lowered from heaven, full of non-kosher food.

"Help yourself," said a voice.

Refusing was almost more than he could bear, but he couldn't bring himself to do it.

"Who are you to call treif, what God has called kosher?" asked a voice.

Three times the vision was repeated, and while Peter was puzzling over its meaning, three men called and asked him to accompany them to the house of a Gentile, who wanted to hear about this new "Way" he had been preaching all over Jerusalem. Suddenly the vision made sense. Food taught one church leader a vital lesson, that all people, whether Jew or Gentile, were equal in God's eyes.

My favourite story of how food can become a symbol concerns Mrs Lack's cake. It was a tale I came across in David Michell's account of his boyhood experiences during the Second World War. Michell, the son of missionary parents, was born in China. In 1942, when he was only eight years old, the Japanese invaded the China Inland Mission School he was attending at Chefoo in north-east China, and interred all the staff and pupils in the Weihsien concentration camp. The children were separated from their parents for several years, and the teachers did their best, in almost intolerable conditions, to shield them from the worst of the misery, and create for them as normal and as bearable an environment as possible.

One day two of the teachers announced that they were getting married. There was little cause for celebration in the camp, and Beatrice Lack, the school cook, recognising the importance of the occasion, decided to make a wedding cake. The effort, recorded in her diary, is an extraordinary tribute to the unquenchability and ingenuity of the human spirit under extreme pressure. "We made up our minds," she wrote, "that as the cake was about all we could give, we would give our best." She collected the ingredients wherever she could find them, and improvised when she couldn't: slivers of apricot stones for almonds, grated bits of orange and pumelo skin, some nearly two years old, to provide the flavour, a few real sultanas from Red Cross parcels, a little dripping scavenged from one of the kitchens, oddments of spice and cinnamon, and lots of Chinese dates to make the mixture sweet. The baking took five hours in a kerosene tin oven. The decoration, a Gothic arch, was made out of a strip of a milk tin, and covered with white tape and artificial lily-of-the-valley, worn for five summers on a dress.

The children enjoyed that cake in a way they had never

enjoyed any cake ever before. It became a symbol of joy
in the midst of misery, triumph in adversity, hope in
despair, the light of God penetrating the darkest hell. And
no doubt, in the years to come, they would never again
eat a piece of wedding cake without remembering.

The best lessons about food are often learned through
hunger and deprivation, another reason why fasting has
its place. To help us appreciate one major, daily blessing. After all, God could have designed it otherwise.
Sustaining the body did not have to be a pleasurable
experience as well. It could have been achieved by
osmosis, and watching some people shovelling down
their grub, half gaga in front of the television set,
I'm tempted to wonder whether it isn't. But the right
food, served and eaten thoughtfully, in good company,
can turn a simple meal into an occasion, an occasion
into an act of worship, worship into a communal
celebration. The Jews recognise that fact every week
when the family gathers together for a Sabbath meal.
The bread, broken and shared out, represents the labour
of man's hands, the cup of wine, passed around the table,
represents rest and rejoicing. They look appetising, smell
wonderful, taste good, and are unforgettable. Is it simply
coincidental that the two most important symbols of the
Christian faith are taken orally?

GRACE AFTER MEALS

Grace begins with a reading of Psalm 126.

> Blessed are You, O Lord our God, King of the
> Universe,
> who feeds the whole world with goodness and grace,
> Thank You for all You have given us.
> For mercy and relief,
> deliverance and prosperity,
> consolation and support,
> life and peace,

For dealing kindly with us so that we have never been hungry.

Let us never take Your generosity for granted,
But always be dependent on Your hand alone.
May this table remain well supplied with food and drink,
May it be a source of blessing like that of our father, Abraham, and our mother, Sarah.
Let the hungry come and find food and comfort.
May the Lord bless this family and their home.

SOME JEWISH SPECIALITIES

CHICKEN SOUP

Make at least one day before serving, because the flavour is better on the second day.

1 boiling fowl, including giblets (or cheat by using giblets, feet, wings and 2 stock cubes)
3 pints of water
1 whole onion
2 carrots, peeled
3 celery stalks
1 whole leek
1 whole parsnip
salt, pepper

Put the bird, salt and pepper into a large soup pan. Cover with the water and bring to the boil. Uncover and remove any froth with a spoon. Add all the remaining ingredients and simmer for at least three hours. Remove the bird and the vegetables and refrigerate the soup overnight. (The chicken can now be removed from the bone, eaten cold with salad, or served with a sauce. Discard the vegetables, except the carrot.) The next day remove any fat and reheat the soup, adding a few fine egg noodles if desired, and the carrot, chopped into small pieces. Strengthen with an extra stock cube if desired.

CHOPPED LIVER

Originally invented as a way of using up the giblets used for the chicken soup to make a cheap and tasty starter to the Sabbath meal. Serves 6.

200g grilled chicken livers (or the liver used in the soup, if sufficient)
1 medium onion
2 hard-boiled eggs
2 tbsp. margarine (a substitute for chicken fat!)
salt, pepper

Fry the onion in the fat until golden, then add the other ingredients, put through a mincer, and mix until well blended.

LOKSCHEN PUDDING

I tease my friends that you can only make this scrumptious, lethargy-inducing pudding when the "lokschen" is in season. But lokschen is simply the Yiddish word for "noodle". So use any kind of ribbon noodles you prefer. It can be cooked for several hours, or even overnight, without spoiling it in any way. Serves 6.

100g ribbon egg noodles, boiled until tender, then sieved
1 egg, whisked
50g sugar
25g melted margarine
2 tbsp. currants
grated rind of ½ a lemon
½ tsp. cinnamon
pinch of salt
to line the bottom of a greased bowl: chopped apples, covered with a layer of golden syrup or honey

Mix all the ingredients together and place on top of the apples. Cook for at least 45 minutes on gas mark 5, 375°F, 190°C, or preferably for much longer on a lower temperature. The pudding should be set on the inside, crisp on the outside.

6

Harvest

"We plough the fields and scatter." Except that very few of us do. Any child today could be forgiven for thinking that our food begins its life in the local supermarket. Few, in our urbanised existences, have the faintest idea of what is involved in sowing, ploughing or reaping. Yet we sing the old hymn as lustily as ever at every Harvest Festival, whether we live in the highest tower block of Manhattan or the centre of London, and present the fresh offerings of the earth, canned, frozen or commercially wrapped, at the altar.

My first experience of the mystery of Harvest was at the Church High School where I was a pupil. Strange idea, some have said to me subsequently, for a Jewish Mama to send her daughter to a Christian school. But education has always been high on the agenda of the Jewish community, in the miracles it can accomplish, second only to chicken soup. And if the Church could provide her daughter with the best possible education, then we would take what it had to offer, and opt out of the bits she didn't want, the "religious bits". No religious education, unless it was Old Testament, and definitely no Act of Worship. No singing any of those dreadful Christian hymns, no kneeling the way "they" do, and no praying in English. God, apparently, objected to being addressed in any language other than his native ancient Hebrew.

I became terribly confused. Once a year, at prizegivings,

the entire school sang together, on a raised stage, for the dubious pleasure of friends and relatives. One year, one of the songs was a setting of a psalm. I excused myself from practices. I wasn't allowed to sing those kinds of songs, I said self-righteously to the music teacher. She never questioned my reasoning and I went back to my classroom, and got on with my homework.

"Why aren't you at singing practice?"

The Deputy Headmistress poked her head around the classroom door, perturbed to see the solitary figure bent studiously over her desk.

"I'm not allowed to sing hymns," I said.

"But it's a psalm," she said gently.

"Yes, but . . ." was all I could stammer. I didn't know how to explain that sung like that, in English, to churchy-sounding music, it seemed vaguely indecent. What would Mama say if she saw me singing that sort of song in public?

To my relief, the teacher shook her head and left the room, a look of amused disbelief on her face.

It was years later that my mother told me that when they were children, she and a cousin had once won sixpence each for singing "Jesus wants me for a Sun-beam" at a Salvation Army talent competition on the beach. Their parents, who only realised what was happen-ing when the winners were announced on the tannoy system, promptly disowned them.

Despite school my brushes with Christianity were few and far between, until I was in my late teens. "Just say you're Jewish," Mama said, and I did, every time I needed an excuse to get out of anything I didn't want to do. "Jammy so-and-so, isn't she?" said my school friends, as they slogged away at their essays in religious education. Tolerance is a wonderful thing. Mother said the school would be understanding, no more anti-Semitic than most other establishments, and not very religious. She was right. The only problem I had was when I was still in the junior school. I was splashed with muddy water

from a playground puddle. "You killed Christ," they
shouted at me. I didn't know who he was. I hadn't killed
anybody. Not that I knew of. So I went home puzzled,
with a dirty tunic. And said nothing. But woke night
after night, in the small hours, haunted by their angry
words and ugly expressions.

Mother could have sent me to another institution committed to turning hoydens into young ladies, a Catholic
Convent School, called "La Sagesse", known locally as
"La Sausages". It was a favourite with the Jewish
community at the time, out of a sense of solidarity
with another oppressed minority group. But the girls
were taught by nuns. Mama had never met a nun, except
courtesy of Hollywood, and suspected their powers of
persuasion, if Audrey Hepburn or Deborah Kerr were
anything to go by. Perhaps there was a hint of *déjà vu*,
but she didn't want her daughter, destined to make the
match of a lifetime, wanting the wrong sort of veil.

So the Church of England had the benefit of my presence instead, and I was the only Jewish girl in my class,
the only one at Harvest without four apples on a piece
of purple card, wrapped in cling film, or three cans of
baked beans in a cardboard box, on her desk. At the
sound of the bell, the girls gathered their treasures, and
clutching them tightly to their ever-expanding chests,
marched into the Assembly Hall, where they sang a turgid
"We plough the fields", and marched out again, yawning,
having deposited a large pile of rather battered tins and
bruised produce on what passed for a stage. I suspect
it was all a rather meaningless exercise, one which had
been outgrown long before puberty passed into genuine
adolescence.

Nor, I have to say, has the ritual increased in meaning
for me in recent years, despite my increased understanding. Harvest was not an event we anticipated with much
excitement when Peter was a curate in West Yorkshire.
Standing in the old Norman church with its timbered
beams and ancient stained-glass windows, I could imagine

hordes of medieval peasants tramping over the worn flag-
stones, bringing their sheep and goats and other offerings
to church, and felt part of a great historic tradition. But
once out of the building, the centuries dissolved away,
the rural idyll vanished, swallowed up in a vista of moun-
tainous slag heaps. Coal, not cows, now gave value to the
land, and I wondered whether it would not have been
more appropriate to find a heap of it on the altar, rather
than oranges, bananas, and the occasional courgette.

It was these "new-fangled" fruits and vegetables which
caused all the trouble in a very traditional mining community. The produce was supposed to be shared out
amongst the needy, the elderly and the infirm. The trouble
was that they didn't seem to appreciate how needy they
really were. They certainly weren't needy enough to accept
a courgette. "What are they anyway? What do you do with
them? I don't eat that kind of thing. I only eat sprouts.
What did you give Mrs Smith down road? A cabbage? She
doesn't want cabbage. It'll only give her wind. You should
have given the cabbage to me. I don't have a problem with
wind. I'll eat a cabbage if I'm stuck for sprouts."

One year a red pepper found its way into the display
left on the altar. We all knew it was a potential disaster,
but no one had the courage to give it a decent home. It
wasn't right somehow to appropriate the Lord's offering
for one's personal use. So we tried to palm it off on one
or two of the unsuspecting recipients of our bounty, who
all, to a woman, gingerly removed it from their parcel
as if it were a grenade, and handed it back. One or
two threw it back, in disgust. Even the local nursing
home rejected our poor capsicum. "We couldn't use one
of these, dear," said the matron, pointing discreetly to
some unidentifiable part of her anatomy, "it will do a
lot of damage – down here."

Kiwis suffered a similar fate. "What's that?" eying it
suspiciously. "Not one of them passion fruit? We don't
want none of that, not at our age, do we, Dad?"

For a moment there's a flicker of something resembling

life in Dad's eye, the dying ember finally extinguished when Mother turns her withering gaze upon him.

"No, no we don't, Mother. That's right."

"What else have you got? Oranges'll do nicely. Good for Dad's bowels. And I don't want two less than Nellie Hardcastle this year."

It was a marathon, a discouraging, disheartening marathon, distributing the harvest offering. All except the year the miners were on strike. That year food was scarce and people were hungry. We asked for tinned food only, kept a vast store, and distributed it over the months, finding time and time again, beyond the possibility of coincidence, that we knocked on someone's door exactly at the moment when they had put the last piece of coal on the fire and were wondering what they were going to give the kids for tea. I was very conscious of having a warm home and a full stomach, knew then that I was rich beyond measure, beyond respectability. That year Harvest made sense.

Materialistic little creature that I was, I never really appreciated Sukkot, the Jewish equivalent of Harvest, either. In fact Sukkot, meaning Tabernacles or Booths, is much more than a harvest festival. "You shall live in booths for seven days, so that future generations will know that I made the people of Israel live in booths when I brought them out of the land of Egypt." It commemorates the forty years my ancestors spent wandering around the Sinai Peninsula. No small achievement, considering the fact that the Egyptians couldn't hold out three days when they found themselves trapped there in 1967 during the Six-Day War. "I gave you food, drink and clothing," God reminds his people, just in case their gratitude has worn a little thin with time. "Even your shoes didn't wear out." On such rough, stony terrain, that was a major miracle. A bad time in the history of Jewish cobblers.

When I was a child I desperately wanted to spend a week in a sukkah, a sort of makeshift tree house at ground level, made out of planks, branches, twigs, bits of carpet, and any other spare materials that are

to hand. Sukkot was supposed to be a celebration of
nature, a special moment when human beings, overawed
by the great canopy of the night sky, are stripped of the
conceit of considering themselves masters of the universe.
I thought it must be terribly romantic to sleep out beneath
the stars, just as my ancestors had done, a sort of glorified
camping holiday. But with a father who didn't know
one end of a screwdriver from another, and a mother
who couldn't sew a button on, my chances were slim.
Inventiveness, creative genius, had hardly been bestowed
in any noticeable quantity on my family, and even if it
had, how could Mama keep one of those things clean?
Or the house, if we were all tramping in and out?

So we had to be satisfied with occasional visits to
the mega-sukkah at the synagogue, though a communal
booth just wasn't the same. Sadly, since the three "Pilgrim
Festivals", Harvest, Passover and Pentecost, when all the
people went up to the Temple in Jerusalem for a huge
communal binge, are regarded as fun, rather than holy
occasions, work is not taboo, except for the first and
last days. So Hebrew classes were compulsory, three
times a week, as usual. The only difference was that
for light relief, we were spared an hour of regimented
translation work, and marched out into a large canopied
contraption, leaning for safety against the synagogue
wall. For a full ten minutes we were allowed to sit on
old wooden benches, under a ceiling of trailing plastic
grapes and greenery, drinking lemonade and eating sweet
biscuits. Having of course made, loudly and in unison, the
appropriate prayer of thanksgiving.

"Which one is it?" we hissed at each other, "What's
the blessing for biscuits? Or lemonade?"

"Try the one for lemons."

"There're probably no lemons in it!"

"Does a lemon grow in the ground or on a tree?"

And woe betide us if we got the wrong one. There was
no law preventing a child from standing in the corner of
a sukkah.

It was all supposed to be a huge treat. The Rabbi, usually engaged in the classroom in demonstrating the effectiveness of corporal punishment on naughty boys, beamed at us all over his beard with festive tolerance. It was more like a leer, and we ungrateful wretches, unused to such rabbinic benevolence, used to gorging ourselves on a great deal more than plain, sweet biscuits, giggled uncontrollably into our plastic beakers. The boys burped lemonade loudly all the way back to the classroom.

Few of my classmates had a sukkah at home either. The Jewish community in which I was raised was prosperous and comfortable. They had no desire to remind themselves of the hard living conditions, either of their forefathers in the wilderness, or of their parents who had fled the pogroms of Eastern Europe. They wanted to forget that they had once been poor immigrants, thankful for a roof over their heads and the means of earning a meagre living. Which strikes me as a pity. For sitting in the sukkah the wealthy are supposed to remember their humble origins, be grateful for what they have, be sensitive to the fragile existence of every human being. For everything we have we owe to divine bounty. "In the day of trouble He will hide me in His sukkah," says the psalmist. Living in a sukkah is a reminder that material possessions are flimsy, shaky and temporary. It is a symbolic gesture, a placing oneself beneath the permanence of divine protection and care.

I suppose I could hardly blame my parents and their friends for their reluctance. The rules governing the construction of booths are extraordinarily complex. The roof must be made of material grown from the earth, not mined, it must be cut down, not connected to the ground, and not subject to any ritual impurity. It would have made matters considerably easier if there had been a do-it-yourself sukkah kit on sale, a sort of glorified wendy-house, which could be erected and taken down every year, like a plastic Christmas tree. And, like a Christmas tree, the sukkah is supposed to be decorated as beautifully as possible, inside, not out, with wall hangings, pictures, flowers and sweets. Some communities in Israel give prizes for the best. Tables and chairs and beds are moved in, so that the entire family can live there for the duration of the festival. A precarious existence for those who live in apartment blocks and attach their sukkah to the balcony or build it on the roof. A chilly existence if the first autumnal frost is in the air. So perhaps one communal sukkah at the synagogue, built and decorated with loving care by all the members, is not such a bad idea after all. It might even be the kind of project which breaks down barriers, and builds relationships.

All three of the Pilgrim Festivals have an agricultural theme. Passover marked the harvesting of the barley, Shevuoth, or Pentecost, the harvesting of the wheat, and Sukkot the final harvesting before the rain of winter. It was their familiarity with the Old Testament texts about celebrating a final harvest, which led the Pilgrim Fathers to institute a day for Thanksgiving, when they first arrived in the States. For the Jew thanksgiving is a command; ingratitude, even for courgettes, peppers and other vegetables, a cardinal sin. The very Hebrew word for Jew, a contraction of Judah or Judean, means thanksgiving. It is a religious duty to rejoice on festivals. "You shall have nothing but joy," says God, and that's an order. Like any of us, he doesn't much enjoy having to contend with a load of miserable, unappreciative sinners. Though judging by some church services that may be hard to believe.

I was sixteen when I first went into a church. It struck me as terribly drab and dull after the whitewashed crispness, the stunning contrast of gold, silver, crimson and scarlet of the synagogue. The stone and plaster was grey and icy to the touch. The saints stared mournfully down from their stained-glass windows at the tiny congregation, lamenting their pitiful attempt to make their voices heard.

"Oh Lord, open thou our lips," piped a tiny voice at the front.

"And our mouth shall show forth thy praise," came the

warbled, rather tired, response from an exceedingly elderly choir, and a few hardy members of the congregation.

I thought everyone was about to nod off. With boredom.

"And make thy chosen people joyful," they intoned, reluctantly, voices trailing off into a kind of a dirge.

I had never heard anything sound less like joy.

Then nor has my Mama ever quite grasped the principle of entering into the religious festivals with zest and happiness, to show God how much he was loved and appreciated. Like a demanding child, he is simply a bit of a nuisance, who needed placating. Like most other men.

"Another festival, oy vey, more cooking, more cleaning, more work."

"What does this one mean?" we used to ask her when we were children. We always knew she wouldn't know the answer.

"I can't remember."

"Then why do we celebrate it?"

"Because we have to. It's our duty."

Useless to tell her that that was exactly the point. God wanted gladness not duty. How much that passes for religion falls into the same trap? Though, for her, there is admittedly a little more joy nowadays. She spends the festivals with my brother and sister-in-law.

The Jewish way of life provides lots of opportunities for feasting, merry-making, music and dance. It was the Hasids who reintroduced dance into Judaism in the eighteenth century, primarily for the men. Dance in Judaism has never been seen as effeminate, a woman's prerogative. Nowadays everyone gets up out of their seat and dances on Simchat Torah, the eighth and last day of Sukkot, when the scrolls of the law are lovingly removed from the ark and are carried around the synagogue. In Israel they dance around after the law in the streets. So seriously is the command to rejoice taken, so independent of personal circumstances, that some even danced in

Auschwitz, carrying rocks on their shoulders because they had no access to the scrolls. "They taught us how a Jew is supposed to behave in time of trouble," said the writer, Elie Wiesel. "For them the commandment to rejoice on your festival was an impossible commandment to observe – but observe it they did."

Sukkot is a time to look back and be grateful for God's protection and provision, a time to pray for the present, for rain, for rain is the key to life in the Middle East, and it is also a time to look forward to the future, the coming of the Messiah.

Jesus went to the Temple at Sukkot, on the seventh, official last day of the feast. It was Hashanah Rabbah, the Day of the Great Hosanna, the day when the people cry out, "Hosheanu, Lord, save us, send us the Messiah." In their hands they held a lulav and an etrog, the lulav made of palm branches, tied together with a golden thread, the etrog, a lemon or other citrus fruit, symbolic of the promised land. While the congregation were waving their palm branches, the choir of Levites sang psalms 113 to 118, known as the Little Hallel or Praise, sung at every important festival. When they reached psalm 118, at the climax, "Save us now, we beseech you, O Lord. Blessed is he who comes in the name of the Lord, we bless you out of the house of the Lord," there was a mighty blast on the shofars, and water drawn from the Pool of Siloam was poured from a golden pitcher on to the altar, while the people prayed for earthly and spiritual rain. With the waving, singing, water splashing, and trumpets sounding, it must have been fairly noisy in the Temple, unlike most churches I have ever attended, and, as the whole occasion rose to a crescendo of messianic fervour, Jesus stood up, silence fell, and he said quietly, but with complete authority, "If any man thirst, let him come to me and drink. He that believes in me, out of his innermost being will flow rivers of living water." If, throughout the festival, there had been a great deal of whispered discussion, and even heated debate, about who he really was, he left them in no doubt now. When, six months later, the crowds thronged the streets of Jerusalem to await his arrival for the Passover, when they waved their lulavs at the man on the donkey, and shouted, "Hosanna," or "Hosheanu, save us now," were they not recalling the events of that extraordinary day?

This gives the average Harvest Festival or Thanksgiving Day celebration a new dimension altogether. Here is the opportunity for a great communal celebration, a chance to decorate our homes and churches until they dazzle, even more than they do at Christmas. The Jews carried torches into the Temple. The golden candelabra were lit. The building blazed with myriad lights, a brilliant focus for the whole of Jerusalem, shining out for miles around, guiding the pilgrims as they travelled from afar. The Church could become a beacon. Autumn is expiring slowly. Winter beckons with an icy claw. Let's stave it off a while longer. Away with the dreary little plastic bags containing four oranges and a kiwi, three carrots and a pepper, our token, rather half-hearted, offerings, which reveal confusion about the validity of such a festival in a non-agricultural age. Now is the time to consider ways of caring for the poor and hungry of the neighbourhood. It is also a time to invite them to a grand celebration of God's goodness, a chance to make the maximum noise, to have a barn dance to end all barn dances, a thumping, rip-roaring good time.

Sukkot is the one occasion Jews hope and pray to share with non-Jews one day, in fulfilment of the prophet Zechariah's extraordinary apocalyptic vision. "Then all the survivors from the nations which have attacked Jerusalem will go there each year to worship the Lord Almighty as King, and to keep the feast of Tabernacles." Impossible though it may seem, war in the Middle East will come to an end, all nations will live together in peace in a messianic age, and celebrate the festival together.

At the moment our "earthly tabernacle", says the New

Testament, our physical body, is as fragile and temporary as a sukkah. Everything we have and are will vanish. We have no permanent home here on earth. We are waiting for one to come. As a minister's wife, forced, because of my man's calling, to move around more often than I might want, I have taken great comfort from those words. A home-loving girl at heart who likes to put her roots down deep, I wither when I'm uprooted. Whenever the going gets a little rough I long for home, to be where I belong, with the people who know and love me. The problem is, after so many moves, I don't know where home is any more. I sometimes feel rootless and lonely. And I'm grateful to a wise monk who suggested that my condition might be spiritual, rather than geographical. At my age, apparently (and I don't know that I'm all that grateful for those few kind words), many begin to feel a perfectly normal dissatisfaction with the securities of this life, in preparation for the next. A physical move only accelerates the process, and though it may be stressful, isn't necessarily a bad thing. Even Jesus himself came on a temporary visit the first time. "The Word became flesh and tabernacled among us."

But one day, God will tabernacle with human beings for ever, "He will wipe away all tears from their eyes. There will be no more death, tears, grief or pain." On that day there will be a celebration to end all celebrations, the great "marriage feast of the lamb". The Rabbis say that people do not know what rejoicing is until they have been in Jerusalem on the last day of Sukkot. The Torah is paraded through the streets under a bridal canopy. Everyone dances round it, holding lighted candles in apples, performing acrobatic feats. It would be so easy, on a flight of fancy, to wonder whether in fact this might not be a foretaste, a pale reflection of that cataclysmic event yet to come. I have the feeling that when the Messiah returns, on what the Jews await as his first visit, he may well arrive in time for the feast of Sukkot.

HARVEST IDEAS

The very adventurous might like to have a go (or encourage their more inventive offspring to have a go) at making some kind of "sukkah" – either by erecting a quasi-tent on or in a conservatory or porch, in one corner of a sitting-room, or in a small bedroom, then decorating it with all kinds of greenery and flowers. For young children, eating a special harvest meal in their "den" may be a real treat. Let them entertain you to tea and biscuits, or wine and savouries.

RECIPES

It is traditional to symbolise the richness of the festival by eating stuffed foods, for example peppers or aubergines stuffed with a minced beef filling (see below), or baked apples stuffed with cinnamon and raisins. All kinds of melons are served in the sukkah too, and can be filled with chopped citrus fruits.

HOLISHKES
An adaptation of stuffed vine leaves. Serves 4.

1 firm head of a large winter cabbage
1 onion finely chopped
500g minced beef
4 tbsp. long-grain rice
50g margarine
100ml chicken stock
salt, pepper

the sauce:
small can of tomato puree
3 cans of water
4 tbsp. brown sugar
juice of a large lemon

Blanch the cabbage head by boiling it whole for five minutes, covered, then plunging it into cold water. Chop off the tough stalk end, then carefully peel off 12 leaves. Fry the onion in the margarine until tender, then add the rice and cook for a further three minutes until opaque. Add the stock and cook until it is absorbed. Then mix it with the meat and seasonings. Spread each cabbage leaf with 1 tbsp. of the filling, fold up like a parcel, and place, in rows, in a casserole. Mix all the sauce ingredients together and pour over the bundles. Cook for two hours at gas mark 2, 300°F, 150°C, then uncover, turn up oven slightly and brown for half an hour.

WINTER

I'm not a winter person, which is probably why autumn fills me with a sense of dread and foreboding. Once Sukkot is past, I fetch those long-forgotten winter clothes down from the attic, try them on again, revelling in the fun of what seems like a brand new wardrobe and, a quarter of an hour later, long for the season to melt into spring as quickly as possible.

I keep telling myself I was made for hotter climes. I'm a martyr of the diaspora, a victim of my ancestors' sins, and mass anti-Semitism. Whenever the Jews were persecuted in one country they sailed to another. For hundreds of years they kept sailing straight past Britain. The grey climate and even greyer-looking land-mass, sitting beneath a yellowish pall, was hardly an attractive proposition. In fact, as soon as they saw it in the distance, they hastily turned their boats round and sailed in the opposite direction. Until there was nowhere else in Europe to go.

If you were really lucky, you acquired a ticket to the United States. Many of my relatives thought they were destined for the real "Goldene Medina", the turn-of-the-century equivalent of a promised land flowing with milk and honey. For years the sight of a skyline dominated by the mighty Statue of Liberty had filled their every waking dream. But their luck ran out in London. Their tickets were fake. England would have to do, at least for a while.

So I have my ancestors and their persecutors to blame for dark, dank British winters. I could emigrate to Israel, but despite its weather, one's own country, whatever its problems, has a way of worming itself into one's affections. Quite simply, as two of my cousins who, inexplicably to my mind, returned to their native, "cleansed" Frankfurt in 1946, explained, "One lives where one belongs." And must therefore take the rough with the smooth, learning what waste is involved, what ingratitude, in wishing the months away. The old Jewish approach is to savour the moment, for each is unique, a gift from God, which will never come in quite that way again. Here is a challenge to revel in the delightful, distinctive features of the season: a brisk walk on those cold, crisp, shimmering days when the colours melt into each other at the edges and the ground crunches beneath your feet. Thawing out afterwards, cheeks on fire, with a steaming cup of coffee clutched between reawakening fingers. The long dark evenings curled up on the settee with a box of continental chocolates and a good film on the television. Tartan, mohair and corduroy, baked potatoes, soups and stews, the smell of smoking pine, the lights of a house at dusk. So many simple gifts, so many pleasures to enhance the moment, delight the senses, and make us feel fully alive. So often unnoticed, unappreciated, as we wait for winter to ease its grip.

I'm happy as long as I'm warm. I hate being cold. If I'm forced to function in a freezing environment my whole system closes down and my mental capacity is reduced to the level of a hibernating hedgehog. Perhaps we were really designed to hibernate in the winter and we're fools to fight what comes naturally. We push our systems which then succumb to coughs, colds, bronchitis and the flu, we push our cars to travel in abrasive, unfriendly conditions, we push our bodies into all kind of evening activities and meetings, when all they want to do on a dark evening, after a busy day at work, is close down.

The Christian tradition, reflecting its ancient Greek pedigree, tends to be ascetic. We have hang-ups about inactivity, about sitting still. We have even greater hang-ups about warming our homes, and our churches. In most countries where temperatures fall to sub-zero the inhabitants work with the climate, not against it. Anglo-Saxons believe they're made of hardier stuff. They soldier on, expecting life to continue as normal, even when the world is an ice rink or there's three feet of snow on the ground. Furthermore, to run the central heating for longer than the customary two hours morning and night is a sign of immense inner weakness and flabbiness of spirit.

My husband tells me (to the accompaniment of our children, in unison, playing the melancholic lament of a pair of wailing violins – their usual response to their father's hard-luck childhood tales) that when he was a lad, during his three years forced labour at an English boys' boarding school, committed to training the Christian leaders of the next generation, he had to crack the ice in the basin first thing every morning, before he could wash. Then he scraped it off the inside of the windows so that he could see out, dressed in ten seconds, holding his breath, and ate a vast breakfast of rib-cloying porridge and other carbohydrate to coat and protect the body on the inside. Things could have been worse. The tradition of ice-cold showers in boys' boarding schools had just been abandoned at his school. Presumably the powers-that-be thought the system rigorous enough to transform hordes of unbridled infidels into Christian gentlemen without that particular little exercise.

He did leave the school with his faith reinforced, but that had little to do with surviving in almost sub-zero temperatures, and a great deal more to do with the friendships he formed. In fact those years filled him with an abiding intolerance of cold places. Expending all one's inner energy on keeping warm, rather than on creative projects and relationships, has always seemed to him a futile waste of time and resources. He carries a radiator key in his pocket permanently, bleeding the thousands of non-functioning systems wherever they fail to keep the nation warm. Why human beings allow air locks to accumulate in their pipes is for him one of life's greatest sources of bewilderment.

The theological college we attended in Nottingham had major central heating problems. The "vicar factory" was permanently cold. Every one of Peter's lectures began with its own mini-ritual. A word of prayer? Certainly not. This earnest young vicar-in-the-making took out his key and bled the radiators. Wherever he went blood-thawing, marrow-warming gurglings and rattlings followed him.

They called him the "College Bleeder", but blessed him for it.

Since then successive church boilers have filled the gap which the college central heating system left in his life. When we were last weighing up the pros and cons of taking on a new parish we rang a close friend for his wisdom.

"Does the church in question need a new boiler?" he asked.

"Why?"

"Because if it does, I should take it as a clear sign of God's guidance."

It didn't. But we still moved, and discovered that the boiler needed replacing after all.

Peter's intolerance of cold churches isn't simply a matter of personal preference. If a church is physically cold, it might just as well be socially and spiritually cold. A cold building is unfriendly, unwelcoming, uncaring. It says, "We'll freeze your blood and your bones, and freeze your spirit too, given half a service." It says, "Keep your coats and parkas on, stay muffled in your bonnets and scarves. Wrap yourself up in your own little world and don't attempt to reach out into anyone else's." When human beings take off their coats, they make themselves at home. They relax. They meet each other.

Some years ago I was invited to lead a retreat for clergy wives. I have become very reluctant to take on any speaking engagements which involve spending a night away because it usually means eight hours of enforced torture: roller coaster beds, lumpy bedding, mirrors three foot above my head, no socket for the hair dryer and curling tongs, and, worst of all, hours of restless, sleepless shivering in a dank, cold bedroom. This particular retreat was no exception. I was glad when the first rays of grey morning light forced their way between the gap in the curtains, and I could heave my stiff and aching muscles out of bed. Wrapped in coat and shawl, my teeth chattering, I crawled out of the accommodation block and down the path to the chapel for the pre-breakfast communion service. And found, when I got there, that the chapel had not been heated. It simply wasn't worth spending money on thirty-five women for an hour, was it? Our breath froze in front of our faces as we sang the opening hymn. I spent my hour fuming and raging against the ungenerous nature of Christians, instead of enjoying the generous presence of God.

I have never been cold in a synagogue. Coats are removed as people come in and are left in the cloakroom. In temperatures which make the Sahara seem pleasantly cool, the congregation, possibly there for several hours, unwinds and enjoys the environment and the company. The whole building, warm in atmosphere, with white-washed walls, golden pine, rich carpets, jewel-coloured windows and glittering ark, beckons and invites. There are no pictures. Jews fear transgressing the commandment which says, "Thou shalt have no graven image," so they make no representations of God or man. But the men wear skull caps and prayer shawls embroidered in a thousand shimmering, metallic threads, and the women wear jade and cherry, buttercup and fuchsia. And where there is intense colour, pictures no longer seem necessary.

My earliest childhood impressions of churches were of cold, drab, dingy, unwelcoming buildings, and when I eventually took the plunge and allowed myself to be carried into alien territory, it bore out the worst of my expectations. I was reminded of a set for a gothic horror movie and expected Dracula to rise up from behind one of the stone slabs at any moment. It surprised me at first that no one had removed their coats, and I wondered whether they planned on staying or, for some reason, were ready to make a quick getaway. Until I realised how cold it was and my fingers were so numb that I was almost unable to fumble my way through prayer and hymn book. I was lost and no one made any attempt to help me. No one moved out of their own frozen little world. How many happy hours the women while away in the synagogue finding the place for each other. Most Jews, like me, can read ancient Hebrew fluently, but are not too good with the translation.

I wonder to this day what impression our churches make on visitors, whether they see ascetic Anglicanism or cold Calvinism, the hard, unwelcoming face of an alien culture, or the warmth of true belief. Peeling paintwork, bare walls, crumbling cement, rotten woodwork, dusty banners, and even a jumbled mass of yellowing pictures, which would be gladly received by the local museum, don't announce to the world that the inhabitants of this building love being there and are comfortable and creative in it. And often, since most visitors to the church are attending a wedding or a funeral, the building is all they see of us, all they know of our faith.

So there's more to a church boiler than first meets the eye. I have had a love-hate relationship with many in my time. Arch-rivals in my husband's affections, yet they have become for me a symbol of the way the practical and the spiritual can and must be integrated.

Winter cold can keep human beings apart, or it can break down barriers and bring them together. One Saturday morning early in the December of 1990, snow began to fall on the West Midlands, and it fell and fell until the motorways and main roads came to a complete standstill, cars strewn across the carriageways, the shops were forced to close, telephone cables sagged and snapped, trees bent and cracked and there slowly descended upon the city of Coventry a profound and peaceful hush. Coventry, where Peter had his first parish, is not a city with much sense of community. Its history was all but wiped out in a single night in November 1941, when every familiar landmark was decimated by Hitler's bombs. After the war came the invasion. From every corner of Britain descended armies of workers looking for their fortune in the car factories. They made money, not relationships. And the new city, channelling its way north and south, west and east, sprang up without facilities, shopping centres, or parks. Planning policy focused on stimulating a proudly modern city centre. All the rest was housing, and more housing, with no focal point, no meeting place, no heart. Neighbourliness played no part in this model city of the fifties.

But those few days of snow in the nineteen nineties flushed the inhabitants out of their houses, to dig their way towards civilisation, to visit the elderly, to share their food and warmth with those who had no electricity. Next-door neighbours who had never met shared candles and mugs of coffee. Sworn enemies, who had fallen out years before over the exact demarcation of the dividing fence, or the behaviour of next-door's children, took up shovels and worked side by side. Everyone on our normally frenetic main road into town came out in wellington boots. People who had ignored me week after week when I had passed them in the street stopped for a chat. "It's just like it was during the war," the older ones said.

Then why did the goodwill melt away with the snow? I went on saying hello to people I passed in the street, but they walked straight past, eyes down. The moment had gone. Relationships were put away with the bad weather.

"God is more interested in right relationships than in right doctrine." It's one of my husband's most frequent sayings from the pulpit. And my favourite. It's so much easier, so much speedier, to keep our theology, rather than our relationships, correct and in good order. But if the latter fall apart while the former remain intact, what then remains? A cold, hard kind of a God in a cold, hard church. An edifice without life, structures without warmth, a disparate group of people without real human contact.

Winter provides ample opportunity for that defrosting contact human beings so badly need, not in endless meetings, heaven forbid, but in the home, by a flickering fireside, around the table, sharing a casserole and a loaf and a story or two. Winter is long Sabbath evenings, bread and wine, candlelight, Hanukkah and Christmas. The Jews maximise the usefulness of the season, the season which should perhaps hem us indoors a little more, so that we have the opportunity to re-evaluate the pure delights of hearth and home.

7

Money, Money, Money or If I Were a Rich Man

Then why do we put up with being cold? My Canadian mother-in-law told me that the Canadians certainly don't. Nor do the Scandinavians, or the Swiss, in their freezing temperatures. It all boils down, in a manner of speaking, to a rather embarrassing subject. Embarrassing that is for those who have plenty, and therefore no need to mention it. It isn't sex. That comes later. It isn't death. I've already tackled that particular little taboo. It's the subject which now draws the ultimate demarcation line not only in the American, but also in the British, class system. If you can talk in public about your annual income without the faintest hint of discomfort, without fear of criticism or pity, you are definitely not middle-class. But if the word "money" makes you feel decidedly squeamish, if spending drives you into a profound anxiety state, and heating your home seems the ultimate in unnecessary self-indulgence, while budget plans, savings accounts and trips to the accountant make you positively purr, the chances are, whatever your background or nationality, that you could now become an acceptable member of the British bourgeoisie.

Money. It perverts reason and destroys relationships. It's the subject which more than any other has helped to define the British stereotype of their American cousins. I was once asked to speak at a ladies' meeting in

Bournemouth on the south coast. We lived in the north at the time, so it would have been a round trip of about 700 miles. "Your husband could drive you here," the letter said, "and we would give him a cup of tea." There was no mention of any other hospitality, no offer of expenses, no fee to cover child-minding and, of course, no stamped-addressed envelope for my reply. I wrote back and told them the price of the return train fare. If they were willing to pay it, I was willing to speak at their meeting. I never heard from them again. This labourer manifestly wasn't worth hiring.

On the other hand, one of my father-in-law's lasting memories of a preaching tour of the United States was the way one pastor locked the doors of his church and refused to let the congregation leave until a board at the front, set out for the speaker's expenses, was covered in dollar bills. The Americans, said my father-in-law, had ways and means of making the preacher feel wanted. Even if those ways and means were hardly a free-will offering.

British congregations found his story distasteful. Americans, they tutted, do rather show an unfortunate lack of sensitivity in matters monetary. Better the preacher should starve than Christians contravene good taste by offering expenses, or, heaven forbid, a decent fee. I gave up much public speaking many years ago, in the early days of our marriage, when I could not afford the journey. A friend of ours once returned expenses sent him by a student organisation which would have barely put a litre of petrol in his car. Their need, he told them, was obviously greater than his.

Now I'm a freelance journalist and broadcaster. The grandeur of our large Victorian vicarage, much as we love it, tends to give a rather exaggerated impression of the means of its inhabitants. An average stipend barely heats a modern box, let alone a miniature palace. We depend therefore rather heavily upon my earnings. Hard-headed businesswoman that I am, do I relish the cut and thrust of selling myself, parrying with producers, negotiating the best deals? I do not. When asked what I charge for a script I whimper and whisper and mutter something inaudible beneath my breath. I am coy and shy and develop a sudden fascination for my shoes. Nice people don't talk about money. The BBC never mentions the word. Not the religious department at any rate. Nor do the countless Christian organisations who invite me to speak to them. It wouldn't be quite right. Christians work for love, for the kingdom, or for the pure aesthetic pleasure of it. Don't they? They don't have mouths to feed or fuel bills to pay. And after all, a married woman always has a man to support her. Perhaps I should be paying the BBC for the privilege of working for them? And though the first thing I need to know is the fee, I'm far too nice to ask – or just too plain inhibited.

But where do my inhibitions come from? Not from my Jewish background, that's for sure. There's an old joke about a Jewish man knocked down by a car.

"Are you comfortable?" asks a bystander who has wrapped him in his coat.

"Well, I make a living," comes the reply.

It is hardly surprising, after centuries of grinding poverty, of exclusion from professional life, of insecurity and persecution, that the Jews should develop an obsession with survival. And money means survival. My maternal grandfather Abe was a second generation immigrant. His father, like so many other first generation immigrants, had managed to convert his basic skills into a small family business, a furniture business, which he then handed on to his sons. Grandfather Abe was a gambling man, a weakness which cost his family dear. Running a business provided the same excitement as a flutter on the dogs or the horses. A happy rivalry existed between him and every other Jewish businessman in the north-east of England. Whenever he caught any of the family engaged in conversation with a stranger, he would always ask,

"Who is he related to? And how much does he earn?"

"Dad!" my mother would say witheringly, for she was the third generation to be born in Britain, and had picked up a few of the refinements of assimilation.

"A fat lot of good you are to me," he would say, "when you never bother to find out the essentials."

And money, whether we choose to admit it or not, is a fairly essential commodity in our society. It provides opportunities and choices, a sense of personal worth and value. It opens doors. The lack of it ensnares the poor in a stranglehold of powerlessness and rejection. For many years after their immigration Jews were denied membership of those twin symbols of British acceptability: the Golf Club and the Tennis Club. By the sixties, when their wealth had finally endowed them with a veneer of respectability, the walls of Jericho came tumbling down. Money bestowed status. But, unlike their counterparts in the Germany of the Third Reich, they have never been foolish enough to think that it also granted a guaranteed immunity from future rejection.

Although Jews are as prone to the snobbery of one-upmanship as anyone else, perhaps more so, after years of subjugation, Grandpa Abe wasn't interested in status. He simply enjoyed playing the gambler's game of seeing who could earn the most. If status had been his goal, the professions would have been his target. For the professions bestow real respect, and the chance to give something back to a country which has provided security, and freedom from persecution. Which is why the Mama at a large Jewish function is heard to wail, "Is there a doctor in the house?"

"Yes, madam, I'm a doctor," says an earnest young man, rushing towards her, stethoscope at the ready, looking for the patient.

"Oy," she says, "have I got a daughter for you!"

And why my father accepted so graciously the news that his son-in-law was to leave teaching to become a minister of the Church.

"He'll be a professional man," said my father to my mother reassuringly, while she was having a bout of near hysteria on the sofa.

The fact that a minister of the Church is the lowest paid of all professionals had, at that point, escaped his notice.

Many Christian organisations, in fact, pay their fulltime workers a pittance. When my husband was a deacon in the Free Church the elders were invited to the home of one of the trustees, to discuss the new minister's salary. They arrived at an expensive, gracious detached house, set in its own spacious grounds, a BMW parked at the top of a sweeping drive, and were shown into a large, lavish sitting-room, filled with the best furniture.

"The man we're inviting to be our pastor," said the Church leaders, sunk into their armchairs, plates of dainty sandwiches in their hands, "is at the top of his profession and is leaving it for us. We plan to pay him the equivalent of a top teacher's salary."

The honourable trustee all but choked into his coffee cup.

"That seems more than just a little extravagant," he said.

"Why?" they asked.

"Well . . . well, I'm a solicitor and I'm payed a solicitor's salary. A pastor should be paid a pastor's salary."

"Which," they then replied triumphantly, "should, if we're going to follow what it says in the New Testament to the letter, be double your pay."

I have met pastors and ministers forced to live in grossly substandard accommodation, with such a small income that they cannot afford a basic annual holiday, enduring the sort of "hair-shirt" existence their congregation would balk at. But they are supposed to live a holy life on behalf of us all. We wouldn't want anyone going into church work with impure motives. Spoiled by too much luxury. Another example of dividing the spiritual from the practical, and in the end, as weariness and resentment grows, the holy thing sullied by filthy lucre, or the lack of it, is relationship.

"Let me be neither rich nor poor," says the ancient Proverb, "for if I am rich I might think I don't need you. And if I'm poor I might be tempted to steal and bring disgrace on your name." There's great value in having just enough. Though the variations on the definition of "enough" seem infinitesimal. Jews will never admit to being anything more than "comfortable", in case God is playing a little game with them. There could be some unexpected surprise around the corner, as there has so often been. So don't tempt fate. Many a Jewish man whiles away the long hours in the synagogue lamenting the precarious nature of business, his business. Bankruptcy stories were a familiar backdrop to my childhood. I knew, long before I understood why, that any house I ever had would be in my name, not my husband's.

"And then no one will ever be able to take it away from you or your children," Mama said.

"Oh," I said, mystified, but happy to be a woman. Women lived secure in their kingdom. Men went to prison.

I also learned that dying was not the worst thing a man could do to his wife. Dying and not providing for her was the ultimate failure. Husbands after all are replaceable. And usually discovered on Mediterranean cruises. That's why she needs the legacy.

Unfortunately the attitude of the Jews to money, their openness on the subject, their obsession with its tendency to come and go, is often regarded by outsiders as crass rather than natural. The money-grabbing caricature acquired over the centuries, and carved in stone by Shakespeare's Shylock, when the means to make more than a comfortable living was limited to money-lending, dies slowly. Probably because non-Jews have found great relief in transferring all their own angst and guilt about their greed on to the Jew. But like any other people they can be immensely mean, or immensely generous.

Whichever, they rarely do things by half. As a susceptible teenager in the Church, I quickly learned to acquire verbal inhibitions on the subject of my pocket money, and what I did with it, in case I became a caricature of myself. And had to conquer my inhibitions and force myself to discuss the subject when I got married.

I shall never forget the evening my intended told me what percentage of his salary he gave away and intended to go on giving away after our marriage. I was nearly speechless with shock. Nearly, but not quite. I was planning to give up my job, as our leisure hours would have been incompatible. But how could we repair and decorate our new home, how could we eat, if the wage earner was merrily giving so much of his earnings away?

"Well, I don't see why I should change my policy, just because I'm marrying you," he said.

There then ensued the first of many heated discussions on a subject which has never ceased, throughout our married life, to provoke interesting and lively debate! Jack Dominion, the marriage counsellor, claims that money is the single greatest cause of marriage breakdown. If couples cannot be totally open in this area of their lives, how will they trust each other in any other? Peter and I have called an uneasy truce. He still gives away more of his salary than I give away of mine. He has more faith. And he is usually vindicated. To this day I have no idea how we managed to spend two years at a theological college without any regular income, without any real scrimping or scrounging (though Peter would want me to say that he never had his shoes repaired).

But if you were to come to my home, I would kill the fatted calf, in the great Jewish tradition. There would be an expensive joint, or chicken, with all the trimmings, even if the family had to starve for the rest of the week. And Peter, if he knew what I had spent, would probably have a nervous breakdown. I also find it much easier to give away extraneous nice things than he does, on the basis that if my fellow can use and enjoy something more than I do, they ought to have it. Giving appears in many different disguises.

So does taking. In the niggling attitude of some churches, historically obsessed with fund-raising, robbing the country of the good news, because its committees are more worried about how to make ends meet. In the penny-pinching refusal to pay labourers their hire, showing real respect and appreciation for their gifts and effort. In the rampant materialism of the West in general, blissfully unaware of the pain and despair of the "have-nots". And sadly, when it comes to money, we seem to be much better at taking than giving. Which is probably one good reason why we try and avoid the subject altogether.

Of course Jesus did tell us not to let our right hand know what our left hand was doing. So, afraid of being showy, for good measure, we keep both hands well beneath the pew. The sound of small change clinking on the collection plate never ceases to amaze me. It means that the congregation is emptying its purse and pockets of its leftovers, an amount which will barely heat the small square foot in which they stand. It means that there has been no forethought about how much to give. It means some poor committee spending hours of nervous energy wondering how and whether to find the resources to satisfy the endless demands of the monster of a building handed down to us from previous generations. All over Britain churches and chapels lie derelict, or are converted into warehouses and offices, mocking symbols of a faith which appears to have lost its fire. And now, because of economic recession, because nothing, not even investments, is as safe as it seemed, the Anglican Church faces an enormous crisis and is having to cut back its number of ministers, as well as its buildings.

Whatever happened to the Old Testament principle of the tithe, giving away ten per cent of one's income? The Jews don't risk waiting for a voluntary contribution. They extract it. Once a year a bill from the local Hebrew

Congregation lands on the doormat. The charge is for a seat in the synagogue, and use of all other associated facilities, including burial. My father, who tended towards agnosticism and rarely took advantage of any of the facilities on offer, objected violently every year, when the bill from the Orthodox congregation arrived. The problem was that he had started to attend the Reform Synagogue, and they sent him a bill too. Why should he buy shares in two opposing companies, when he wasn't sure he knew who the director was? And then my mother would remind him that if he wanted to have an eternal resting place next to her, then he must contribute towards the plot in the proper place, the Orthodox cemetery, which was where she would lie. And he always conceded, driven, I suspect, by the necessity of peace with her in this world, rather than the next.

Every year the dues were greater, to keep pace with the cost of heating, lighting, decorating, repairs, the Rabbi's salary and expenses. There are many advantages in having such a system. It is a reminder of the practical responsibility involved in being part of a community, whatever your financial circumstances. No nebulous spiritual attachment here. On the other hand, and herein lies its major disadvantage, it does necessitate being well-off. Rich and poor pay the same, whatever your ability to pay. If you're having a hard time, why should everyone else have to suffer for it? Though I must say that every synagogue has a large charitable fund for those who need help instantly and anonymously. And I suspect that under this system the Rabbi rests more easily in his bed than his Christian counterpart. No fund-raising problems disturb his beauty sleep.

The tithe never seems to have caught on in the Church. Tony, a minister friend of mine, recently wrote to his bishop. The diocese had discovered that the average annual giving from each individual church member was 2% of his or her income. Small wonder the diocese was in dire straits, threatening to cut back all kinds of community projects, where the Church was vitally needed: in youth work, broadcasting, industry. Could you, do you think, the Bishop wrote in a public letter to his flock, in this time of crisis, see your way to committing yourself to 5%? Tony was horrified. If you only ask for 5%, he wrote to the Bishop, that is what you will get. If you ask for the amount set down in the Bible as the norm, the tithe, you might then get the 10% we need so badly to do the work God wants us to do. But the Bishop demurred. After all, one couldn't push the people too far.

Never has my husband preached about giving away a minimum 10% of one's income without a ripple of panic working its way through the congregation to the exit, where any unfortunate church member who happens to be manning the doors has their ears well and truly bent.

"How can anyone, in these difficult times, give away such an amount? It's irresponsible. Madness."

Peter understands their sense of confusion. He was unemployed for several months, struggled with his tithe then and on many other occasions since, but has always paid it. And survived. He always replies that he would love to make it easier for people, but wasn't responsible for laying down the basic principle.

The problem is that money has a way of worming itself into the very heart of our beings, until it is embedded so deep that we cannot let go of it without a fight. It has a way of subjugating us until all our values are turned topsy-turvy. That was brought home to me the day there was a car crash outside our home. Neither driver was hurt, but one of them, a young woman, in deep shock, kept lamenting the state of her car over and over again.

"You're alive, thank God," I said to her, "no one is hurt. The car is only a heap of metal, only money. It's replaceable. You're not."

But I appeared to be speaking another language. The inanimate box was more important than the person in it.

A friend of ours who is a university lecturer receives regular visits from what he refers to as "men in macs", checking out the records of students who have applied to join the civil service. One day his curiosity got the better of him and he asked the visitor what exactly he was looking for.

"In what areas are 'your people' most vulnerable, most likely to be at risk?"

"In their twenties, it's alcohol," came the reply, "in their thirties and forties, it's money. Sex doesn't rear its ugly head until they reach their fifties."

It's at the age when we rear our families, worry about their education, fall foul of the mid-life crisis and the haunting spectre of not being successful, that money exercises its greatest allure. Despite the fact that Jesus told us not to store up wealth, saving is regarded as an almost Christian virtue. Television advertising reminds us that it is the only real way to secure a happy, picture-book, rosy-round-the-edges future. It panders to our fears of being left destitute in old age. Sadly, it contains an element of truth. Society will not take care of us in later life. Grandfather Abe's gambling streak produced a harvest of problems. In a rash moment he ploughed all the profits back into the business, and the gamble failed. He died before the business was sold, leaving his younger brother in dire financial straits. When the brother died suddenly, his wife, my Great-aunt Sadie, was left without the means to live as she had been accustomed.

The family rallied. Each month a son, a daughter, a sister-in-law, a nephew, a niece, a cousin, took it in turns to pay the bills. Which were many. Sadly, Aunt Sadie had a passion for clothes. She also had a passion for the casino. They may well have been aggravated with her spending, but no Jewish family would leave an aunty with debts. And it taught me a valuable lesson. That when we give, we cannot dictate the terms. No patronising the recipient. No telling them what they may or may not do with their gift. As in one church I heard of which provided the minister's wife with a home help while she was pregnant, so that she could rest. Then criticised her every time she appeared in public for not resting. She became a virtual prisoner within her own home.

We are victims of our alienated society. Unlike members of the Jewish community we have no means of knowing that we will be supported in our need, and cannot live as we would like in an ideal Christian world. We have to "put a little by". It makes sense, but we dare not let it become our only security. We dare not let money dominate us like that.

A lesson Peter and I learned the hard way, but now, looking back, I am glad we did. A few years ago we had money problems. Debts? Not a bit of it. A certain book of mine sold rather well and for the first time in our lives we had what seemed to us like substantial savings. And they caused us more heart-searching than any amount of scrimping to make ends meet. We didn't know what to do with them. We couldn't decide upon the right way to proceed. We dreamed terribly altruistic dreams of buying a cottage for the use of all the poor church ministers who couldn't afford a holiday, and for us, of course. In the end, for the first time ever, and as a temporary measure, we approached a financial adviser, who advertised in several reputable Christian magazines. He invested our money in a company called Barlow Clowes. Our problems were solved overnight. Mr Clowes needed our money to fund his luxury lifestyle.

One night in 1988 the television informed us that all our savings had disappeared somewhere between Cheshire and Gibraltar. Worse, the press intimated that those who had been foolish enough to invest in such a company did so out of greed, and deserved their lot.

It cushioned the blow when we reminded ourselves that our losses were as nothing compared to the elderly and retired who were divested of lump redundancy sums, pensions, the very means of survival. But we felt silly, ashamed to admit we had had savings, and ashamed to admit the way we had lost them. On the whole friends were very supportive. As we suspected, one or two, perhaps to the more left of centre, wondered, tactfully of course, whether we ought to have had investments. Ought they have a mortgage? A car loan? Ought we own dishwashers, washing machines, video recorders, all the paraphernalia of a materialistic age which is supposed to make our lives so much easier and more pleasurable? I do. But I admire my friends who will not be pushed into it, and think carefully before they purchase.

During the months which followed we had bouts of real thankfulness that we had been rescued from our "problem". And bouts of real depression as we came to terms with what felt like a bereavement. God had to perform a surgical operation deep down inside us to remove our treasure, and it left us with an inner crater. Fortunately the manipulation of the knife was so swift we hardly had the time to fight or squeal. And when, some years later, the government decided to make good much of what we had lost, it was a pleasant surprise, but not a desperate necessity. "Don't store up treasure which the thief can steal." But theft, fraud and burglary happened to other people. Not to us. Not until Barlow Clowes. And it can happen again. We survived, without being tempted to leap off any high buildings, as some did after the Wall Street crash. But having taken a bit of a tumble none the less. We learned the hard way to hold our purses, bank accounts, and credit cards on the open palms of our hands. Hopefully we haven't closed our fists again, for our complex world monetary systems could rob us of all we have overnight. Economic recession hovers like a giant bird of prey over rich and poor alike. And when it strikes, the rich, not the poor, have the most to lose.

The working people we lived with for five years in a mining parish in Yorkshire have no problem with savings. They believe that what they earn by the sweat of their brow they should spend with gusto. I don't think they have it completely right, any more than middle-class squirrels who like to hoard, but there's a certain healthiness in their approach. During the miners' strike of 1986 it was they who gave the most, when they barely had enough themselves, to the Ethiopian Famine Appeal. They knew what it was to be hungry and cold. They were used to spending, happy to be rich or poor. And when we left them for another church their gift to us took our breath away. "The poor are ever liberal," says the old Jewish proverb. Our experience has always been that those who can least afford it are always the most generous.

The secret is to treat all that we have as a loan. There's a story in the Talmud of a woman whose son dies while her husband is away. She doesn't know how to break the news to him when he gets back, and then suddenly an idea occurs to her.

"I borrowed a necklace," she tells him, "and while you were away the owner came and asked for it back."

"And you gave it back, of course," her husband says to her.

"Well," she says, "it was a pretty necklace. I liked it a lot. I didn't want to part with it."

"You have no choice, my dear. It doesn't belong to you."

And at that point she takes her husband by the hand and leads him to the room where their son lies dead.

The story of course has great theological problems. It takes no account of the evil in the world which Christ came to conquer, but the principle remains that all that we have comes from God's hands, and he has the right to do with it exactly as he pleases. Which is why the Apostle Paul explained that he had to learn the secret of how to handle having too much, as well as how to cope with having too little. There is no promise of wealth here for anyone who takes being a Christian seriously.

It is ironic that the subject we find such a tongue-tying taboo should be one that Jesus spoke about almost more than any other. But then he was a Jew! And he knew that here was the real test of how much we loved him.

8

The Relative Problem

The second test is how much we love one another.

Easy to do, in the abstract. When we can hand-pick relationships. "You can choose your friends, but not your family," or so I've been told. By non-Jews. For any Jew will tell you that choice in this matter is an unknown luxury. You are landed with both – by a freak of birth. Responsibility for the entire Jewish community rests upon your shoulders. Every other Jew throughout the world can rely on you in an emergency. Nearer to home, your "mishpahah", or relatives, who have a right to your commitment, if not your love, seem to span out in an ever-increasing circle, for there are your father's cousins, and your mother's cousins, your cousin's cousins, and their cousins, not to mention your wife's family and her in-laws and their cousins and relations. After several generations of intermarriage the chances are that you are related to almost everyone else anyway. And no matter how much you fall out and feud, and Jews do for we are a very volatile people, in the end, every one of them is your mishpahah. And you have to live with the fact that some strange destiny has thrown you together and there is no escape. You belong.

The original tale of three men in a boat comes from the Talmud. One of them, for reasons unknown, suddenly begins to drill a hole beneath his seat.

"What are you doing?" his two companions shout.

"Don't worry," he says, "I'm only drilling under my seat!"

The moral of the tale, told by Rabbis throughout Jewish history, is that all Jews are in the same boat.

"To be Jewish", said one scholar, "primarily is to be part of the group."

"I may not be a good Jew, but I am a proud one." I heard that so often as a child. It meant, "I may well break all the laws, I may let God and the system down, but I never fail the community by trying to disassociate myself from it." Which is why Messianic Jews, or whatever we choose to call ourselves, are branded as semi-traitors. For hundreds of years baptism has been the ultimate slap in the face, an abnegation of birthright by someone ashamed of their own people.

"Look in the mirror, girl", my Mama said to me, when I tried to explain to her that belief had nothing to do with my sense of racial identity. "Look at your nose and tell me you're not Jewish."

"I am Jewish," I said to her, "I'm not ashamed of the fact. I'm not going to have plastic surgery. The Jesus I believe in was as Jewish as I am."

And I knew, too, that in the event of another holocaust, God forbid, I would suffer the same fate as my fellow Jews. The fate of many small groups of Jewish Christians throughout Europe during the Second World War. If Hitler didn't spare great musicians or artists, no other warped embodiment of evil was going to distinguish between Jews who believed Jesus was the Messiah, and Jews who did not.

A similar, though not so obvious, hostility exists between ultra-Orthodox, or Hasidic, Jews and those who are much more liberal by persuasion. They have very little in common. I remember the aggravation my father felt every Saturday when he saw the Hasidic community of our town, dressed in black frockcoats and top hats, out in the local park for their Sabbath stroll.

"Must they dress like Polish noblemen of the last century? Must they stick out like pork sausages at a kosher butcher's?"

But though my father believed in assimilation, and they believed in separation, though their appearance and behaviour made him cringe, ultimately, as far as outsiders were concerned, a Jew was a Jew, in whatever disguise, and there existed between my worldly, fun-loving father, and these pious, serious-minded gentlemen the affinity produced by birth into a minority, persecuted race.

Christians are born, the second time around, spiritually speaking, into a minority, sometimes persecuted, race. So what happened to the sense of affinity, of inescapable belonging? Why are we so often a disparate mass of isolated individuals with no sense of corporate identity? I sometimes wish we could have the equivalent of a Jewish nose – a distinguishing feature which would convey instant recognition. Oh I do toot madly, leap up and down on my seat and wave frantically every time I pass a car with the familiar fish symbol on it. The occupants usually stare at me as if I have taken leave of my senses. Why put the traditional Christian symbol on your car in the first place, if you're too inhibited to acknowledge a traditional Christian greeting?

"Am I my brother's keeper?" The question was left dangling in the air in the Old Testament. The answer, in the New, is a resounding "Yes". If, as the parable of the Good Samaritan shows, I am responsible for a complete stranger, then how much more for whoever sits next to me in the pew. They're family, flesh and blood, relatives even, oy vey. And you're stuck with your family. However much they make you cringe.

The "righteousness" of right relationships comes through hard and bitter work, is born of tears, sweat and self-denial. It's so much easier to get our Christian doctrine right, and reject those who disagree with us. That's how the denominations were born. There's an old story that a rather lively (Jewish for extremely heated) debate broke out between the followers of Hillel and Shammai, two leading Rabbis who lived at the time of Jesus. The hostility was resolved when a voice from heaven declared, "Both sides speak the words of the living God." My father always taught me to look for the element of truth in every argument. Sadly we tend to assume that if I am right, everyone else must be wrong. But two people can have radically opposing views, yet both, in some way, "speak the words of the living God". The problem is meeting in the middle. Each time we move to a new church my husband spends his first few weeks as an arbitrator, sorting out a host of fraught relationships. Kick over the stones and out scurries an army of grubs. The only difference between the Church and virtually every other organisation in society, from office to factory, is that the Christian grubs tend to scuttle about underground.

Working in an office for the first time, six years ago, opened my eyes to a micro-environment I never knew existed. I felt as if I had come of age. To think that all over the country existed thousands of miniature kingdoms with their own language, legislation, culture and political systems. Each with its own intrigue, in-jokes and power struggles. I loved the banter, the teasing, the easy camaraderie. I loathed the groaning, griping and back-stabbing. It can be a very creative environment, when positive ideas are bounced like coloured balls from one to another. It can be immensely destructive, when the balls all fall to the floor and are used to trip each other up. Where human beings are, the best democratic system can be destroyed by petty arguments and grudging resentment. But most offices do not even aspire to democracy. They opt for a hierarchical system in the workplace, ruled by dictators, and dependent, for its effectiveness, on their benevolence. Which is counter-productive, for it brings out the worst in most of us. Who wouldn't rather be a chief than an indian, given half a chance? And the thirst for power does very odd things to the nicest of people. It makes them grasping and greedy and underhand. It destroys relationships. I sometimes came home feeling sad and tainted.

I learned very quickly that the one who wielded the greatest power was she who shared the boss's bed. Which taught me a valuable lesson about being the minister's wife. I had always stoutly maintained that I was a member of the congregation like any other, a lay person with no special favours or influence. I was naïve. Like it or not, I had a special hot-line to the vicar. I could modify his sterner judgements. Or aggravate an already difficult situation. I suddenly realised that unless I consciously recognised the power I had, I would never use it carefully, wisely or fairly.

The lust for power can be a very destructive force in any church. It reared its head before Jesus had even had a chance to die.

"My boys are good boys," said the mother of James and John, "When you become King, let them sit on either side of you."

She was a Jewish Mama. What should she want but the best for her boys? If they weren't going to be doctors or dentists, let them be top politicians. She was barely out of the room when the other disciples started carping and complaining. Strange how fast brotherly love disintegrates when status is threatened. No one, even then, seems to have grasped how radical Jesus was. Service, not status, was to be the mark of his disciples. They were to lay down the right to power, as he did.

Jews are not very good at hierarchies. Not because everyone wants to be the boss. But because everyone thinks that they are. There's a saying that the President of the United States visited the President of Israel. "You, Mr President," said the President of Israel, "have an easy life, for you are president of millions of people. But I am president of a million presidents."

It throws a different complexion on synagogue life. Corporate identity rather than individualism means that everyone is equal. The Rabbi, for example, particularly in

Orthodox congregations, has no authority. He is a teacher, not a leader of his congregation, benign but ineffectual, too learned to be bothered with practical responsibilities. That pleasure is left to democratically elected representatives who have to steer their way through six opinions for every one member of the congregation, then stand down, exhausted, after a thankfully short term of office.

Hierarchical structures in the Church seem to me to be as doomed as any in a secular institution. A large family has to have its leaders, some employed full-time, on behalf of the congregation, which hasn't the time to run the church and do their own work, but if service is their hallmark, so is humility, sensitivity, and self-effacement. They support the structure from underneath, not dominate it from above. Too often individualism has produced authority figures who impose their views by dint of a powerful personality and lead the people into sect mentality. The truth is that all have equal status with Grandma, who is probably the far greater saint.

Respect for my grandparents, my duty towards them and towards all other relatives, who relied on our visits, was one of the most important features of my childhood. I particularly remember the dreaded weekly visits to my maternal great-grandparents, who had fled from the pogroms of Lithuania. They spoke an amazing, broken English, with a heavy Geordie accent and I couldn't understand a word they were saying. While he sat alone in the corner, singing Hebrew songs to himself, in time to the rhythmical motion of the plunger which forced a piece of lemon up and down his glass beaker of tea, she would take a fold of my cheek between her bony fingers and shake me about like a rag doll, until my eyes smarted. I thought it must be some strange Lithuanian form of affection. And then I would be made to eat, and eat, and eat. And the food tasted strange, and the house smelt strange, of lavender and must and Eastern European spices. But it was no use saying I didn't want to go, any more than I could refuse to accompany my parents on any family visit.

My weekends were completely tied up. Chosen friendships had to be fitted around family duties.

But I did develop a very special attachment for my relatives, especially my childless aunt, who was always dressed from top to toe in purple, including her eyeshadow, and for whom I was more of a surrogate daughter than a niece. And when I first found myself in a church it seemed a very lonely environment by comparison. I was twenty-one, and had just been baptised. Links with my family had been temporarily severed while they came to terms with the situation, and I desperately needed surrogate aunts and uncles, parents and grandparents. But no one adopted me. And yet, when I visited the local synagogue in my first year at university, I had been inundated with offers of lunch. "Unthinkable for you to eat alone on Shabbat," they said, "it's only what I would expect your family to do for my daughter in the same situation."

What the Jews see as their duty, Christians call, "having someone round for a meal". The latter is optional, the former is not. And that despite a New Testament command to practise hospitality. In a religion of lay people however, the home is more important than the synagogue, a temple in miniature, not a castle with moat and bailey. Sharing it is as automatic as breathing. There must be room at every meal table for the widow, orphan, or stranger, the single and the student from out of town. Do for others what you would want them to do for you. It's a cardinal rule in Judaism.

My brother will do a detour of sixty miles to give a widowed great-aunt a lift to a bridge party. He may moan about it, but he will do what he has to do, what is expected of him. But try and find a volunteer to do a four-mile round trip to bring an elderly person to church every week, and it may well be a problem. We simply do not have that sense of responsibility for our "relatives".

Never has Western society been so alienated or fragmented. The old communities where everyone left their doors open and popped in and out of each other's homes have vanished. Mobility has meant the end of having granny or aunty next door, for the nuclear family moves away from its roots and survives alone. As do those who are left behind. Self-sufficiency is the order of the day. And this provides the Church with an unprecedented opportunity to create the radical, loving, inter-dependent community God intended. It isn't good for anyone to try and survive alone, the widowed, the single, the single-parent family, not even the nuclear family. Our expectation of marriage has become unrealistic. It is seen as the ultimate symbiotic relationship, two people living in a vacuum with their two point five children, each supplying all the other needs, where once it existed as part of a community, nourished and enriched by all kinds of outside support. Children thrive on relationships with older people, as much as older people benefit from being with children. The nuclear family needs input from single people as much as single people need adopting. In the Church there is no shortage of surrogate grandparents, aunts, uncles and children, no shortage of potentially life-enriching relationships, if we are prepared for the commitment, the duty, involved. The Christian is called to make the Jew jealous, says the Apostle Paul to the Roman Church. There is a high standard of loving, communal care to beat.

But sadly, instead of sharing our lives and homes the way the Jewish community does, instead of creating a network of extended families, where all belong and have a profound sense of commitment to one another, our Western individualism tells the congregation they don't need to meet, let alone support, each other. Religious broadcasting doesn't help. It offers you your own private, non-relational, religious experience at home. My husband can almost guarantee at a funeral visit, that when the bereaved say, "He was a good Christian, he always watched the religious programmes on the telly," it meant that the deceased had usually fallen out with everyone at his local church.

Jewish family life, it must be said, and here is its major drawback, can ensnare a person in a web of such tight emotional ties, that it is almost impossible to break free. A few years ago my mother thought we should persuade my mother-in-law to give up her apartment and go into a retirement home.

"She doesn't want to just yet," I said.

"But it's not fair on you."

I couldn't help but wonder whether she would have been so worried about us if it had been her future which hung in the balance.

Then she said the words which robbed me of mine for more than a moment.

"Well if all else fails to make her do what you want," she said, "I should try emotional blackmail."

Many a Jewish Mama would have thought of the possibility. Only mine would have said it. I must say she had a very good teacher. She would never have dared to omit telephoning her own mother, who lived twenty miles away, at least once a day.

Finding an appropriate Mother's Day card for her every year is becoming an increasing nightmare. The sloppy, saccharine, sentimental stuff which passes for appreciation never seems quite right.

"Thank you, Mother," said one card, "for your silent presence."

Should I send it, covered in exclamation marks? A nice touch of irony? I thought not and put it back on the rack. The spilt guts involved in forming a meaningful relationship with a parent is hardly done the greatest of justice by a sickly verse in a card.

I fought my way free when I was baptised. I thought I would never hold out against the barrage of "You can't love us if you do this," and "We won't love you," but I did, and as I established my own independence, the relationship with my parents deepened. I had waited four years, until I was twenty-one, to prove to them that my faith was more than an adolescent whim. I had also agreed not to go to church during that time, braving a mass of pressure from Christians, who told me I was compromising my beliefs. Emotional blackmail is not a solely Jewish prerogative. I wanted to show my parents that I was prepared to bend over backwards to honour them. It never ceases to amaze me how lightly non-Jews take the commandment. Yet somehow there has to be a balance. Honour, duty and responsibility on the one hand, personal integrity and autonomy on the other.

Jesus didn't find it easy. Mary had to learn on several occasions that she couldn't slot him into her stereotype of the ideal son. It began at his barmitzvah, the moment when every Jewish boy becomes an adult, and he disappeared on his own into the Temple, leaving his parents to look for him. At the wedding in Cana he told her quite forcefully to mind her own business. And once, when something important commanded his attention, kept her waiting outside, an unthinkable way for a Jewish boy to treat his mama. But at the end, as he hung on the cross, in immense pain himself, he worried about her, and what her grief might do to her, and asked John to look after her for him.

Finding the right balance may cause a great deal of effort and pain. It may mean counselling, inner healing of raw wounds, careful, but plain, speaking. It is not passing off on to our parents the blame for our problems. It means understanding why they behaved as they did, so that we can forgive, and go on forgiving, sometimes through gritted teeth.

Forgiveness is the key to coping with relatives. Not always easy to receive it. Positive agony to grant it. But Jesus made it clear that there cannot be one without the other. And what better opportunity to ensure that both the giving and receiving are in good working order, than on the Sabbath?

9

Shabbat Shalom

The first thing to remember about the Jewish Sabbath is that it is a total-rest day. Not religious-observance day. Not spiritual-boost day. Not even see-the-minister-and-sort-out-all-my-problems or the problems-of-the-church day. It is a day for being, not doing, a day for enjoying God's best gifts: home and family, community and fellowship. All work is strictly forbidden. On Shabbat rich and poor, employer and employee are absolutely equal, free from the domination of their weekly drudgery, free to be themselves, invested with the dignity due to all humanity, without the artificial divisions imposed by the workplace.

With circumcision, though they do seem rather uneasy bedfellows, Sabbath is one of the two signs of covenant, of God's special relationship with his children. It marks them out. Makes them different from all other people. Orthodox Jews regard it as a chance to sample the joys of the world to come, which, they say, will be one long Sabbath. How will anyone feel at home in heaven if they don't fully enjoy Sabbath here?

Sabbath here lasts a full twenty-four hours, not the mere fifteen hours or so which constitute a Christian Sunday. A complete change of gear needs mental and emotional preparation, the chance to breathe, unwind. Sometimes the run-up, with its wonderful sense of relaxation, seems more important than the event itself. A

Jewish Friday evening is special. When I was a child, it was the pivot of the entire week. Nothing was allowed to interfere with this family time. No Rotary functions, no night-clubbing, dancing or dinner parties. Tonight my parents were at home. For us.

From six in the evening an open fire blazed in the dining-room hearth. Sabbaths to me are always winter. Perhaps because they were at their cosiest. The heavy velvet curtains, shut tight, severed us from all connection with the world outside. No television tonight, nothing but profound silence, broken only by the ticking of the clock and the occasional spit and crackle of an exploding piece of coal in the grate, as we sat reading, waiting for my father to finish his evening surgery.

"Where is he?" Mama would complain, if he hadn't appeared by seven, removed his white doctor's coat, and taken his place at the head of the table. "He knows what night it is," as if he had deliberately encouraged his patients to find extra ailments, just to spite her.

Usually she lit the candles before he arrived. "They should be lit at sundown," she said.

"We should be home by sundown too," we moaned. "Other Jewish children leave school early on Fridays." Our non-Jewish friends thought it worth converting for.

"It's not necessary," she snapped.

"Yes," we said.

We had learned not to ask why almost as soon as we could speak. There was never any rationale for her arguments. For her, being Jewish was a matter of feelings, not reason.

She stood staring vacantly at candles and began to whisper the traditional prayer to herself, a look of something almost resembling piety smoothing out her fine features and skin for just a moment.

"What are you doing?"

"Trying to pray."

"What about?"

"Never you mind."

Small wonder that my childish mind associated the prayer at the lighting of the Sabbath candles with making a wish when you blew out all the candles on a birthday cake.

"You're supposed to wave now," I once said to her.

"Who to?"

"Not to anyone. You welcome in Shabbat as if it were an important visitor. A bride or a queen."

At Hebrew classes they had shown the girls how to make the appropriate sweeping motions over the flames and I had been terribly impressed.

"Then you hide your face in your hands, ask God to send me a good husband, and when you open your eyes, hey presto, all is light and the Sabbath has come."

"All this waving sounds a bit surplus to me," she said. "And besides, you're perfectly capable of finding yourself a husband one day. As long as he's Jewish."

Had she known what lay ahead, she might have prayed harder.

Tradition has it, and this may stick in a feminist gullet, that Mother lights the candles because Eve, the first mother, extinguished the light of eternal life when she disobeyed God and gave Adam fruit from the forbidden tree. The fact that Adam needed little encouragement seems to have escaped attention. One candle represents "creation", the other "redemption", and though it may be pushing the point to its limit, I have heard it argued, by Christians, not Jews, that this could be symbolic of the fact that woman is now involved in the redemptive process, since Mary gave birth to "the Light of the World".

The tradition for lighting candles probably arose many archaic, pre-electric centuries ago, when the sound of the ram's horn filled the air, announcing Shabbat, "a time of rest", and everyone cheered and went home faster than on any other day, with that unique, Friday-night feeling fizzing in the pit of their stomachs. As the sun went down they lit their lamps, and hung them in the window, so that light shone out into the darkness of the Gentile community from every Jewish home, making it clear that tonight was like no other.

The principle of a sabbath rest, of course, pre-dates Judaism. God set human beings the best possible example of how to control stress. After six days' hard labour creating the world, he sat back and spent a day taking stock of what he had done. Kiddush, the Friday night Sabbath prayer, begins with the familiar Genesis story. To this day I can still hear my father's gentle, lilting voice saying, "Vay'erev vay'voker yam hashishi – And it was evening, it was morning – the sixth day." I never ceased to be amazed at his sincerity, for a man usually so lacking in piety. But this important ritual, setting the mood for the evening and even the whole weekend, was one he loved.

After Friday evening, Saturday was a let-down. For a child. It was one long list of "can't"s and "don't"s. Knitting was forbidden. A minor restriction, except that it provided the only excitement in my grandparents' home on a Saturday afternoon. Reading was allowed. So there was always the *News of the World*, an exceedingly illuminating newspaper – for a twelve-year-old. While I was being initiated into the world of rape and adultery, my grandmother smoked, contravening a subdivision of the "shalt not light a fire" law. She stubbed out her cigarette in the nearest receptacle, usually the pot of one of my grandfather's beloved azaleas, whenever a relative passed in front of the large bay window out on their Sabbath walk. She waved graciously. He opened half an eye, groaned, and went back to sleep, head on hand, slumped in front of the horse racing. Watching television was forbidden. Not that he saw very much. But he had had a little flutter. Handling money was forbidden. His horse had come last again. Did he want sympathy?

I grew up believing that religious laws were meant to be broken. If they spoilt the fun. Most of the Jews I knew travelled to the synagogue by car. Of course the Rabbi knew his congregation had not got up at the

crack of dawn to make a six- or seven-mile trek on foot.
Why bother parking round the corner? But if you were
a child, however, the rules had to be strictly obeyed,
otherwise the Big Ogre in the Sky would strike you
with a thunderbolt. When I was about twelve I realised
I had never seen a thunderbolt, and felt exasperated
with the sham. It obliterated the positive side of my
heritage. I wanted to throw off every restraint, every
hypocrisy, the whole of Judaism.

When it comes to religious observance, human beings
love hedging each other in with dozens of manmade
regulations. Until we have to decide whether to break
out or submit and die. Either way there is a danger of
throwing out the proverbial baby with the bath water,
the faith which appears to imprison us, or our integrity.
Christians can be faced with this dilemma. The vital,
irrepressible, inner freedom of Jesus Christ was one of
his most immediate attractions for me. It came as a huge
shock to discover later that some of his followers conform
to a set of rules as comprehensive and demanding as any
proscribed by the Talmud. Particularly with reference to
Sundays. I had a friend at university who insisted on
wearing a hat to church, because her mother expected
it. Even though Mother was more than two hundred
miles away. We walked along the streets of Manchester
together every Sunday morning, I in my gaudy, Jewish
gear, she in chameleon-brown, head down, shoulders
hunched, a picture of discomfort and embarrassment.
What a strange pair we must have made. I felt alternate
admiration for her determination to honour her mother,
and anger with a mother who would submit a child she
loved to such an endurance test.

I remember the horror of being discovered at my desk
by a fellow Christian student on a Sunday. I might just
as well have been caught in the act of pilfering. I tried
in vain to cover up a French essay. Working? On the
Lord's day? Rules always made me defiant. I now see
that the principle of not working was a good one. I

needed a day away from my books, a day for reading and relationships, a day different from all others. At the time it simply seemed yet another form of Judaism.

A Rabbi once said that the sabbath laws were like mountains suspended on hairs. The sages spent hours discussing such momentous perplexities as: is carrying a handkerchief transgressing the commandment not to bear a burden on the Sabbath? The answer: yes, if it is carried in the pocket, no, if it is tied around the neck, for it counts as clothing. Christians have tended to assume that Jesus preached a radical new approach to the Sabbath. But it is not as simple as that. When he said that the Sabbath was made for man, not man for the Sabbath, he followed a ploy he, as a Pharisee, regularly used, quoting them their own Pharisaic teachings, reminding them about Sabbath joy, not abolishing the law. When he encouraged the disciples to pluck ears of corn, it was not a casual infringement of sabbath law. It was an emergency. They were as hungry as King David, when he ate the holy bread in the Temple. As for healing on the Sabbath, nowhere is it proscribed in Pharisaic law. Inflexibility, dogmatism, putting systems before people, not sabbath observance, was the butt of his anger.

Regimenting a Sabbath is one danger. Ignoring it altogether because it seems too much effort is another. One church I knew had their Sunday morning service as early as possible, "to get it out of the way, so that we can all have the rest of the day to ourselves". In the book of Isaiah the prophet, God has to remonstrate with his people for doing their own thing on that one special day. "If you honour it by not doing as you please, or speaking idle words, then you will find joy in the Lord." That is a promise I rather like.

Sabbath is potentially a wonderful gift, from God to his people, and from us to each other. No gift is as precious these days as the gift of time. Which is why I am totally committed to keeping Sunday special, a day like no other day, when the pace of life slows to tortoise-speed, there are no shops, no hustle and bustle, nothing to remind us of our normally frenetic existence. Even the Jewish law forbidding the use of a car has its value. No motor car, no engine noise, no fumes. We might even catch, for once, the song of a bird, the buzz of a bee. We might even smell pure, fresh air, or the scent of a rose. We're forced to walk and when we walk we think. We pass other human beings. We make eye contact, stop to talk, become aware of our world in a new way.

The ideal of Shabbat is that a person is free to do the things which are normally overlooked, like playing silly games with the children, reading a good book, having a lunchtime nap, talking to a spouse, a child, a friend, without the pressure of the next event. The Jews, because they have Friday evening and the whole of the next day, have both family and community time, which alleviates any conflict there might be between the two. We today have a weekend.

We have tried hard as a family to preserve some kind of "Shabbat". Our treasured Friday night family ritual is more under threat as the years go by and the children get older and want to be out with their friends, and the church demands Peter's presence. I still light my candles to remind me to pray for my children, to remind the family that weekends are for rest and togetherness, to remind visitors that tonight is special. There is a light which goes on shining, no matter how dark the world around us. We still have kiddush, the familiar bread and wine.

By sundown I try to have an empty desk. Clearing my notes and files into neat little piles all over my study does me a great deal of psychological good, even if it achieves very little. Soon after that, or whenever it is practically possible, family and guests gather around the meal table. I, or Abby, my daughter, light the candles. She has been involved in this favourite tradition since we could trust her to hold a match without setting the house on fire. Occasionally there is a present for each child, usually the edible variety. Traditionally the father is then supposed to pay his wife the highest compliment by telling her she has all the qualities of the proverbial wife. "An excellent wife who can find?" he reads aloud to the assembled gathering. Somehow I seem to have missed out on that particular little piece of liturgy all these years. That's the penalty for having a husband who doesn't know the rules of the game.

We drink wine, symbolising joy and life and blessing, rest and relaxation. And then the bread, the produce of a person's labour. Or in our case, a parson's labour.

Ever since Sarah, the matriarch, the first great Jewish master-chef, baked her mouth-watering meal and water hearth cakes for the visiting angels, long before the miraculous raising powers of yeast were discovered (in Egypt, ironically, at about the same time my Jewish ancestors were building Pharaoh's luxury homes), Mother is supposed to bake this staple food and offer it as a mark of hospitality to her honoured guests. On Friday morning, as she kneads and works the dough for the chollah, the traditional sweet, plaited loaf, she prays blessings on all her family. In our liberated home, Dad is the baker, the result of cookery lessons taken when he suddenly decided that he had had enough of waiting for the major wage-earner to come home and make him his evening meal. In fact, one Sunday, when, through some inadvertent error, there was no bread for the evening communion service, and all the shops were shut, the vicar nipped home and baked his flock a loaf. All in a clergyman's day. I wanted to know which members of the congregation he was praying for when he was pummelling the dough. I suspect he had hit upon a very satisfactory way of dealing with ministerial stress.

Work is becoming an increasingly rare privilege in our world. We pray, as we eat the bread, for those who have none, and no food. And we remind each other that Jesus told us, when we ate bread and drank wine, to remember him.

Saturday is Saturday, sleep-late, meet-the-children, share-project-with-spouse, cook-the-Sunday-lunch day, a hiatus between Friday night and Sunday. It is a semi-Sabbath, but then so is Sunday, for a minister's family. Two half-Sabbaths have to make a whole.

Sunday is an institution. It remains completely free for the family, both the blood and church variety. Traditional Sunday lunch is almost always shared with others. People ask me how I manage to cook for eight, or ten or more. But I operate on the Jewish principle of having as much as I can prepared in advance. Then I don't spend Sunday, like almost every other day of the week, slaving over a hot cooker. My friends marvel at how amazingly well-organised I always seem to be in the kitchen. Christmas fare is often in the freezer by the end of November. By March my shelves are filling up with Passover coconut pyramids and spicy Easter biscuits. It is more habit than organisation. Thinking ahead is an auto-response, inspired by a long-held tradition, which actually works rather well, and gives me a relaxed, rather than a fraught, Sunday with friends. And what Sabbath would be complete without good food?

An older friend told me a while ago that she was so fed up with the work involved in making a roast dinner on a Sunday, that she and her husband have now settled for a quiet omelette. I have nothing against the humble egg. I sympathised with her, but wondered whether something special wasn't lost if Sunday, and the omelette, remained unshared. After all, Sabbath meals for the Jews often consist of cold meats or fish, or one-pot casseroles left stewing for hours. If only, now that she was so tired, others began to invite her out for Sunday lunch. Or if we had occasional communal church lunches, so that everyone had a chance of sharing a Sabbath lunch, once in a while.

There is a lovely way to end the Sabbath, called "Havdalah" or Separation. Two twisted tapers are lit, and a goblet is filled to the brim with wine, so that it pours over into a saucer. As the wine is spilt the Sabbath departs, and everyone thanks God for the overflowing cup of blessing they have just received. The tapers are extinguished in the pool of wine and everyone takes a long hard sniff at a bessamen, or spice box, which is passed from person to person. The idea is that the fragrance of the Sabbath will sustain them through the pressures of the week. It's the perfect way of saying a sad goodbye to a lovely day. Last week, Sabbath and next week are perfectly integrated and somehow it all makes Monday morning more than just a little bearable.

KIDDUSH, A SERVICE FOR THE SABBATH EVE

1. Lighting the Candles, *said by Mother, and her daughters.*

Blessed are You, O Lord our God, King of the Universe,
Who brings light out of darkness,
And whom we honour with these lights on the Sabbath.

*Add here any other prayers, meditations or readings with the theme of light, creation and redemption,
e.g. Matt. 5:14–16.*

2. The Blessings, *said by both parents, laying their hands on their children's heads.*

To the sons: God make you like Ephraim and Manasseh.
To the daughters: God make you like Sarah, Rebecca, Rachel and Leah.
To both: (extempore prayers, followed by) The Lord bless you and keep you, the Lord make His face to shine upon you, and give you His peace. *(This is a chance to give them a small treat.)*

The father may then read Proverbs 31:10–13 especially for his wife, as a token of his love and appreciation. (He may also bring her flowers!)

3. The Wine and the Bread

And it was evening and it was morning – the sixth day.
And the heaven and earth were finished.
And on the seventh day God rested from His work.
And God blessed the seventh day and made it a special day,
because He himself rested from His work.

Father, or his sons, raises the cup of wine, the symbol of rest and rejoicing and says, Blessed are You O Lord our God, King of the Universe, who created the fruit of the vine. *Everyone takes a sip.*

Blessed are You, O Lord, our God,
whose commandments make us holy,
In Your love You gave us a Sabbath rest
to remind us of Your creative work
and our redemption from slavery in Egypt.
Your love also provides us with times of refreshment and recreation.

Blessed are You, O Lord our God, who makes food come out of the earth.

The chollah (symbol of the labour of a human being's hands) is broken, not cut, into pieces. A knife too closely resembles an instrument of war and Jews are supposed to deplore violence, longing for swords to be beaten into ploughshares. The pieces of bread are sprinkled with salt, and passed to every adult and child.
This is an opportunity to thank God for the gift of work, "You shall gain your bread by the sweat of your brow," and to pray for those without work, and without bread.

We also remind ourselves that Christ said, "When you do this, remember me," and finish the occasion with a few songs, while the meal is being served.

SABBATH RECIPES

CHOLLAH

A 3000-year-old recipe, developed by the Macedonian bakers of Perseus II. It is plaited so that it looks as if its arms are folded, and at rest. Makes one large plaited loaf.

480g strong white flour
15g fresh yeast
2 eggs
2 tsp. salt
3 tsp. caster sugar
2 tbsp. oil
200ml warm water

Heat the water until warm, not hot, place in a mixing bowl and add one-third of the flour, the sugar and the yeast. Mix until smooth, cover with a tea-towel, then leave about 20 minutes, until frothy. Add all the remaining ingredients, and knead by hand or in a mixing machine with a dough hook until smooth. Place the ball of dough in a greased polythene bag and leave in the fridge for 12–24 hours.

Take the risen dough from the fridge and leave half an hour at room temperature, then divide it into three pieces and roll the pieces into long sausage shapes. Press all three strands firmly together at one end, then plait firmly, and place on a greased tray.

Put the loaves in a greased polythene bag and leave to rise in a warm place for about half an hour. Take the dough out of the polythene bag and brush it with egg yolk. Scatter with poppy seeds if desired, then place in the oven and bake for 15 minutes (gas mark 7, 425°F,

220°C) then turn down the oven (gas mark 5, 375°F, 190°C) for a further 30–45 minutes.

CHOLENT

A one-pot meal consisting of anything with the stamina to stand up to 24 hours in the oven. It originated in Poland when the bitter European winters made a hot meal on the Sabbath a necessity. Serves 6.

2kg boneless brisket or pot roast
500g dried butter or lima beans or pearl barley, soaked overnight
3 chopped onions
6 potatoes, peeled and chopped
2 tbsp. oil or margarine
salt, pepper, paprika, ginger and garlic
1 bay leaf

Rub the joint with all the seasonings, then brown in the oil with the onions and potatoes. Place all the ingredients in a deep casserole, cover with boiling water, and seal with a tight-fitting lid. Bake very slowly (gas mark ½, 250°F, 130°C), overnight if desired. Add a little extra water if necessary.

10

Just Like a Prayer

My right hand was poised in mid-air, soup spoon awaiting its descent into the steaming, mouth-watering concoction under my nose, when my companion across the table suddenly said, "Let's say grace."

She folded her hands, bowed her head, closed her eyes. And I, reluctantly, lowered my spoon and followed suit.

"Everything all right, ladies?" broke in an anxious voice, before she had even managed to say, "Dear, Lord . . ."

Our heads jerked up in perfect harmony. We blinked and saw the waiter staring into our food with worried concern.

I was tempted to say, "Well actually there's a fly in my soup," but instead we feigned innocence and said nonchalantly, "Fine, it's fine, thank you."

As if he were the one behaving in an unusual manner.

Unconvinced, he examined the soup again, then backed like a defensive spider into the shadows.

That was one of many occasions when I have felt uneasy about traditional attitudes to praying. When, a few seconds later, I broke the bread roll on my side plate, it occurred to me that a Jew would simply have muttered the thanksgiving for bread under her breath, and perhaps even handed a piece to her companion as a sign of sharing.

Nowhere are people more tempted to hack off what they see as the spiritual side of themselves from the

mundane and earthy than when it comes to praying.
There was a series on the television a few months ago
about women and religion. One programme featured four
women of different faiths at prayer. The Hindu sat quietly
before her home-made shrine. The Muslim took out her
prayer mat. The Christian sat in silence with her Bible.
The Jewish woman was getting her little boy ready for
nursery school as they said morning prayer together.
There were constant interruptions from a glove puppet
which the little boy had on his hand, who was Mrs
Mandelstam, his teacher.

"Why do we need to thank *Ha' Shem* (the Name)
every morning, Davey? For a new day? For lots of new
things to do? Yes. Oh, hello, Mrs Mandelstam, what's
the class going to do this morning? Painting? That's nice.
Shema, yisroel, adonai, elohenu, adenai echod. My, Mrs
Mandelstam, what a big mouth you have. You must let
me fasten Davey's buttons. Hear O Israel, the Lord our
God, the Lord is One."

The Christian prayed more like the Hindu and the
Muslim than the Jew. Despite the fact that Christianity
grew out of Judaism. Despite the fact that Jesus, the
Jew, when asked how to pray, didn't fold his hands,
close his eyes, or construct a long, extemporary piece of
verbiage. "A man's words should be few when address-
ing God," says the Gemara. Jesus simply reminded his
followers of one of the most earthed and gutsy prayers
in existence, short, to the point and firmly rooted in
everyday experience. Which is why I, still wearing my
"L" plates, a remedial in this area, dare to join the host
of spiritual giants who have written about this particular
subject.

For the Jewish woman there was no difference between
talking to God and talking to her child, between prayer
and play. Far be it from me to suggest that we never
need silence or stillness, but sometimes it isn't practicable.
When my children were small I despaired of even going
to the toilet in peace, let alone of finding a few quiet

moments for prayer. Thoroughly indoctrinated with the evangelical notion of a "Quiet Time" I felt guilty and depressed about my failure. Sure that God would remove his blessing. As if he sat in heaven waiting to see who had and had not clocked in for work that morning. And in my case, there would certainly be no bonuses for overtime.

Anglo-Catholic books on spirituality only compounded my sense of depression. Most of them were written by men. It was all right for them to recommend silence and meditation, I said to myself, as I fed and changed the baby, threw her in the buggy, took her out and changed her again because she had filled her nappy, then raced the mile to playgroup with a reluctant, foot-dragging toddler, already fifteen minutes late.

I wish now that I had remembered the way I was brought up, when prayer wasn't a separate entity in its own little box, something to be done on its own, apart from everything else, but was instead fully integrated into the daily routine. Getting out of bed, brushing your teeth, driving, eating, seeing the sun, or the rain, even going to the toilet, with their relevant blessings, all provided the stimulus for communion with the divine.

Life, for the Jew, is perpetual prayer, like breathing, spontaneous, natural, almost subconscious. They do not kneel, close their eyes, and rarely do anything a person wouldn't normally do in the course of an ordinary day. Except that a man will stand and face Jerusalem in the morning when he binds on his phylacteries. He may rock backwards and forwards, known as davening, and he'll mutter, or sing to himself under his breath. The Hebrew word for meditating is "hagah", which also means to murmur. Verbalising your thoughts, not silence, is the Jewish means of maintaining concentration. So he will go on rocking and murmuring when the kids or the wife burst in on him to complain about each other, ask for the bus fare, or enquire what time he intends coming home that evening. After all, almost every conversation has its diversions and distractions.

Prayer in the synagogue continues even when there is such a racket all around him that the Rabbi can hardly hear himself think, let alone pray. But he knows that his congregation will dip in and out of the service, one minute joining in the unsynchronised, communal muttering and chanting which is prayer, the next discussing the unpredictability of business, the weather, or the performance of the football team. Which is another kind of prayer. It was always one of the greatest mysteries to me how, amidst this apparently unco-ordinated cacophony, everyone managed to say amen together at the right time. But the synagogue is the community's meeting place, not a place for private devotion. If you want silence, why come to schul? Go find it at home. Jesus himself, when he wanted quiet, headed for the mountains. He knew better than to expect it from the Temple.

"You and Rabbi Mandel were having a really deep conversation in schul the other day," Mama said to my brother, a few weeks ago. "Anything interesting?"

"When? You mean as I was waiting to read a portion? He was thanking me for the season ticket I got for him."

"It takes three minutes to say thank you for a football ticket?"

"It was hard to get. Oh, and then he told me to get a move on with the reading, because Naomi had his favourite Shabbas meal waiting for him at home."

No religious ceremony around the table in a Jewish home is ever halted because Grandma is discussing a new way to cook a chicken, or Grandpa has fallen asleep – while leading the service. That was a regular occurrence in my grandparents' home. At least five minutes might pass before anyone realised that the occasion had ground to a halt. Then the chatter would stop while Grandpa was prodded, punched and shaken awake, and start up again the moment he began to read from the prayer book.

When my uncle led the Passover service, and Mama and Grandmother were deeply engrossed in conversation, he would stop altogether and time them to see how long it would be before they realised we were all listening to them. It infuriated my mother.

"Get on with it," she would snap.

"Or else the meal will be ruined," Grandmother would chime in.

It was becoming impossible for a mother and daughter to have a chat in peace these days!

But say "prayer" to a non-Jew and there's almost a Pavlov's dog response, head down, eyes closed, vague attempt at suitably pious expression. Opening a meeting with prayer is one of my particular little foibles. A dozen or so worthy committee members gather in a front room to discuss the independent lifestyle of the church boiler, the pigeon droppings on the porch, the inadequacies of the parish hall plumbing, or some other vital issue which makes up the average spiritual and intellectual stimulation of the people of God. They laugh and chatter and unwind as the steaming mug in their hands defrosts the senses numbed by the daily drudgery at the office, school or factory, and loosens the emotions and the tongue with its tingling warmth.

Then a voice says, "Let us pray," and this is a signal for the gathered throng to go into holy mode.

Some stare at the ceiling, some study the pattern on the carpet, others screw up their eyes as if blinded by a sudden light.

And an angel in heaven says, "Jump to it, Sir," to the Almighty, in case he hasn't noticed that his presence is required.

There is a very fine dividing line between superstition and prayer, between placating a deity and acknowledging the omnipresence of a loving Father. And the change which comes over us when we "say a prayer" seems to suggest the belief that one minute God isn't there, and the next minute he is, when we ask him nicely. Like shop floor workers requesting a visit from the managing director.

The Jews can fall into the trap of superstition too. My little niece knew that the words of the Shema, "Hear O

Israel, the Lord our God, the Lord is One," were to be the last words on her lips before sleeping. The problem came when her two cousins were sharing her bedroom. She had to repeat the prayer eight times before the chatter ended, and she was only spared a ninth repeat by being the only one left awake after the eighth rendering.

Severing prayer from the rest of life begins in childhood. I was horrified when Joel, at three, started to put his hands together, close his eyes, bow his head and say grace in better parsonical voice than ever his father could manage. That was how they did it at Sunday School. And then, instead of thanking God for the warmth of the sun, the wind in his hair, the giggles of the little girl next door, he began to say, "God bless Mummy" and "God bless Daddy", prayers I knew would cease as soon as he realised that grown-ups didn't say them. Of course they didn't. Not unless they were loopy. Or thought that God was an automaton, swallowing the information, spewing out responses.

Presumably making children close their eyes and fold their hands together was a way of teaching them to switch off from outside distractions. But I have a sneaking suspicion that it actually teaches them that God exists only in their own heads, and that talking to him is a rather weird activity, which they can drop, along with any belief, when they're old enough. After all, how many adults do they see sitting around with folded hands, bowed heads and closed eyes? My children always found it hysterically funny when a teacher told them off for not closing their eyes while praying.

"How did she know, unless she didn't close them herself?"

I realised, when my children were small, that if traditional prayer wasn't working very well for me, it might not for them and began experimenting with a more Jewish approach, to enable them to discover a sense of God's presence everywhere, all the time. We never taught them to "say their prayers" at bedtime. We prayed with them every morning in one bed together as a family, trying to weave it into conversation about the events of the day, without changing our tone of voice, or the kind of words we used. Let's be honest, I was often the "sleeping partner" in this activity, dozing through it all, vaguely aware of the gentle murmurings of Peter reading a Bible story, imbibing the atmosphere, I told them, through my skin cells.

When it came to "family prayers", we did not want to inflict a boring endurance test upon them. Or set up an unnatural situation, divorced from the rest of their daily lives. So we wove prayer through and around special occasions. Along with the preparation, candles, fun and good food, it was simply a part of Kiddush around the table on Friday evenings, enhanced by the bread and wine. With the symbol of mankind's labour in our hands, it was natural to pray for those without work, and without food. In fact, for a number of years, the sight of a plate of steaming food on the table seemed to be a trigger for Joel to pray his way halfway round the world. Every lesson we teach our children has its drawbacks.

But so many people grow up and leave childhood behind, finding prayer a very difficult thing to do. Instead of the most natural. Strange, when many of us are never lost for words in normal circumstances. Could it be the invisible nature of the company? Hardly, when most of us relish the opportunity to dominate the discussion. So perhaps the problem lies in the word "normal". Perhaps we don't regard talking to God as a "normal" thing to do.

I have been experimenting with various types of prayer for a number of years now, instinctively feeling that we should follow life's flow instead of fighting it. Enjoying silence as a sacred gift if it was given, allowing noise to dominate if it had to, without resentment or frustration. My ability in the latter was put to the test one day when I was due to speak at a major event in Birmingham city centre. It was the first time a woman had been invited to preach at this particular gathering, and I felt that my entire sex depended on my performance. But there had been almost no time for preparation. For instead of small children I now had a career, and a parish, and teenagers, reports and scripts, shopping and cooking, committees and visits. I had of course told God in passing that I would very much appreciate his pulling out the stops, but felt I needed a little time and space to gather my wits. The house was pandemonium, Peter holding a meeting, noisy youngsters coming and going, so I decided to head early to Birmingham, find a quiet café, and discover that inner stillness I craved.

"But everywhere was closed. The only café open was a fast self-service Wimpy Bar, with pop music playing loudly. I could handle that, hear God despite the competition, I told myself. It was all a matter of attitude. I found a quiet corner, settled down with a psalm and a burger, and sighed happily. At which point the air was split with the sound of police sirens. Two panda cars screeched to a halt right outside the window, half a dozen policemen burst through the doors. Several youths leapt to their feet, somersaulted over tables and chairs. The police gave chase around the café, until the youths were brought to the floor with a crash, and handcuffed at my feet.

"He leads me beside still waters."

The police waited for reinforcements, then marched their resistant booty out into the cars.

It was time to go.

I felt amazingly prepared. For our inner, spiritual awareness is somehow more acute when integrated with the harsh reality of the world outside. Dozens of daily occurrences, important or insignificant, can sensitise us to a God who is everywhere, and in everything. A God who is in a child's drawing as well as the *Mona Lisa*, a hand-knitted jumper as well as the laser, a joke as well as a classical novel, fast food as well as a gourmet dinner. Glimmers of the divine breaking through the greyness of the daily grind.

It was not simply in my own communion with God that I searched for a more natural, earthy approach.

Praying with others, particularly my husband, required a much greater integrity. We were told, before we married, that we ought to pray together regularly as a couple. "The couple who prays together, stays together." The theory is fairly sound. When you feel like murdering your spouse, it's difficult to cope with the company of any third party, let alone God. It puts you under a certain pressure to sort out your differences. Either that, or prayer is turned into an imposition, which you resent or refuse. Peter and I agreed before our wedding that instead of burying our problems behind a spiritual veneer we would confront them together, and never let the sun go down on our anger. It has always worked well, largely because I can stay awake much longer than he can, which means that by about four o'clock in the morning I can usually win the argument.

Praying together can become a rather superficial, meaningless ritual, or simply a grind. We would spend an hour or so, at the end of the day, catching up with each other's news, then feel we ought to pray, so repeat everything we had just said in pious language. As if God had turned his hearing aid off until then. We now try and have a more three-way conversation, often in the dark in bed together. We involve the Almighty in our chatter from the beginning, handing over the problems, the fears and the people we love, as we discuss them. Occasionally saying a much-loved, familiar prayer together, such as "Defend us, O Lord from the perils and dangers of this night", because at midnight, after a busy day, when the brain has long given up in protest, it is much easier to rely on someone else's inspiration than expect one's own grey cells to deliver something vaguely resembling coherency.

It seems too that the Church has set off on a new adventure in prayer. We are rediscovering some of the old traditions, lost in time: Celtic prayer, blending chanting with work; monastic exercises which settle the mind and aid meditation, the use of candles, sung harmonies, and varieties of liturgies and extemporary forms, which stretch the creative imagination. There is an increasing dissatisfaction with the kind of rigid formalisation which locks individuals into their own motionless, emotionless, little worlds. We might even be tempted to rock backwards and forwards like the Jews, to sway as they do, when pronouncing the Levitical blessing on the congregation, to dance as they do, for pure joy, like King David, at Simchat Torah. Our bodies are a valuable asset, not an impediment. In Taizé in France, young people, overwhelmed by the sense of God's presence, often stay prostrate on the floor for hours after the services are over.

When Paul the Apostle talked about bowing the knee before the Father in some of his letters to the early Christians, it was a radical idea. Jews didn't kneel. Today a gesture like that has lost the sense of awe and wonder it once conveyed. And we need to think of new, sometimes radical, ways of expressing the love song which wells up within us. Which is, after all, what prayer, in its essence, is all about.

A NIGHT PRAYER

Almighty God,
As this day comes to a close, I humbly thank You for
  all the blessings it has brought me.
For the life and power You have given me,
For human companionship and fellowship,
And above all, for Your saving and uplifting presence.

If I have been unkind or impatient,
Insensitive or idle,
If I have forgotten You,
Or failed to do what You wanted me to do,
Forgive me,
For You know just how weak and frail I am.

Do not take Your Holy Spirit from me.
But as I lie down to rest, let me feel that nothing separates
  me from Your love.

May Your presence hover over me in the night.
May I sleep, cradled in Your peace.
And if I wake, let me find comfort in the thought that You,
the Guardian of Israel, neither slumbers nor sleeps.
Into Your hands I commit my spirit, my rock and my
refuge.

Hear O Israel, the Lord our God, the Lord is one.

A PRAYER ON WAKING

O Lord my God, thank you for Your presence with me
during the stillness of the night.
You who in Your great wisdom create all things, and care
for the creatures You have made,
Thank you for waking me up to a new day,
For all its potential,
The good things to be enjoyed,
The opportunities waiting for me.
Help me to be worthy of all Your gifts,
To be dutiful, thoughtful and kind,
To pursue only the happiness which comes from pleasing
You.
In the turmoils and distractions of the day,
Let me rest and rely only on You, the God of all truth.

Hear O Israel, the Lord our God, the Lord is one.

Both prayers are taken from *Forms of Prayer for Jewish
Worship*, edited by the Ministers of the West London
Synagogue of British Jews.

II

There was a Catholic, a Protestant and a Jew . . .

And you can guarantee that the punchline will be about the Jew. Which is really rather odd, when you think how funny Catholics and Protestants can be. Perhaps it is because the Jews find it so much easier to laugh at their own foibles. In fact they write the majority of Jewish jokes themselves. "Why did the elephant sit on an orange outside the synagogue? He was waiting for the Jews to come out." My daughter's first Jewish joke. At five she thought it was hilarious.

Real Jewish humour is often much more pointed. Like the story of the prisoner in the concentration camp who is told he will be spared the gas oven if he can tell the commandant which of his two eyes is made of glass. He chooses the correct one.

"How could you tell?" asks the commandant.

"Easy," says the Jew. "In the glass eye there was a glimmer of compassion."

Non-Jews might find jokes about concentration camps rather distasteful, but how else do human beings come to terms with something as horrendous as the holocaust? Jewish humour can be very black, or filled with pathos, because it is a means of coping with immense suffering, a vital tool in the fight for survival.

Suffering is one of those awkward experiences. The very word suggests a display of explosive, negative emotion, which makes the average Anglo-Saxon a little uncomfortable. It doesn't fit neatly into the theological package of a loving God, who wants only the best for his children. So we tend to run from it, and the feelings that go with it.

The problem is that they don't go away. Not while illness exists, robbing those we love of their wholeness and happiness. Not while death removes them to a place where we cannot reach them. I have learned to keep my tears in check at funerals. I hang on to them for dear life, press them down inside, pat myself on the back and tell myself how good I am. I'll treat myself to a really good howl on my own, later. But later doesn't come. Partly because life continues and I'm too busy, partly because I cannot recreate the right emotional environment. I can set off into the countryside, climb the highest mountain, and open my mouth, but all that emerges is a feeble squawk. Better than nothing, but it doesn't seem to disperse the solid lump sitting in my middle.

Yet we applaud those who control their emotions. A church warden and businessman told a friend of mine that he met many Jews in the course of his work. He tried very hard to get on with them, but what he really found hard to swallow was their emotionalism. They were so volatile.

"You wouldn't have liked Jesus very much then," my friend replied. "He certainly wasn't afraid of emotion. He lost his temper at the Temple, and made a scene. He cried in public. He stirred up the crowds until they made more noise than spectators at a football match."

Jewish history is awash with tears. The earliest book in their Scriptures tells the story of a man who lost everything he cared about most, and was left to try and make some sense of the faith he thought he had. Job's friends tried to cheer him up with a pat on the back, a "Now, now, then", and a word or two of accepted theological wisdom, unacceptable in practice, as our theory often is. He needed to work through his despair. They needed to stay with him. Preferably in silence. When it comes to the subject of suffering we are in danger the moment we open our mouths. How to explain the inexplicable? Only now, more than fifty years on, do Jewish theologians dare attempt to formulate a theology of the holocaust, that without it, grossly inadequate as the explanation may seem, there might be no Jewish homeland. Ultimately, Job himself reaches a point where he can see his own suffering in the context of a massive cosmic scheme, and takes some comfort from that.

The most famous of all Jewish books manages to capture the utter wretchedness and misery human beings can feel, without any attempt to explain the great universal "why?" "Why have you forsaken me, oh my God?" There is silence. No answers, only promises. God will hear. God will answer. I have to admit that one of the most excruciating experiences for a Jew in the Church is to hear all that oozing, raw emotion reduced by an Anglo-Saxon congregation to a form of genteel chanting or recitation. The psalms burst with the heights and depths of human experience, and without one how can we appreciate the other? Sorrow and joy, despair and hope are interwoven into an immense outpouring of yearning for a being who condemns us to the misery of his absence, then, when we least expect it, startles us with the wonder of his presence.

At first glance the Church does not appear to reflect the breathtaking sweep of the psalmist's mood swings. We can be awfully jolly or awfully dreary. Either way we skate smoothly over the real churnings inside the human breast. I'm not sure when Christianity and feeling first parted company, but displays of religious emotion are, for our sect-fearful society, totally unacceptable. On one occasion I was making a television documentary about a centre for spiritual healing. We filmed the weekly communion service, during which one or two members of the congregation felt free, in a not entirely unrestrained way, to express their affection for the Almighty.

"Quacks!" said the cameraman. "Nutters, the lot of them."

"Why?" I asked him.

"Well, it's not normal."

"But you wouldn't have felt uncomfortable if you'd been at a football match, would you?" I asked him.

He smiled sheepishly and shook his head.

"Or if the congregation were all Muslims, or Sikhs?"

He admitted he wouldn't. But that was different. Christianity should be safe, bland, inhibited, unthreatening.

So Christians have been forced to submit themselves to a conspiracy of repression, unable to express today the bitterness, bafflement and bewilderment which haunted the psalmist so many centuries ago. There is a wonderful moment in the film *Shadowlands*, the story of the life of the writer and academic, C.S. Lewis, when he is walking with the college chaplain shortly after his beloved wife, Joy, has died.

"At least you have your faith," the chaplain says to him.

Lewis stops dead.

"And what good is that," he asks, "when frankly, this whole thing is a mess?"

Lewis understood that there could be no inner wholeness, no shalom or genuine integration of reality and belief, unless suffering, unless the inexplicable, was confronted head-on. "What chokes every prayer and every hope," he said, "is the memory of all the prayers we offered and the false hopes we had."

I have never, when teaching my children to pray, been able to assure them that every prayer would be answered. How could I? How could I then explain that six million of their people had been destroyed for no other crime than being Jewish? And that the God who had chosen them as his people so many centuries ago, had appeared to have abandoned them to the worst possible nightmare? But at the same time they have two thousand years of Jewish history to remind them that despite such horror, despite suffering and pain of untold proportions, God and faith and hope go on. Lewis discovered, in time, that there was no answer because God himself was the answer. Rather like the writing discovered on a wall in Auschwitz, which said, "I believe in the sun, even when it is not shining; I believe in love, even when I cannot feel it; I believe in God, even when he is silent."

Perhaps it is not the why of suffering which counts, but what we do with it. "Pain is inevitable," said one American writer, "but misery is optional." Positive action, channelling the emotional flood, seems to be a part of the healing process. The early pioneers of the new nation of Israel drew immense energy from the pain of the past. All the years of Jewish rejection, from Biblical times, through the Crusades, the Spanish Inquisition, the pogroms in Eastern Europe to the holocaust, inspired their determination to make the land blossom and flourish. But after they died a new generation took control, who, instead of putting the pain of their national memory to positive use, were fed by its bitterness, so that it produced fear, suspicion and hostility. The abused child grows up to abuse, unless the wounds are healed. Who will heal the raw and gaping wounds of Israel?

Of all the television documentaries I have made, one in particular stays in my memory. It was a programme about the Compassionate Friends, an organisation formed by two couples who had each lost a young son, to support parents bereaved of their children. Although I was an "outsider", although I had never experienced the almost unbearable grief of losing a child, I felt enfolded in the warmth of the people I met, as if their own sense of loss had taught them to reach outside themselves and value human contact.

"I have a robust kind of a faith," Joe Lawley, one of the founders and a wonderfully earthy Scot, said to me. "I don't let God get away with it. I tell him what I think of him. But then he's big enough to take it."

The president of the newly founded branch for the parents of murdered children told me that he used to march up and down the path from the back door to the gate shouting and swearing at God, "telling him he couldn't do this to me, take away my daughter, my only child".

I asked him how he had managed to continue as a deacon in his local Baptist church, saying the Lord's Prayer, forgiving those who had sinned against him?

He said it was hard at first, but then, "When I got to court I saw the parents of the boy who had done it, and I saw that they were suffering so much more than I was. How could they live with what their son had done? I just had to go across to them and comfort them."

In the end it cost him his marriage too. But he had an unshakeable faith in a God who was duty-bound to play fair, and would, in the end, enable him to find new life. "God waits long," says the Talmud, "but pays with interest."

By the time the programme was finished I expected to feel depressed. I didn't. I felt enriched, and that is a tribute to the people who took part. Grief can turn people into givers or takers. It was a lesson I was fortunate enough to learn from a group of givers.

Suffering has made the Jew resilient. And laughter has always been the best vehicle for making endurable the unendurable. Insults hurt less when they're self-inflicted. Nothing is sacrosanct. Not suffering, or death, or sex, and certainly not religion. There's a story about a Chief Rabbi of historically anti-Semitic Warsaw, who found himself seated at a civic banquet next to the Bishop.

"*Hors d'oeuvres*, Rabbi?" asked the Bishop impishly, handing him a plate of spiced ham.

"Thank you, Your Grace," said the Rabbi, "but I think you know that in our religion ham is forbidden."

"Shame!" said the Bishop. "What a silly religion. When ham is so delicious."

After the banquet was over the Rabbi said a polite goodnight to his neighbour and asked him to convey his good wishes to his wife.

"Wife?" laughed the Bishop. "Don't you know that my religion forbids a priest to marry?"

"Shame," murmured the Rabbi, "what a silly religion. When a wife is so delicious."

Such are our human foibles that all religion has its "silly" side. We would see it more easily if we didn't take ourselves quite so seriously. Speaking at a large interdenominational meeting recently, I told the joke about the little old Jewish lady walking through the park, when a man leaps out of the bushes, opens his mac and exposes himself. "Hmmphh," she says, "you call that a lining?" Someone wrote to tell me she thought I had been coarse. She was probably right. But she had missed the whole point of Jewish humour. Sadly, this is a coarse old world we live in. We and our children face potential trauma every time we go to a park. But I feel fairly certain that because of that joke, my children are better prepared for it than many. Laughter has already removed the fuse.

When we have a good look round, there's plenty to amuse us in church. In his last ministry my husband had to wear what is known as a cassock alb, a sort of long, white, hooded tunic. Self-conscious at the best of times, the idea worried him.

"What do you think of it?" he said to me, standing in front of the mirror, when he put it on for the first time.

He's a very tall, very thin man.

"Well, if you want my opinion," I said to him, "all you need is a yellow bobble hat, and you'll look like a walking candle."

Which did much for his ego. He doesn't like uniforms at any time. Not even what he calls the medieval angel kit he has to wear now. He thinks they make a man pompous. And pompous people can never see how funny they are.

I learnt an important lesson about God's sense of humour from a lovely Irish nun called Sister Philly. She was sent, by her Order, to Coventry, to join a group of Sisters who lived in a small terraced house in Foleshill, serving the ethnic community. She was terribly nervous, and very anxious to please, both her new Sisters, and her Asian neighbours. And was a little nonplussed when, on

her first day, one of the Sisters asked her to nip down
to the shops to collect a few groceries.

"Take the car, Sister," she was told. "It's parked
outside."

She picked up the keys, found the car, and, trembling
a little, tried to fit them into the lock. With no success.

"Dear Lord Jesus," she prayed, "If ever you've helped
me, help me now."

Miraculously, barely were the words out of her mouth,
when the key slid into place, and the car door opened.

"Thank you Jesus," she breathed with relief, and got
in behind the wheel.

Suddenly there was a tap on the car window, and
looking up, she saw one of her Asian neighbours. As
she hastily wound down the window he said to her,
"Excuse me, Sister, but I think that is my car you are
trying to drive."

To this day, Sister Philly told me, giggling, she never
knew why God played such a joke on her. But it does
put our self-analytical agonising over what makes God
answer prayer, and how, as humans, we can organise a
few more miracles, into a new perspective.

Nothing, not even the most important aspects of our
faith, are immune from the comic, if we're able to laugh at
ourselves the way the Jews do. Not even the Communion
Service. Last Christmas Day my husband hit on an ingenious way of creating a quiet atmosphere for the service.
No small feat when half the congregation are still opening
their stockings and the other half are worrying about the
food in the oven. He gave the sound technician a cassette
of a well-known cathedral choir singing carols.

"Play that as people come in," he said, "It will put
them in the right frame of mind."

It did. The problem arose later, as the congregation
went forward to take communion, and the sound technician, working on the doubtful principle that what worked
well once would work even better a second time, decided
to switch the cassette on again. Out from the speakers

blasted, "We all want figgy pudding, we all want figgy pudding, so bring some in here."

I walked out to, "We won't go till we've had some."

Small wonder that the child kneeling at the altar next to me whispered to her mother who was eating the bread, "What are they giving us today?"

I was in a state of near hysteria, but as I looked round, no one else even managed a smile or a titter. Perhaps they hadn't registered what was happening. Because they didn't anticipate being amused. Not in church.

If only we could send ourselves up more. How many crises would be defused, how many relationships improved, how many church council meetings turned from a nerve-wracking strain into a pleasant evening out? Laughter is a barometer. When the laughter stops at home, the situation is serious. It means we're too busy. Too intense. Sinking under stress. It's a signal that we need to create some space for each other. And it is the same with a church. The congregation which has lost its sense of humour is in serious trouble. "This year," I said to one congregation I was speaking to, "let your annual general meeting be the opportunity for a really good communal belly laugh." They looked at me as if I had just arrived from Mars.

Jesus was a funny man. Sadly, our cultural barriers prevent us from entering the world of his particular humour. Imagine someone trying to take a splinter out of his friend's eye, when he cannot even see properly for the log in his own? Like everyone else in Jerusalem, he told shepherd jokes. As the Americans tell Polish jokes. And the British tell Irish jokes. There was once a shepherd who abandoned his entire flock to go looking for a daft sheep who was lost. He must have made the disciples laugh. "Eeeh, Jesus, it were the shepherd who were daft." They probably thought they knew the punchline. "And when he came back the whole flock had been eaten by wolves?"

Part of an oppressed people in an occupied land, he knew, as the Jews have always known, that humour is a wonderful way of venting frustration. It provides a sense of balance. And without balance human beings lose their humanity.

It was a lesson I once learned from a squashed banana. I had been working in London and was rushing to catch the five o'clock train home as I usually do. As a hick suburbaner I enjoy my occasional trips to the great metropolis, but when you are a working mum what glamour has the bright lights, the shows, the theatre, the exhibitions, when instead, you could be at home doing the mending, and the cooking, and feeding the rabbit? So there I always am, while other aliens finish their meetings, return to their hotels and prepare for their evening's entertainment, rushing to the station, so that I can be home for eight, change, like Cinderella, out of my smart suit into my shmatters, make the supper and tuck the kids into bed.

On one occasion I only just made it and the train was pulling out as I leapt on board. It was absolutely packed and I ploughed my way through carriages, falling over bags, dogs, outstretched limbs and other human paraphernalia, desperately looking for somewhere to rest my aching body. And have something to eat. I had hardly had the time to grab a bite all day and was absolutely famished. I suddenly remembered the large, luscious banana lying at the bottom of my briefcase. I had put it there that morning, before leaving home, in case I might feel a little peckish. That moment had arrived.

Eventually I sighted a spare seat tucked away next to a window and not wanting to disturb the passenger on the corridor side too often, decided to root around in my case for the precious banana, and for the can of drink I had just bought at the station, before I heaved it on to the luggage rack and sat down.

It had been a long, hot day. Only when my hand touched a mound of slushy mush at the bottom of the case did I realise that my poor banana had failed to survive it. My fellow traveller responded to some unintentional signal and stood up to let me past. Then sat down promptly when she saw one half-dead banana in my hand. I beat a hasty retreat to the toilets.

Five minutes and one drowned banana later I was back, and after yet another prolonged wrestling match with my case, found my can of drink, hoisted my belongings on to the rack, and finally took my seat. Time for a nice, refreshing drink. There's a knack to opening a metal can. I haven't got it! I tugged and tugged on the metal loop, which finally gave way in one great jerk, spraying orange juice all over the private papers of the gentleman across the table.

"I'm sorry," I said, and proceeded to mop him up with a tissue. It was covered with blood. Whose? Mine! I stole myself to look down at his papers again and saw drops of blood all over his pristine sheets.

"I'm sorry," I said again, wrapping up my finger and mopping his papers frantically.

He muttered some vague acceptance of my apology. The companion on my right looked away in a hurry. The traveller opposite her buried himself in a book.

I suddenly had a terrible urge to laugh. What else was there to do in a situation like this? Instead we sat po-faced, in silence for three hours, four expressionless dummies, locked into our own private little worlds. Not a word of sympathy. No smile of understanding or acceptance. No sense of being fellow human beings sharing the same disasters and embarrassments. If we had laughed, we might have given something to each other, might even have enjoyed each other's company, learnt a thing or two. Instead we never met.

"There was once a Catholic, a Protestant and a Jew . . ." One of these days the punchline will be about the Catholic. Or better still, about the Protestant. I can always live in hope.

12

Let there be Light

Winter is Christmas, that wonderful, glistening hiatus between sepulchral autumn mists and the first crocuses of spring. That ultimate celebration of light in the darkness, hope in despair, personified and personalised in the incarnation. That now commercialised, grotesque, greed-pandering parody of all a festival should be.

As a child it was the only festival I envied my non-Jewish friends. They didn't appear to celebrate any others. Apart from handing out a few chocolate eggs at Easter. Fantasising from the outside about the mysterious world hidden behind the closed curtains of every non-Jewish home in our town, I thought Christmas must be the most joyous occasion imaginable: happy families nestling cosily around a flickering open fire, fairy lights twinkling on a sweet-scented tree, undreamed-of delights, wrapped in crêpe paper and tinfoil, and topped with satin bows, spicy, melt-in-the-mouth mince pies, familiar carols sung softly in harmony around the piano. A vision which owed far more to Charles Dickens than reality. I knew nothing of the near murders which ensued when Mother-in-Law became helpful in the kitchen, Granny left her hearing aid at home, Billy rode his new bike over the baby, Dad wanted to watch the ballet instead of *Superman III*, and Daphne announced she'd become a vegetarian. It would have amazed, even shocked me if I had known then that the majority of the population lived in dread of this major event in the Christian calendar, submitted to it with stoic resignation, and endured it in an uncomfortable, tranquillised, stomach-stretched, semi-inebriated state.

The grass is always greener on the other side! I never realised then that the great Jewish festivals such as the Passover, celebrated primarily in the home, integrating familiar food, wine, singing, story-telling and family-togetherness, were far nearer my fantasised ideal Christian Christmas. We did celebrate Christmas, in a fashion, because it was a national holiday, and because many Jews have the distinct feeling that they are fighting a losing battle.

"Mummy, do we believe in Father Christmas?" my five-year-old nephew asked last year.

"Of course we don't, Daniel," she said. "We're a Jewish family."

"Well that's funny," said the little boy, "because he's coming to school on Tuesday."

My mother cooked her kosher turkey like the rest of the community. How would a Jewish butcher survive, without Christmas? We were amused, one year, to see on the television that Israel was doing a roaring trade selling Christmas trees to the Christian West. But we had no tree, no decorations, and our presents were never wrapped, just left in a pile at the foot of the bed, as if Father Christmas wasn't prepared to put himself out for Jewish children.

To be fair to my parents, Christmas hadn't exactly excelled in providing them with the kind of positive, happy memories which add a special dimension to celebration. When I was nine my paternal grandmother, as many people might like to do, took her own life on Christmas Day. I'm not alone, it seems, in my idealised childhood fantasy of other people's Christmases. For some, the reality is unbearable. In her case, life had long lost any meaning without the partner she had loved. But how I wished she had come to that conclusion on any other day of the year.

Many years later, just a few days before Christmas, my

mother's younger brother, only twenty-seven, a brilliant television journalist, and more like a brother to me than an uncle, fell down the stairs in his apartment in Peru, and died of a brain haemorrhage. That was a Christmas I have tried to forget. My mother never will.

Small wonder that it is not her favourite time of year. "Christmas again, oy," she sighs down the telephone, "your father's birthday, God rest his soul. All the awful memories, they keep on flooding back."

She catalogues them, and asks whether it isn't the same for me.

It isn't. Not that I don't remember. It's simply that they have been supplanted now by the joy of the occasion, and by a rather special, once-and-for-all Christmas gift from above which fills me with thankfulness. Even when I wash his bristles from the washbasin and help his dirty socks on their journey from the bedroom floor to the laundry basket.

Peter asked me to marry him on 23 December, my father's birthday. We had dinner at a very expensive restaurant. I guessed he might be in love by the potential size of the bill. There was chestnut soup on the menu, turkey and all the trimmings, and old-fashioned plum pudding. The whole place was bedecked in holly and mistletoe. Carol singers in Victorian costume serenaded us. And how he looked at me! The dining-room, shimmering in the candlelight, blurred softly around the edges.

And then he popped the question. Not in the restaurant. He waited until we were sitting in his car, parked outside Woolworth's in Bolton High Street. Though he swears he didn't. He maintains I had already agreed to marry him by then and he was simply trying to find somewhere a little more private to elicit a fuller, less verbal, response to his offer. I only vaguely remember that, but I had had two very large glasses of wine.

And I was very nervous. This moment had been etched and resketched by a very vivid imagination in almost every waking dream for nearly four years. Living with the fantasy was far easier than confronting the reality. I had loved Peter almost from the moment I met him. But he was a very earnest, intense young man, and not ready to commit himself to a relationship. So I waited. And I waited. There were other men, gentle, considerate, attractive men, romantic walks, hand-in-hand in the moonlight, proposals. I turned them all down. Was I mad? But none compared with my "Mr Right". I was in great danger of wasting away my life, mooning after the impossible like a lovesick toad. The minister of the church I attended decided that matters should be brought to a head. He suggested that we gave the Almighty a deadline: four months, until Christmas. If, by then, there was still no spark of life from the object of my desires, I was to leave the town and find a job elsewhere.

And there I was, three days before Christmas, in a close encounter, in Bolton High Street, with my dream-come-true. He maintains that around September time he had been praying alone, when the idea that it might be time to find himself a wife simply popped into his head.

"But who?" he asked. "I haven't got a girlfriend."

My name somehow materialised in his mind, and the feelings to accompany that seed of an idea grew slowly over the next four months, without our seeing anything of each other. Not the most flattering of romantic beginnings. Once his mind was made up however he pursued me with the single-mindedness which earned his brewing and banking ancestors their millions and the minister had to suggest that I might prefer an old-fashioned courtship to being swept off my feet. I didn't. And we were married seven months after that first Christmas date.

My husband is and will always be one of the best Christmas presents I ever received. I ruminate on the fact every time I wake up in the morning, turn over and gaze at the dishevelled, open-mouthed heap with whom I share the sleeping, as well as the waking, hours of my life, if I could manage to switch off the sound of a revving motorbike from the other side of the bed. "You, my darling," I whisper under my breath, "are the ultimate in God's generosity to the human part of me!"

To whoever doubts God's sense of humour I have but one word: marriage. Yet for me it was a very special way of healing the hurtful memories of so many miserable Christmases past, so that I could begin to celebrate the festival with the exuberance it deserved.

Peter's parents lived abroad, and having both had years of spending Christmas alone, we were determined it should be a high spot in our calendar, a festival of thanksgiving for the greatest gift of all: God with us. And yet, over the years, it has become extremely difficult not to join the weary masses, dragged into Christmas kicking and screaming, pulled one way by a society gone mad with materialism and meaningless carol singing, yet another way by a Church pandering wearily and unimaginatively to tradition and expectation, and yet another by a nagging inner voice which tells us it's all a load of pagan claptrap anyway, since Jesus was probably born in September, in a heatwave.

I do suspect that Jesus was born at Tabernacles, in the late autumn. The Biblical data and symbolism seem to fit. But that doesn't spoil Christmas. A nine-month leap backwards to the conception takes us to the end of December. And after all, Jesus' birth was not miraculous. It was absolutely normal. It was his conception which made him unique.

There are other reasons why I am convinced that celebrating the Messiah's entrance into the world in December is not simply the unfortunate legacy of a pagan past, a throwback to the winter solstice. The early Christians, who were Jewish of course, saw a definite association between the Feast of the Dedication of the Temple, Hanukkah, and the coming of the Messiah. Hanukkah celebrates not so much the dedication of the original Temple, but an event which took place a great while later, in 164 BC. Antiochus Epiphanes, ruler of Syria, had pillaged and occupied Jerusalem. He had invaded the Temple, carrying away all the glorious treasures made so lovingly in the time of Solomon the Great. And then, to show his utter contempt for the Holy One of Israel, he sacrificed and cooked a pig on the altar, pouring the broth all over the scrolls of the law, polluting the entire sanctuary.

On to the scene, with all the drama of a Hollywood movie, came Judas the Maccabean. Waging ingenious, guerilla warfare he finally succeeded in driving the Syrians out of the Temple, and Jerusalem itself. Before the people could give thanks for their deliverance, the Temple had to be cleansed. A single phial of holy oil was found hidden behind a stone in a wall, barely enough to keep the holy flame flickering for a day. But it lasted eight days, a miracle, just long enough for the priests to consecrate a new altar. The Temple was finally rededicated with huge rejoicing on the 25th of Kislev, the Hebrew equivalent of December.

"Destroy this Temple and in three days I will raise it up," Jesus said. His words have new poignancy in the light of the fact that in his day, in one corner of the Temple stood a pile of stones, the old altar, sacred, but polluted, left until the Messiah came to tell the people what to do with them.

"Are you He who is to come, or shall we look for another?" the crowds asked him.

Perhaps they were hoping that their chance had come at last to tidy up the mess in the corner. Whatever they thought it seems that they, unlike the early Church, missed the link between an inanimate temple made by man, therefore limited geographically and historically, and the living Temple of God, which came down from heaven and has no boundary in space or time. There seems little doubt that the first Christians went on celebrating the event on the 25th of Kislev. Which became the 25th of December.

One winter, when Jesus was walking in the Temple at the Feast of the Dedication, the crowds asked him again whether he was the Messiah. It appears to have been their favourite question. Though, however he said it, they never heard the answer. As at Tabernacles the Temple would have been a blaze of light, not because it was a pilgrim festival, summoning the people to worship from far and wide, but because of the miraculous event it commemorated, God's supernatural intervention to give light at a time of great darkness. It is possible that this was when Jesus said, "I am the light of the world: he who follows me shall not walk in darkness, but have the light of life." He certainly said, "You are not my sheep because you don't hear my voice. My sheep hear my voice. I know them and they follow me."

Hanukkah was always exciting when I was a child because it was the one occasion we could take the menorah, the eight-branched candelabra, down from the shelf, and use it. The other fifty-one weeks of the year it was only dusted. We stood it proudly in the window, leaving the curtains open a smidgen so that the neighbours could see it. If they could have their Christmas Trees, we would have our nearest equivalent. The only problem was that tiny candles take a relatively short time to burn, compared to the electric variety. None the less, each night we lit the front candle, known as "the Servant", and used it to light the other candles, one on the first night, two on the second, three on the third, until, by the last night, all eight, and the servant itself, were left to burn. And we said: "My soul was embittered during my subjugation to the Egyptians, but God saved his people. The oppressor came and took me captive into Babylon. But I was saved after seventy years of hell. Haman tried to destroy us then, but was foiled and became the victim of his own pride. The Greeks defiled all the oils, but from one remaining flask you performed a miracle for your beloved. Bring near the day of Salvation, that we may be saved. Thrust the evil one into the deep darkness, and send us seven shepherds to look after us."

At that time, of course, I made no association between Hannukah and Christmas. But now the symbolism of the

"Temple", living on earth, the "Servant", spreading light throughout the world, the "Shepherd", coming to protect and lead his sheep, shouts at me for recognition. And gives Christmas a new dimension.

I began to think about how Jewish festivals are celebrated with their familiar psalms, flickering candles, traditional food, wine glowing crimson in the silver cups, and the recounting of the legends of God's miraculous intervention in history to save his people. Those moments created a sense of occasion, of continuity and destiny. They contained that special element so often missing in the Christian home at any festival-time: a sense of wonder. How to recapture it for Christmas, that was my dilemma. How to combine a time for play and a time for wonder. Noise and silence. Hilarity and quiet reflection. How to play with all of the senses, sight, sound, touch and smell, to create a sense of awe at the joyful realisation that God is Emmanuel, with us for ever.

There are countless possibilities, and no one way is right for any individual or family. For us Christmas Eve, after a candlelit carol service at church, is definitely a time for fun, with games, charades, and a huge casserole bubbling on the stove. Christmas Day, now that the children are older, has become more serene. We walk, listen to music, read, and eat once the sun has set, and the atmosphere has mellowed into a contented, tongue-loosening tranquillity. I've tried to encourage that by experimenting with colours, filling my dining-room with crimson and emerald, and sweet-smelling spices, in an attempt to convey something of the majesty of the special guest, who has deigned to come and celebrate his birthday with us. And then there are so many symbols available, some old, some new, some linked to Hanukkah: piles of coloured stones, myriads of candles placed in a window, shining out into the darkness, plastic, furry or, better still, olive-wood sheep sitting beside the tinsel angels.

Many families share their Christmas with friends and relatives who would not be particularly pleased by the introduction of any spiritual element into the occasion. But as Judaism proves, worship in the home doesn't have to be overtly or obnoxiously "religious". Aunty Gladys may rightly balk at a half-hour prayer-meeting, but she is less likely to object to the singing of carols by candlelight, accompanied by little Jimmy on his recorder, or any other instruments at hand. And if he insists on getting out the new drum set, thank God for his musical instincts, switch him off by sending him upstairs to rehearse a Christmas play, and switch on the recorded professionals. There are countless Christmas legends which can be acted out or read around the table: Baboushka, The Little Cobbler, The Spider's Web, stories handed down through the generations, which have their own message, and teach never-to-be-forgotten lessons about love and generosity.

Anything which makes the occasion more in a child's mind than the opportunity for rampant, unleashed greed and self-acquisition is vital. A lesson I learned in a way I will always regret. Many Christmases ago, when Peter was a student at theological college and money was scarce, I had found, in a jumble sale, a bag full of Dinky toys, the perfect stocking-fillers for our three-year-old Joel. We cleaned each car, tractor and bus, carefully and lovingly, wrapped them in coloured tissue paper and placed the stockingful at the foot of his bed on Christmas Eve. We were sharing a house, and the festival, with another family with four children.

At six o'clock on Christmas morning everyone was wakened by loud whoops and screams of delight from Joel, who tore from room to room like a miniature tornado, throwing the tissue-wrapped parcels from his stocking on to the beds of the other children, shouting, "He's been, he's been. Father Christmas has been. And he's brought me a present, and one for you, and one for you, and one for you." Then he sat down on our bedroom floor to open the one present he had kept for himself, and gasped with delight and gratitude when he pulled off the paper and saw the very battered secondhand lorry.

Peter and I went round the other bedrooms taking back his other presents, and we brought them to him and put them beside him on the floor. He looked at us in bewilderment.

"All for me?" he asked slowly, and there was no pleasure on his face.

With a sinking heart I knew that we had destroyed something very precious. The little lorry had lost its lustre. One cream cake is a treat. Several eaten in a single sitting make you feel sick. Materialism had sated our son and spoiled his pleasure. Jews give their children one present a night for the eight nights of Hanukkah. I now saw the sense of it.

Joel had discovered instinctively that it was more satisfying to give than to receive. We turned those values upside down.

"I hate that story about me," my strapping, frighteningly materialistic teenage son says now. "I was so stupid."

"On the contrary," I say to him, "you were right. It's we who are stupid."

The danger is that we all become so sated with the season that we lose our ability to respond altogether. Even the Church tends to sound a little like a record with a needle stuck in its groove by the time the great festival arrives. Christmas Eve and Day pass in a haze, with most of the believers in a semi-zombified state, worn out by the shopping, cooking, cards, commercial glitz, and family quarrels, having already attended so many carol services that they have lockjaw. Any spirit of anticipation has long been drowned in a surfeit of saccharine and mince pies. Wonder and awe have been pre-empted by nativity plays and hype. Each organisation has had its own, individual Christmas event, each the exact replica of the other, without any reference to the whole. No possibility here for inspired, integrated planning, building the suspense slowly to a grand climax. The congregation has Christmas-fatigue. One of the greatest festivals in the

Church's year seems more like an endurance test than a cause for wonder and thankfulness.

Peter and I usually try to find a bit of time alone together on the 23rd, to recapture some of the magic and romance of our special day, so many years ago now. And it's a principle which seems to work for Christmas itself too. I try and find a secluded spot, or use time when I'm doing one of those brain-deadening chores, like peeling the chestnuts, to ease my spirit into its proper gear, to try and recapture some of the magic of the special season. Often lighting a candle or opening an advent calendar can provide those few precious moments which bring God back into the centre of events. And once he is there, wonder is a natural response.

A CHRISTMAS/HANUKKAH PRAYER

Blessed are You, O Lord our God, King of the Universe,
     who makes us holy with Your commandments,
Who has the power to work great miracles,
And brings deliverance to all humanity.

These candles
Which we now light
Are in memory of the miracle of our deliverance,
Of the wonderful and mighty deeds
Which You performed for our ancestors
And still perform for us today.
These candles are holy,
For we cannot look at them
without giving You praise and honour, O Lord,
For all the wonders and miracles You have performed,
For the joy of salvation,
And for Your great glory,
Which has come into the world.

May these lights shed their radiance in our home and
     world.

May they rekindle in us and in our children,
The flame of piety and faith,
So that we may be willing to fight more bravely for justice,
   truth and peace,
As we follow You, the Everlasting Light.

RECIPES

It is traditional to eat anything fried in oil at Hanukkah,
as a reminder of the oil which lasted eight days. We
make our own doughnuts and serve them warm with
ice-cream. Just as good, and more savoury, are potato
latkas, a kind of fritter, made originally with cream cheese
to celebrate the famous cheese and wine party thrown
by Judith in honour of the Greek general, Holofernes.
Russian Jews first began to make them with potatoes.
They're scrumptious served hot instead of chips. We once
found our Joel, aged eighteen months, hiding behind an
armchair, with three cold latkas in an empty cornflakes
box he had retrieved from the rubbish bin, stuffing his
face. I wouldn't, however, recommend latkas cold.

POTATO LATKAS
Serves 4–6

6 large potatoes
2 beaten eggs
4 tbsp. self-raising flour (or plain flour with 1 tsp. baking
   powder)
1 tsp. salt
Pinch of white pepper

Grate the potatoes finely and place in a colander. Pour
over boiling water from the kettle and leave to drain
for ten minutes. (The potato may go a little brown.)
Place the grated potato in a bowl and add the other
ingredients. Heat 1 cm depth of oil in a heavy frying

pan and when hot put in tablespoonfuls of the mixture, flattening each latka with the back of the spoon. Cook at a steady temperature for about 5 minutes on each side until a rich brown colour. Then drain on kitchen paper and serve at once.

SPRING

I was standing watching a field full of lambs, an occupational hazard at this lovely, burgeoning time of year for any parent with an animal-infatuated child. Abby has always been besotted with almost any small, moving furry thing, and would love to show her solidarity with the animal kingdom by becoming a vegetarian. But she's already confronting the sad reality, studiously avoided by adults, that principles are easy to have, but exceedingly difficult to live out. The trouble is she's far too keen on gourmet meat cuisine. And that's an occupational hazard for a child of a Jewish mother, reared on chopped liver and chicken soup.

We were spending a few days in dank North Wales, our spirits sinking beneath a bulging canopy of perpetually moist, black-grey clouds, and had stopped, at her command, to oooh and aaah and coo at the new life in nature's maternity hospital. The sight of an entire field heaving joyfully with a mass of leaping, woolly creatures, raised her dejected spirits into a paroxysm of delight. And that despite the brotherly taunts of "mint sauce" coming from the back of the car.

It was while we were standing watching, buttoned up in our kagouls like a party of Muslim women in purdah, that I began to wonder how lambs ever became sheep. No one in their right mind would ever coo at a sheep. A sheep isn't cute. A sheep isn't fun. It isn't even terribly interesting. So how does a frisky, frolicking, free spirit become the dullest, daftest, most disappointing of all the farmyard animals?

And I suddenly understood, as never before, what a perfect, though uncomfortable, parable nature provides for the potentially disappointing progress of the human species. "Send us seven shepherds," demand the Jews at Hanukkah, painfully aware of their utter defencelessness. One is provided. One who grasped the symbolic importance of sheep, long before I did. And knew our need for direction, as well as protection. Incapable of independent, sensible thought, likely to follow each other into the middle of the motorway, sheep are hardly the best example of all that's noble and intelligent in the animal kingdom.

Whenever I play the party game which requires matching the photograph of the cute little baby to the balding, bespectacled middle-aged man with paunch and double chin, it always comes as a shock how much human beings change as they grow. Must lambs also lose so much in the transition to maturity? And what if Christians, full of play and wonder when they are born, thrilled by the sensation of new life surging through veins, soul and spirit, suppress that natural childlike exuberance as they grow up into what passes for maturity? And if, in acquiring a veneer of respectability, we despise that early spontaneity and playfulness, haven't we lost some vital prerequisite for celebration?

Spring itself is a massive symphony of praise. The whole created order wakens from its winter sleep and rises up to celebrate the creator. Human beings were made to celebrate on a grand scale, loudly, openly, joyfully, free from inhibition. Except that the very idea frightens us a little. And so we stuff it into our boots, shove it up our sleeves and zip up our spirits. And become a herd of boring old sheep, following each other's lead, terrified of busting out of the safe restraints of conformity, unable to set free the frolicking lamb inside. While the Lamb, not the Sheep, of God sadly regrets our unwillingness to dance after him over the hillsides.

A long time ago the first realisation of what it meant to be reborn seeped through the channels of my being into the darker areas of mind and soul like mercury, pushing out in its wake all guilt and shame, regret and despair. At last, with all questions answered, all hopes fulfilled and with a lorryload of fresh promises, I could live. So this was abundant life, this gurgling in the pit of the stomach, this giggling in the spirit, the sense of weightlessness, of slight drunkenness. Sadly, I'm now quite a sober being really. A sheep among sheep, though

I kick like a mule from time to time, and manage an occasional frolic on special occasions.

Such as Easter. Perhaps that's why spring is my favourite season, a time of resurrection and new beginnings, new shudderings beneath the earth and flutterings in the trees. All that has withered and wilted, decayed and died suddenly emerges bright and new. And as I celebrate the Passover, because as far as I'm concerned Easter is unthinkable, unintelligible without it, as I give myself completely to the great Jewish celebration of freedom, I remember how it felt, over twenty years ago, to be aware for the first time that I was totally, utterly, joyously free.

13

A Little Bit of Shmatter or
It's How You Wear It that Counts

During our trip to Wales we visited almost every factory
shop and warehouse we passed, particularly those prom-
ising bargains in Welsh woollen goods. My nose never
can resist a snip. It tweaks irresistibly whenever it sees
a certain four-letter word: "SALE". My mother-in-law
used to say that it made me a wonderful shopper, much
like the paragon of a wife of the Proverbs. At least, that's
how I interpret her meaning.

The main object of our mill visits was to buy Peter
some new jumpers, and thus prevent him from becoming
the proverbial vicar of pilled-pullover-with-holes-in-the-
elbows tradition. None the less I virtually had to drag
him in. Why do men always wait until their jackets are
in shreds, their shirts frayed, their soles holey and their
trousers virtually indecent before they submit themselves
to the painful and surgical procedure of replacing them?
And then I'm the one who has to dive among the piles
of possibilities, fishing out potential purchases.

"This one?"

"Too thin!"

"This one?"

"Too short!"

"This one?"

"Too flimsy!"

Suddenly my eyes fastened on a half-hidden mass of

scarlet, jade, gold and royal. I tugged and pulled and dragged out an exceptionally snappy little number, which I held up for him to see.

"Your colours, my dear, strong and striking to enhance your dark good looks."

He stared at it and me in disbelief. Why does my husband always think I'm pulling his leg?

"Much too bright," chimed in Mother-in-Law, suddenly appearing at my elbow, "for a minister of the Church."

And she held up a rather muted beige and cream affair for his admiration.

He reached out his hands reluctantly, one to each of us, like a convict waiting to be manacled, and we placed our respective choices on to his upturned palms.

Then he tried on each in turn, and I could tell, from the way his lips twitched at the corners when he looked at himself in the mirror, that there was a slow but mounting enthusiasm for the multi-coloured creation. But the beige and cream had its attractions too, namely its conventionality. It would blend nicely into the scenery at ministers' fraternals, sparing him the struggle of being conspicuous. How tempting to stick to the safe and easy path. He reached for the price tags. They were identical. No help there.

He tried them both on again, and again, until my mother-in-law, gasping for a cup of coffee and aching to sit down, reluctantly admitted that the colourful jumper, "though a little jazzy, was quite nice too".

Undaunted by faint praise, he was at the till in a flash, waving his credit card.

While we indulged in coffee and bara brith in the polished log-cabin of a café upstairs, a bright-eyed little old lady whose face was framed in a halo of white curls timidly approached our table.

"I'm sorry to interrupt you," she apologised, "but I was watching you all downstairs and I have to ask. Which of the jumpers did you buy?" Peter reached down into the parcel propped against his chair and pulled out a riot of colour, blinking as the full impact of his purchase dazzled him again.

"Oh, I'm so glad," cried the little old lady, clapping her hands with delight. "You've made my day," she said, and skipped out of the café door.

Colour enriches our lives. It's one way of compensating for a grey climate. But how little we make of it. Whenever I travel by train I join the "Grey Suit Brigade", an army of professional men in uniform whose conversation seems to reflect the way they look.

"Had a good weekend, Bob?"

"Yes, thank you."

"Do anything interesting?"

"Much the same."

"Kids all right?"

"Much the same. Johnny has a bit of a snuffle. But it's the time of year."

"Now, about last month's accounts . . ."

I don't make a habit of listening in on other people's conversations, not when they're as boring as that. Which they often are on commuter trains. The Orthodox Jews thank God they're not a woman. I thank him that I'm not a man.

I can't say I was ever Margaret Thatcher's greatest fan, but I have to admit she was a peacock among sparrows, dazzling the political scenario of the world with blue and jade and purple. For that alone she deserves to go down in the annals of history. And though her pearls and diamonds, clips, brooches and beads did get a bit out of hand, they made a positive statement. They said, "I like being a woman. I like a bit of glitz."

The only comment Jesus made about clothes in no way limits his followers to a hair-shirt. In fact he seems to suggest that we could be a great deal more colourful than we often are. "Look at the lilies of the field," he said, "even Solomon in all his glory was not dressed up like one of these." Lilies are not brown or grey or even navy blue. No one can convince me that King Solomon opted for a commuter-style suit and tie.

We don't know what Jesus wore, except that underneath was his tzizit, a sort of sheet, with holes cut out for the head and arms, and worn as a long vest. When people approached him for healing, they touched its tassels, hanging below his robe. Each tassel had a bright blue thread running through it to remind the Jew to obey God's commandments. Only the very Orthodox wear the tzizit today. It has been transmogrified into the white and blue satin prayer shawl a Jew puts on when he prays. The point is that even what you wear has special significance, and should act as a jolt to the memory. Blue is a vivid primary colour, a symbol of purity, adopted by the Church for the Virgin Mary. My husband, wearing his cornflower-blue clerical shirt, in preference for the traditional black or grey, was once asked at a monastery whether he had a special devotion to the Virgin.

"My wife hasn't been that for a very long time," he said.

The irony in our present society is that we have reversed the natural order. Women are allowed to wear strong colours. Men must be subdued. In nature it is the male of the species who wears the bold colours, who prances and preens and makes the greatest spectacle of himself – to attract the female. Throughout history men have worn satin bows and breeches, velvet and brocade, powdered wigs and painted beauty spots. Today the man with the ponytail is a little bohemian, a fuchsia-pink shirt suggests an over-inflated ego, and jazzy jeans a distinct lack of good fashion taste. The word "understatement" has become a compliment in the fashion industry. Judging by our city centres we're all afraid of colour, of standing out in a crowd, of expressing our unique individuality. Men more than women. Apart from church dignitaries in certain denominations, who are allowed to wear scarlet and purple, they are condemned to a rather turgid grey existence, unless they have the courage to break free.

One might imagine that the situation is easier for women. Not so. Our hang-ups are different. We belong to a society which devalues us if we haven't the looks or the figure of Joan Collins. Few of us fit into what are supposed to be "standard", off-the-peg sizes, and assume there is something wrong with us, some parts of our anatomy, which are so substandard or substantial, that every part of us ought to be concealed. When leg-lengthening seemed to be in fashion in one or two rather more off-beat churches, my husband threatened to send me to have both mine done. But I'm now learning to accept the fact that my feet don't touch ground when I sit on someone else's settee or travel by train, and I look rather like a wizened six-year-old. I'm forcing myself to swallow the patronising cliché of the makers of clothing for the smaller woman, that though "petite", I'm probably "perfectly formed". Yes, fortunately the good Lord, though perhaps a trifle neglectful when it came to the length of my legs, doesn't appear to have overlooked any of the other important bits.

Not only do they have the conventional hang-ups to contend with, but generations of pious churchwomen have also been inhibited by the Apostle Peter's admonition not to plait the hair, wear gold or dress up in fine clothing. Instead, he said, put on the inner jewellery of a "quiet and gentle spirit". Peter lived in a culture heavily divided by wealth and status, and what he deplored was making a show of it. It is all too easy to feign superiority. In my professional capacity as a journalist, a woman in a world largely dominated by men, I have discovered that "power dressing" works. What I wear can hold the key to what I achieve. So Peter's words, reminding us that it is what we are inside which counts, contain a vital truth in a world of topsy-turvy values, dominated by superficial judgements.

But this is no excuse for the kind of drabness which for centuries has been associated with modesty and piety. The great Spanish Carmelite and mystic, Teresa of Avila, writing about her mother, said she was a very virtuous woman. "Though extremely beautiful, she was never known to give any reason for supposing that she made the slightest account of her beauty; and though she died at thirty-three, her dress was already that of a person advanced in years."

How unutterably depressing to think that looking old before one's time could ever be a sign of virtue. In fact, Teresa of Avila's mother had twelve children before she was thirty-three. That was why she looked like a shrivelled old prune.

When I first dabbled in the Church, way back in the swinging sixties, I had a luminous red Mary Quant PVC mackintosh, which barely covered my bottom or kept me dry in a downpour, and a matching wide-brimmed hat. I thought, if I slipped into the back of the building, I would be incognito. But no one else was wearing anything faintly resembling my bright red mac and hat, which, to boot, crinkled in the silence. Such was the culture shock that I felt like a lost soul who had inadvertently strayed in when she was looking for the synagogue. Later, when I had become a little more firmly ensconced, though not fully at home, in this alien world, I heard some girls being described as "awfully mish". It took me a while to realise that "mish" was short for missionary, a caricature in dowdy tweed suit and brogues, with hair scraped back in a bun. And many women in the Church at that time were frighteningly, repressively, "mish".

I once met the genuine article at a conference, a missionary to the Jews. We shared a bedroom. I was shocked to discover she was twenty-eight, not forty-eight, as I had assumed. At night she took the pins out of her bun and masses of glorious chestnut hair cascaded over her shoulders.

"Wow," I said to her, as she sat at the dressing table, brushing her thick mane, "you really are pretty."

I saw her blush in the mirror.

"Why don't you leave it down like that sometimes?"

"Oh, I couldn't," she said, in a lovely, lilting Scottish voice.

I detected a faint hint of wistfulness.

"But why not? It's beautiful. You look so much younger."

Smiling, she surveyed her reflection, moved her head from side to side, then sighed and put down the brush.

"It wouldn't be seemly."

I remember wondering what seemly meant. Whatever it was it would not help her fulfil her calling. How would the gaudy younger members of the Jewish community ever relate to this coyly demure, old-before-her-time Granny-Grey?

Equating dowdiness with spirituality seems little different to me to "dressing to kill". Both are for show, one for domination, one for piety. Humility can be as false as pride. My experience in the field of public relations tells me that to be the best advert for the product we want to sell, it's better to look bright, interesting and vibrant, than on our way to the mortuary.

Anyone who watches the Jewish community walking to the synagogue on the Sabbath is in for a treat. Take out the sunglasses, for the streets will be a heaving mass of rainbow-bright colours. Flamboyance is part of the culture. The women perched on the synagogue balcony look, and sound, like canaries in an aviary. And though there may well be a fair smattering of designer gear, I defy anyone who thinks that wearing bright and interesting clothes necessarily means a bulging wallet.

My husband's first gift to me after our marriage was a sewing machine. And I, who couldn't sew a button on, remedial at school in dressmaking, granddaughter of a bespoke tailor that I was, made up my mind to make my own clothes. When you fail to fit into the standard size-range, you have very little choice. When your purse is empty, and you like wearing a variety of nice clothes, it becomes imperative. And I must say that the clothes which were most admired, which gave me most satisfaction, were always my own creations, usually revamps of something several sizes too large picked up in a charity shop. They were unique. There were not thousands like them hanging on pegs in department stores up and down the country. They were truly "me". No one else would have worn them, that's for sure. And now that I can afford an occasional splurge, though I am rarely prepared to pay full price for anything, I don't have half the pleasure which using my own creative energy gave me.

I must say that I am a serious shopper, a professional. I hunt out the seconds and the reductions with the dedication of a Sherlock Holmes. Few friends can keep up the pace. Those who try go into training weeks in advance. Now that we live in a more "rural" environment I suffer seriously from shopping withdrawal symptoms, and a trip to friends in Manchester or West Yorkshire inevitably means I hit the nearest city centre in a big way. It was during one such trip that my friend Rose and I saw the swinging crêpe smocks in Miss Selfridge's window. They were burnt orange and frilly, and very like a certain little number we had worn in our teenybop days in the swinging sixties. Nostalgia rolled over us both in one enormous wave. Silently, reverently, we took two down, she looking at the label and sadly lamenting the change in size since those halcyon, golden days. And we tiptoed quickly towards the fitting-room.

Wonder of all wonders it was empty. No leggy, youthful sylphs to sneer at our wrinkles, protrusions and varicose veins. One of the cruellest tricks of the present age must be the communal fitting room, with the smell of sweaty feet and the sight of bulging white flesh being squeezed into sequined tubes, a public hall of mirrors displaying nudity on a scale unknown in Soho, where schoolgirls stare at their mother's generation in wide-eyed panic, as if to say, "Must we all come to this?" And I want to shout back, "Yes! I never thought I'd reach mid-life either. But now that the rot has set in, I've as much right to shop here as you."

We put the smocks on and stood for some time in an orange glow, surveying ourselves in triplicate, studying the effect. Then we took hold of the hem between our first fingers and thumbs, twizzled and turned, and remembered the dances we danced and the songs that we sung. And laughed as the years fell away and we remembered what it was like to be young, backcombing our hair into a monstrous beehive, whitening our lips, blackening our eyelids and spitting into the mascara. It was good to forget motherhood, wifely duty and the daily grind of work. It was good to be stripped of sobriety, responsibility and the weight of years which burdens us down and stifles our spirits. It was hard to take the smocks off, walk out of the fitting-room and leave them hanging on the rail. They weren't quite right any more. We left the shop with a sigh and a giggle, feeling surprisingly refreshed and renewed. There in Miss Selfridge's fitting-room we had been on a magical adventure in search of a long-forgotten part of our fun-loving selves. And finding the missing part made us that little bit more whole.

What we wear liberates, or enslaves our spirits. It sends out messages that say whether we feel good about who we are, or not. For two years I presented my own daily programme on BBC local radio, and one of my favourite guests was Alison, who ran a fashion shop for larger ladies. She was big herself, and beautiful, smart and self-assured in the bright red and emerald-green suits she wore, carefully enhanced with bold costume jewellery. Small wonder heads turned when she walked into the studio.

"I gave up dieting long ago," she said. "I gave up wanting to be a sylph when I realised that I had never ever been short of a cuddle – from the men! And as for you," she said, looking me up and down, "if you lived in Africa, the relief lorry would be calling at your door."

Jewish Mamas have long known that being big had its advantages.

I do not believe the old assumption that women corrupt men with what they wear. It is a myth which robs so many women of the joy of their own sexuality, ensnaring them in the shackles of their own inhibitions. Male fantasy varies enormously and feasts on what for a woman may be the most innocuous item in her wardrobe. A man can be turned on by a full skirt, baggy jumper, or a high-necked dress, covering every part of the anatomy, except the ankle. One male friend of mine says that there's nothing he likes to see more than a woman with hairy legs. Meanwhile, millions of women throughout the West spend hours and pounds colluding in the extraordinary social comedy of pretending that God made their legs smooth and bald. Whatever his sexual fantasy, controlling it is the man's responsibility. And they do. They are not the weak, vulnerable, potential rapists, seducers or abusers women seem inclined to believe. Rape is not a sexual crime, provoked by women. It is a crime of aggression, performed by very distorted minds, and grannies in their eighties can be its victims.

I still remember the acute embarrassment I felt, many years ago, when an exceedingly intense young man, a fellow student, asked my forgiveness for the "impure" thoughts I inspired. I realise now that I should have been flattered. Sexual fantasies are normal for single young people. Not having them would have been far more worrying. But at the time, lacking confidence as I did, wanting to be a good Christian as I did, I thought it must be my fault. What was it about me that caused the problem, I asked him. He couldn't honestly say. My hair was too curly. My eyes too green. My personality too extrovert. I listened. And as women tend to do, took the blame. He felt a great deal better. I was left tied up in emotional knots. Knots I have unravelled slowly over the years, until now, when I not only enjoy being me, I positively allow myself the luxury of revelling in the unalloyed pleasures of being a woman: mascara, perfume, the silky feel of a new pair of tights, and even painted toenails. A Jezebel, you say. No, it's simply my Jewish nature, and right for me. Mama would always say, "Get your lipstick on, we're going out." After all, who knew what eligible man we might bump into. A girl should always be prepared. Always make the best of herself. And now it's a habit I enjoy. I refuse to fear the sexuality God gave me. I receive it as a gift, resisting all kinds of pressure to conform to whatever happens to be the acceptable image of the time. The greatest compliment I ever received was from a retired minister's wife who said I was totally unsuitable for the part. Presumably, since she didn't know the real me, she had judged by appearances.

A friend of mine called Jan, who is also married to a minister, was delighted when a member of the congregation came up to her after a service to tell her what an inspiration she was to the women in the church. She tried to decide which of the many gifts and talents she had so selflessly and hitherto so thanklessly employed for the good of the church were at last being appreciated. Was it her leadership ability, her preaching, or her praying? On the other hand it might have been her counselling skills. Or her loving, pastoral care and visiting. The patient way she dealt with the constant stream of callers and telephone calls. The possibilities were endless. She could hardly contain her curiosity as she waited in anticipation to discover what it was about her that was changing so many lives.

"In what way am I an inspiration?" she asked.

"Since you came we're all wearing coloured tights," came the reply.

The shalom or wholeness we seek, the integration of our physical and spiritual selves, is about having the confidence to be fully, happily who we are, and giving others the courage to be themselves too. The coloured tights became a kind of symbol, of individuality, freedom and fun. Without realising it, Jan had shown others that it was all right to be a little more daring, a little more colourful, a little more confident, not by preaching or praying, not by anything she said or did, but simply by being who she was.

I am an avowed Colour-Me-Beautiful fan, a system of discovering your own personal colour coding. It revolutionised my wardrobe, opening up possibilities of wonderful colours I would never have dreamed of wearing before, saving hours of time when I went shopping. Taking my husband for a consultation as a birthday treat made a perfect day out. Few men ever take the chance of looking at themselves in the mirror for longer than it takes to shave in the morning. Even fewer stop to think about their appearance. We spent a whole morning just looking at him. For several hours we drank coffee and stared at the reflection in the mirror swathed in purples, magentas, crimsons and sapphires, and saw how they made his face come alive. He was a "winter", which meant that strong, bold, blue-based colours, blended with pale-as-ice colours, were the perfect combination for him. As I had guessed, the gaudy jumper bought in Wales had been a perfect choice. What a relief. We could hardly take it back. He could also wear black and white. Just as well – for a clergyman. I could hardly see the Church altering its uniform to suit his convenience. But it was an experience which boosted his confidence. Never very certain about the looks God had given him (and who is?), it helped him to feel positive about the man who stared back at him in the mirror.

There are times when, like the early Church fathers and mystics, I quite agree that the human body was an odd sort of vehicle for God to create. Its demands get you down. They are so time consuming. It is always requiring fresh fuel and the removal of waste products, its parts have a hopeless propensity for going wrong, and it isn't truly beautiful for long, once age and gravity take over. But God must have known what he was doing. So why not enjoy what he has given us to the utmost?

14

And if I Die for It . . .

There is nothing like letting yourself go every once in a while. The Jews do it often. But especially in March. This is when they let their imaginations, as well as their legs, run riot, and parade and dance through the streets in a colourful array of fancy dress costumes. The excuse for this terribly un-Anglo-Saxon display of behaviour is a woman, believe it or not, who lived well over two thousand years ago. She was a very ordinary little Jewish girl who happened to be in the right place at the right time, and, as Queen of Persia, saved her people from a massacre. In fact the Feast of Esther is such fun that the sages say, though all the other festivals become redundant when the Messiah comes, Purim will continue for ever. Be prepared for a grand, annual fancy dress competition in heaven.

It's a wonderful day to be in the synagogue – for anyone without a nervous disposition or wearing ear-plugs. As the familiar story is read aloud, the children clap and cheer for Mordecai, the hero, and for Esther, his adopted daughter, and hiss and boo and stamp their feet whenever that villain Haman's name is mentioned. They even wave special noisemakers which make a rather rude sort of belching sound. The genuine article would be quite acceptable, as long as it's reserved for the right character. This is the one occasion when the Rabbi is the centre of attention, and everyone hangs on his words.

Congregational participation is at its maximum. I would love this kind of interaction in the Church. So many sermons would benefit from a little heckling. Nodding off seems to be the nearest equivalent, and the only indication of life. No one ever nods off during Purim. Or at any other time in the synagogue to my memory. The gossip and conversation are too stimulating by far.

Purim also means plays, performed for the benefit of long-suffering parents, who smile fondly upon the thespian attempts of their offspring, much like Christians at a nativity play. Except that the children are playing bloodthirsty soldiers, not benign little angels. When I attended Hebrew classes, my unspoken dream was to play the part of Queen Esther, never considering the tubby little figure I squeezed into a school tunic every day. Bulges thwarted my aspirations to stardom. Instead I was always cast, inevitably, as a Persian soldier, and being small even then, wrestled with the visor of an oversized helmet which kept falling over my eyes, so that I couldn't see to make a decent entrance or exit and kept falling over my sword, which trailed along the ground.

Perhaps that's why I became involved in religious broadcasting in later life, to work out my childhood frustrations. The major problem facing any director of religious television programmes is that the star of the show happens to be invisible. It really is terribly inconvenient. All you can do is try and convey the chief player's major qualities by featuring the lives of the lesser characters who interact with him. And that is exactly what the book of Esther does. It appears to be the most irreligious book in the Bible. The name of God is never mentioned. All you have is a story. But the story is a tapestry. A tangled mass of apparent coincidences are intricately and meticulously woven into a picture portraying deliverance. And we are left in no doubt about who or what is doing the weaving: the invisible hand of an invisible God. God becomes visible in the events of the lives of ordinary men and women. No book in the

Bible, by its unique format, more clearly demonstrates the interrelation between the secular and sacred.

Every detail of the story counts. Haman, for example, is a descendant of Amalek, Israel's sworn enemy, whom God told them to destroy. But Saul, the first King of Israel, disobeyed this instruction, saved Haman's ancestors, and ultimately caused tsorus for the Jewish people. Which all goes to show that if you don't handle a situation properly the first time round, it will almost certainly rise up to haunt you again later. Biblical Jewish history is a catalogue of disasters or near-disasters caused by failings such as incredulity, impatience or disobedience, which had taken place hundreds of years before. "If Moses had turned right and not left, we would have had the oil wells," says one old Jewish joke.

God chooses Mordecai, who just happens to belong to the same tribe as Saul, to deal with the incarnation of evil. This time Haman and his offspring are annihilated, thanks to their own sheer stupidity, and the divine edict to destroy Amalek is at last fulfilled.

Mordecai and Esther themselves must be the most ironic choice of heroic characters for God to write into his script. They were not practising Jews. They didn't even like being Jewish. When their people had had the chance to get out of Babylon and go back to Palestine, they were part of a small group who had decided to stay behind. They didn't fancy the hard work involved in rebuilding the country. They were comfortable where they were, thank you, accepted, assimilated. Their dress, their customs, even their names were Babylonian. Like the Jews of pre-war Germany, they didn't see the writing on the wall. In the final analysis the Jew can never be fully assimilated and the appearance of a Haman or a Hitler on the stage reminds them, by blood and tears, of their inescapable heritage and destiny.

So two of the least likely people find themselves key players in a major drama. We know the feeling well. We chug along from day to day in our very ordinary routine, when all of a sudden we become aware of another dimension in our lives. We happened to be in the right place at the right time and the ordinary has become extraordinary. I remember hearing the children's story writer, Patricia St John, speaking about her time as a missionary in Morocco. Once a week she and a fellow nurse would take a trip by bus up into the mountains to hold a clinic in one of the isolated villages. On this particular day the bus driver went way beyond their stop, and had travelled quite a distance before they could persuade him to set them down. They were furious that they now had to walk back several miles in the blazing sun, with bags full of medical treatment. But as the bus disappeared down the road, and they resigned themselves to the marathon ahead, they suddenly noticed a woman walking over the mountains to meet them. She had a small baby in her arms.

"I knew you would come," she said. "My baby is ill. I prayed for help. And a voice told me of two white women who would make him better. This is where I was told to meet you."

Divine intervention in my life has been just as real, if not so dramatic. I remember sitting in the bath one day, the only place for meditation when one has teenage children, and even that isn't sacrosanct, wondering what I should do with my life next. My contract as a researcher and presenter for regional television was coming to an end, and I said, almost out loud, "I really love doing interviews, but I'm not relaxed enough about them. What I would really like to do now is interview people day in, day out, so that I can talk to anyone on air any time, about anything."

The following day the phone rang, and I was offered my own three-hour daily show on local radio. And life became one long interview.

Equally devastating, and timely, was my demise, almost two years later. A new manager decided to make a clean sweep, and I was one of several presenters asked to leave as soon as possible. I now understand how being made redundant can be the biggest single blow to a person's self-confidence. I decided there and then that I had two options. I could take the dismissal as a personal injury, spitting bile at the cause of my hurt. Or, I could accept it as part of some invisible and as yet unknown plan for my life. After all, we ask for guidance. It hardly seems fair to scream and rage when we get it. Tough though it was, and it certainly didn't remove the pain altogether, the latter approach seemed to work. It spared me much of the intense bitterness experienced by my colleagues, and meant that I encouraged my husband in the pursuit of a new job. We would never have moved to our present home without a rather large push from an invisible source.

So Esther, the reluctant Jewess, suddenly finds herself in the King's palace, rounded up as a contestant in a beauty competition. The prize, if you could call him that, is the King himself. She wins hands down, then, thanks to a little bit of timely listening at keyholes by her Uncle Mordecai, alerts her lord and master to an assassination attempt. "But whatever you do," says Mordecai, "don't let on you're Jewish." Farcical in the light of future events. Why else had the invisible hand placed her in the palace? Wouldn't we all like to wriggle out of our destiny at times?

Only when Haman becomes Prime Minister does the plot begin to thicken. Mordecai insults him, and personal pique provokes all the usual anti-Semitic clap-trap. They're alien. They're different. They're unpatriotic. An economic and political burden, for which there is only one final solution: extermination. But he can't decide which day to carry out his dastardly deed. So uses a little bit of magic to help him make up his mind, and lots, or purim in Hebrew, are cast. Nice, subtle irony again. "Man throws the dice," says the Proverb, "but it's God who makes the decisions."

At last Mordecai wakes up.

"Don't think you're safe living in the palace," he says

to Esther. "You won't escape. Anyway, maybe this is why you're there in the first place."

She almost shames him with her response.

She will go to the King, uninvited, and "if I have to die for it, so be it".

It's an extraordinary thing to say. A total self-abandonment. And yet many of the biblical characters say something similar at crisis-point in their lives. Joseph in prison acknowledges that his personal tragedy is largely irrelevant. One day his people will be free. Mary submits to the terrible shame of pregnancy because she knows she is simply a vehicle. It is that moment when we're confronted with our own insignificance and immortality. Perhaps because of a near-accident. Or danger. Or a bereavement. Or the discovery of a hard, unexplained lump in the breast, or the male equivalent, and we convince ourselves we'll be dead before the month is out. Suddenly we catch a glimpse of the immensity of the Almighty, managing thousands of years of history, while we have a mere three score years and ten of them, if that. Our whole perspective changes. In the end it doesn't matter whether he gives us seventy years or seven. They all vanish like a sneeze. And all that remains is the story he is writing, and our tiny part in it. If, like Esther and Joseph and Mary, we consent to play it.

And so they all lived happily ever after. Or did they? I can't speak for Esther, married to such a twit of a man as the King. Nor for Haman who was hanged on the gallows he had prepared for Mordecai. Nor for the Jewish people, with so many more potential disasters to face. But disaster is never the end of the story. Like Hannukah, the feast it follows, Purim is one link in a long chain of salvation and redemption, woven in and out and around the people God loves.

IDEAS FOR CELEBRATING

Why not, some time during the Church's year, perhaps

on the Church's birthday, have a grand "redemption" fancy dress party, when everyone dresses up as goodies or baddies from Biblical history? It has a way of making an old message contemporary.

HAMAN'S POCKETS

A fritter-like pastry, deep-fried and sprinkled with icing sugar.

200g plain flour
1 tsp. baking powder/soda
2 eggs
2 tbsp. caster sugar
1 tbsp. tepid water
½ tsp. salt

Beat the eggs until fluffy, then add the remaining ingredients to make a soft, but non-sticky, dough (the amount of flour may vary with the size of the eggs). Turn on to a floured board and roll out to the thickness of a knife blade. Cut into half-moons by moving a circular cutter down the dough to form crescent shapes, then pinch each crescent in the centre so that it looks like a bow tie with an "ear" on either side. Deep fry until golden brown, then drain on kitchen paper and serve hot or cold, sprinkled with confectioner's sugar.

Purim is also a time for making gingerbread men, or any other edible representations of Haman.

15

Of Sarah, Sex and Espousal

My maternal great-grandmother had a wicked sense of humour. You could tell how risqué the joke from the loudness of her cackle.

When Annie, one of her daughters, told her she was expecting another baby, she promised to keep it a secret, so that Annie could break the news to her brothers and sisters herself. Then she forgot her promise.

"Guess who's pregnant?" she shouted, above the din of the usual Sabbath family get-together.

The room went quiet. Her children, all well past childhood and with families of their own, looked at her in anticipation.

She suddenly remembered the promise.

"Well?" they probed. "Well, Mother, who?"

"Me!" she said triumphantly.

"You!" they chorused, with undisguised horror.

"Yes, me," she said, pulling herself up to her full five feet. "And what's wrong with me? Your father isn't away at the front."

This was no refined, quasi-Edwardian lady. She was far too earthy. But then Judaism is completely open on the subject of sex. How could any religious system, claiming relevance to every aspect of life, ignore the most fundamental instinct in human nature? In fact, one of the Jewish holy books says that after creation was finished, the last thing God did was watch Adam and Eve enjoying sexual intercourse. And that was what prompted him to say his work was "very good". In other words, "That idea of mine has certainly gone down well."

When an angel tells Sarah that she and Abraham will have a son, she laughs at the idea, not, according to the Bible, because she's ninety and too old to have a baby. What she actually says is, "At our age, shall Abraham and I have pleasure together?"

The entire spiritual destiny of human beings hangs in the balance, and what is Sarah thinking about? Sex. Can Abraham actually manage it? But surprise, surprise, there is obviously life in the old boy yet!

My husband's grandfather, a very well-known preacher and evangelist in his time, had children when he was seventy and seventy-two. His bride, I ought to say, was forty years his junior.

Widowed long, he had prayed for a wife, and had a dream of a young woman who came and sat on his knee. In fact, unlikely as it was for an Edwardian lady, she not only sat on his knee. She kissed him. And despite some criticism from his previously admiring audiences about the unseemly nature of the age gap, they were deliriously, passionately happy for the few years they had together. It is a story I like to tell the men. It makes them smile for at least a fortnight.

Sex, for the Jew, is a sacred act. The Hebrew word for marriage, "Kiddushim", comes from Kaddosh, the word for holy. But "holy" for the Jew does not mean "put on a pedestal", removed from everyday life. It means it is a special gift, to be enjoyed and appreciated to the full. Unlike the Christian view of chastity, chastity in Judaism is not the avoidance of sex, but of illicit sex. Within marriage it is to be experienced whenever possible, as often as possible, and is all but compulsory on festivals. The law says a man must give his wife pleasure on the Sabbath. Nowhere does it say that he himself is entitled to it! Hundreds of years before the Christian world woke up to the female orgasm, Jewish men knew their duty.

And since duty isn't always enough to ensure wifely satisfaction, the Rabbi often gives preparation courses, providing the necessary, vital information.

Never is there any suggestion that procreation is the only justification for the sex act. Nor is contraception prohibited, except amongst the ultra-fundamentalist. Some whisper that they only make love through a hole in a sheet, but it is a myth perpetrated by the less Orthodox, who find it hard to imagine that anyone walking around with side-curls and top hat by day, can abandon themselves to unbridled eroticism at night. But I have it on good authority that they do. The only real restriction is during menstruation. Many Jewish women argue that they rather like that guaranteed little rest from time to time, a monthly chance of an early night and a good book. Self-denial, for a few days, can also add a certain sparkle to the resumption of the relationship. Anticipation is a vital part of pleasure.

Theologians have talked for years about a Judaeo-Christian tradition in sexual matters, but there is no such thing. The very idea is a contradiction in terms. The religion which gave birth to one of the most erotic love poems ever written is light years away from one dogged by the idea that sex was the most unfortunate mistake God ever made. It is no coincidence that in my Jewish prayer book, sandwiched between prayers for the Sabbath in the synagogue and prayers for the Sabbath in the home, is the Song of Songs, in its entirety, the only book of the Bible to be quoted in full. I have rarely seen a short quote in any Christian prayer book. Nor is it often the subject of sermons. But then, being full of breasts and belly buttons, that might be a little difficult.

Besides, instead of being a cause for celebration, sex is often relegated to an opportunity for condemnation, judgement and self-righteousness. Sexual sins always appear to be worse than any other. Perhaps because our sexuality, likened in the novels of D.H. Lawrence to the unleashed, uncontrollable force of water, frightens us with its power. And we know how vulnerable we really are. Perhaps because other people's sexual, and therefore obvious, misdemeanours make us feel better about those little weaknesses of ours, which we hide.

The squeamishness on the subject began almost with the Church. The culture in which it grew didn't have much time for the body, its needs, or its pleasures. The real spoil-sport was born in the third century. And he was a man. Men, so a therapist successful in treating sex abusers once told me, have always found it harder than women to handle their sexuality. In his youth Augustine had been what is commonly called "a bit of a lad". Once he became a Christian he was so nauseated by his escapades, so terrified that his sexual urges might get out of hand, that, sadly, he started talking about "the shame which attends all sexual intercourse". He saw it as an enemy of the spiritual life, a sin in marriage, unless it was for the sake of conceiving children.

Augustine's views have haunted the Church down through the centuries. The medieval mystic, Margery Kempe, believed that having to care for her husband when he became senile was a punishment for the "fleshly lust and inordinate love" she had for him when he was a youth. As late as 1926 Maude Royden, a lecturer at Oxford University who fought for women's rights and suffrage, wrote, "I believe the best method of birth control to be abstinence, except when a child is desired." Attitudes which are anathema to the Jewish way of thinking. Which mean that instead of revelling in the glory of intimacy, in its right context, like the Song of Songs, we find it very hard to shake off the idea that it is "not quite nice".

A short while ago Peter and I had a few days away together. When I came back I had a very vivid dream that I was pregnant and, to my surprise, I was absolutely delighted.

"You must have had a good few days away," said a friend when I described my dream.

I muttered a rather ambiguous, bland response.

Now, why was I too prudish to say, "Yes, actually, wonderful"?

After all, we are married. And despite what some church members might like to believe, the ministers' children are not virginal conceptions. Nor does the fun cease once they are born.

On the other hand the last thing couples who are not enjoying the physical side of their relationship want to hear is some bright spark describing its pleasures. At its best, sex can be a spiritual experience, the ultimate communion between two human beings, the visible symbol of God's union with his people. At its worst it can be a disaster. And some people, especially women, may heave a sigh of relief that this great earthly treat will not exist in heaven. Sad and inevitable, in some way, that such a great gift should be so easily spoilt. But there isn't only Augustine's inheritance to deal with. There is the influence of our own culture, the graphic portrayal of the sex act on our television screens, when every couple manage wild, total and simultaneous ecstasy in thirty seconds flat. They have to. It is one of the limitations of the medium. My inside knowledge of it tells me that if there isn't a new twist in the plot every few minutes we switch off. With boredom. Nevertheless, it hardly inspires the idea that the sex relationship, like any sport, may require years of training and practice. And occasional outside advice. For if we do not talk about the immense joy of sex, nor do we talk about the immense sense of failure or frustration it can cause when it isn't working. Despite our so-called "openness" on the subject, sex is more of a taboo than it ever was, and the same web of silence we weave around death, is woven about this vital part of our lives. We dare not ask for help without a sense of shame. When it could, and perhaps should, be the most natural thing in the world.

I know, had she been alive, that my great-grandmother would have been an invaluable source of advice, and tips. She let us know in no uncertain terms that she

thoroughly enjoyed the physical side of her relationship. And the strange thing is, she never really liked
my great-grandfather. They fought like dogs. She was
always convinced he wanted to marry her younger sister, but was forced, according to custom, to marry the
elder sister. But then, for most couples, no matter how
loving, sex, on one occasion, can be an act of profound
spiritual and emotional oneness, and the next, though
enjoyable, simply be a way of gratifying a craving. Like
food, it can be taken thoughtfully and prayerfully, fully
conscious of the richness of its symbolism. Or it can
simply satisfy the appetite. And, says Judaism, the two
different approaches are what divide human beings from
animals. Only humans are made in the image of God. It
is the way an act is performed, and the intention behind
it, which determines whether it is holy or not.

Several years ago Peter and I both decided that our
relationship was feeling a little strained. Neither said
anything to the other, because we couldn't quite work
out what the problem was. Peter went, on his own, to
Israel for ten days. And while we were apart, as couples
do in enforced absence, we thought a great deal about
our sex life. Both of us realised, separately, that it had
become rather same-ish, a little dull. It was a bit like
eating minced beef all the time, when chilli con carne,
or curry, lasagne and moussaka were all on the menu.
He in Israel, and I at home, without conferring, decided
to do something about it once we were together again.
We both prayed for a renewed sense of being God's
gift to each other, which we had felt so strongly at the
beginning.

His return was a second honeymoon, though much
better than the first, because we were more sure of each
other, safer, more confident. We spent an extraordinary
week. It was a journey of discovery, each learning what
the other had imagined in their wildest dreams, each
learning to give, as well as receive, in a new way. The
Hebrew word for intercourse is "yada", from the verb

"to know". God gives human beings the opportunity to know and delight in the hidden recesses of every part of mind and body of their spouse. The very concept took on new meaning for us. And though, sadly, we couldn't sustain the pace for longer, the raptures of those few days have never really died away.

Celibacy, in Judaism, is not a calling. It is a failure. The way of attaining self-control is through marriage, not outside of it. God is the great matchmaker in the sky. There is nothing he relishes more than a game of heavenly pairing. Singleness is an affront to his expertise. A well-born Roman woman, so the story goes, once heard Rabbi Jose ben Halafta saying that the world had been created in six days.

"And what has he been doing since then?" she asked the Rabbi.

"Matchmaking," was the Rabbi's reply.

"Matchmaking?" asked the woman, incredulously.

"That may seem an easy thing to you," said Rabbi Jose, "but in God's eyes it's as difficult as dividing the Red Sea."

Unconvinced, the woman decided to show the Almighty a thing or two, and paired off a thousand of her slaves. Her success barely lasted a night, when a barrage of problems and complaints kept her from her beauty sleep. Perhaps being God was not so easy after all.

Perhaps that is why the Jewish community is so keen to offer him its help in this particular matter. Single people learn to study the seating plan at weddings, long before they take their place at the table, so that they know who and what they are contending with. A friend of mine who had managed to stay single well into her forties always started the conversation by saying to her apparently eligible neighbour, "Divorced, gay or emotionally disturbed?"

The basic belief is that like Adam and Eve, man and woman are only truly fulfilled in each other. There is no strict prohibition of masturbation, not mentioned in the Bible, but homosexual practice is out of the question because it defies the natural created order. Since it marks the beginning of life as a complete person, the marriage ceremony is one of the most festive of all the Jewish traditions.

For obvious reasons I wasn't at Mama's first wedding, except as a twinkle in my father's eye. But I was at her second, and I have rarely had such fun in my life. Lively and attractive as she was, I never thought she would marry again after my father died. But the Jewish community had other ideas. She was invited, by cousins, to meet an "eligible" widower.

"No strings attached," she said.

"Of course, not," I replied.

"I've no intention of getting married. But meeting someone can't do any harm."

"It can't. It may even be a good idea."

And then it was, "We're just having dinner out together. Nothing more. Pleasant company, that's all I want," and methought the lady began to protest too much.

Within days a coy, wheedling little voice asked down the telephone whether I would mind if she got married again.

Mind? I was overjoyed that someone else was prepared to take her off our hands.

"Does he know what he's letting himself in for?" my brother asked me anxiously.

He must, I thought. A Jewish widower in his late sixties must know how the game is played.

"Since when have you ever asked our permission for anything you want to do?" I asked her. She had said it to me often enough! "Go for it."

Within months the family gathered in the home of a cousin, to watch Mama, exceptionally elegant in silver grey and rose, take smiling, unsuspecting Boris, as the second martyr to the perfect Jewish home. They were married in the traditional way, under a chuppah, a canopy of flowers, symbolic of marriages in ancient times, when the bride was brought to her bridegroom's tent.

"Rings?" demanded the Rabbi.

Boris handed them over.

"Are they paid for?"

The extraordinary mixture of dignified ceremonial and farce was almost too much to bear.

"This young . . . er, this couple," said the Rabbi, and the chuppah, supported on poles held by my brother and Boris's three sons, began to shake. My brother swallowed hard and forced down the corners of his mouth.

The ketubbah, or marriage contract, the Jewish alternative to vows, was read aloud, and signed. Failure to observe the contract is a serious matter and can lead to divorce. Mama always claimed she never heard it the first time round. She listened to her rights carefully this time. Then the groom, according to custom, wrapped a glass in cloth and smashed it underfoot. It is supposed to be a moment of sober, quiet reflection on the destruction of the Temple. Instead it has now become a signal for generalised chaos. The room erupted into shouts of "Mazeltov". Everyone hugged and kissed everyone else. Hats slid sideways over eyes or fell to the floor. Mama was a wife again. And looked very pleased about it. Until the Rabbi announced that the young . . . er, the couple would now retire for Yihud.

Yihud, the Hebrew word for seclusion, a compulsory opportunity for the couple to retire in private together, gave a young bridegroom the chance to check out his dues on the contract, if he so chose. And presumably, if there was any question about his partner's virginity, now was the chance to complain and get his money back.

"But I don't know what to do," Boris protested loudly.

"So you'll think of something," said the Rabbi, ushering the reluctant couple into a bedroom.

They had barely had the time to open some of their presents when a short knock on the door announced the arrival of the Rabbi with a trolley laden with tea and cakes. Just as well, my mother said to herself, that she and her new husband had simply been having a little chat.

Yihud, in fact, now simply gives the couple a chance, immediately after their wedding, to have a few moments' space together, to say whatever they want to say to each other, in private. Food is often wheeled in, in case they have been fasting, as a sign of repentance and preparation for their life together.

Meanwhile their guests don't miss the couple at all. They are having a wonderful time. Musical instruments, forbidden in the synagogue, for Jews are in a constant state of mourning for the Temple, are compulsory at a wedding reception. So is dancing. Even the Song of Songs talks about a dance of two companies, possibly referring to an old tradition where the men and women danced separately, the bride brandishing a sword in her right hand, defending herself against all suitors other than her chosen.

God's special relationship with Israel, Christ with his Church, no other relationship is as elevated as marriage. No other relationship as vulnerable therefore. Promiscuity and adultery are not frowned upon because the Almighty is a spoil-sport, who finds sex distasteful and wishes he hadn't bothered to create it, but because he knows the damage it can do, and because he deeply loves those who will be appallingly hurt by its misuse. Jewish law maintains that the marriage relationship must be characterised, above all, by mutual respect and loyalty. When that breaks down, as in the case of Michal, wife of King David, who mocked her husband for dancing for joy before the ark of the covenant, something in the relationship withers. Michal never had children. Possibly because she and her husband never again had sex. He certainly began to take other wives. But when loyalty, respect, trust, and an ability to see the funny side of it, are alive and well, sex is one of God's unbeatable jokes.

THE SEVEN BLESSINGS (OF GOD) AT A MARRIAGE

Blessed are You, O Lord our God, King of the Universe, and Creator of the fruit of life.

Blessed are You O Lord,
who created all things for Your glory.

Blessed are You, O Lord,
who created woman and man in a day.

Blessed are You, O Lord,
who created human beings in your likeness,
established them that they might increase and multiply.
As the barren woman rejoices and is glad
when God blesses her with children,
so blessed be the Lord,
who rejoices when His children are gathered together in
    His presence.

Let all present rejoice,
especially this couple who love each other,
as we remember the joy that was heard
on the day of creation.
Blessed be the Lord
who gives joy to bride and groom.

Blessed be the Lord
who created bride and groom,
mirth and song,
pleasure and delight,
love and peace,
friendship and fellowship.
May the voices of the bride and the groom resound in
    jubilation,
and may the hearts of those who witness their joy be glad.

Blessed be the Lord,
who gives the bride and the groom as a gift to each other.

16

And Singleness, Sensuality, and Symbolism

Exalting marriage and sex as it does, makes Judaism seem very hard on anyone who manages to escape the net and remain single. Not to mention the widowed, or divorced, for divorce has always been recognised within Judaism as a necessary evil. But singleness isn't an issue. Partly because few manage to remain in that state for long. Partly because those who do are automatically cared for by the community, which can never resist a challenge to pair them off. And partly because the Jewish religion, positively encouraging a full involvement of all the senses in the practice of its traditions and rituals, has few hang-ups about sexuality.

Many married people are not fully in touch with their own sexuality. They may have occasional genital contact, but are not at ease with their own body, hide it in unattractive clothing, and repress its immense capacity for sensual enjoyment. How we fear the unleashed, uncontrollable flood of our own sexual awareness. In *Faith Without Pretending* the missionary doctor, Anne Townsend, told the story of her attempt to take her own life and the painful rebuilding process which followed. It seemed as if a traditional form of evangelical Christianity had frozen the real woman within her. Gradually, as the thawing, healing process progressed, her senses awakened. She gave herself time to lie on the grass and feel the warmth of the

sun on her body, inhaling the scent of lavender, aware
of sparrows pecking her arms and the gentle buzzing of
the bees. She walked by the sea, and revelled in the taste
of salt on her lips and the wind whipping her hair. She
picked blackberries for the first time, felt their juices slide
between her fingers and felt well and truly alive.

The problem was that she, along with many of us,
immersed in Western culture, had been reared with what
has come to be known as "The Protestant Work Ethic",
wagging its nagging finger before our noses. And we
have Calvin and the Reformers to thank for that. I
was in Geneva recently, on the city's national fête day,
and stood, jostled by hordes of revellers with lanterns,
looking at the row of sandstone statues erected in their
memory. Part of me was transported back in time by their
academic hats and gowns, their benign and learned stoop,
and I almost felt the thrill of theological excitement their
teaching must have stirred several centuries ago. No more
guilt and penances, no more earning God's forgiveness
to avoid the horrors of hell or purgatory. Peace with
God, by faith in Christ alone. It was all so simple, so
accessible, a new kind of religion, captured by the smooth,
straight lines of the sculptor. But another part of me,
somewhere deep inside, responded negatively to the slight
downturn of their mouths at the corners, and the dour,
rather serious expressions on their faces, surveying with
a certain disapproval the jollifications around their feet.
Looking up at Calvin I knew I would have respected him.
But after basic theological consensus, I don't think he and
I would have agreed about much. His asceticism of course
was a reaction to the excesses of the Catholicism he knew,
disguising the basic Christian message behind a morass of
unbiblical practice. So was Martin Luther's. But as with
any other leaders, the movement they inspired reflected
their personalities, as well as their philosophy. For all
Luther restored a much-needed sense of the undeserved
grace and overwhelming love of God to the Church, he
himself struggled to accept it, and punished his body

with constant fasting, until his intestines, unable to cope with the unpredictability of the daily programme, gave up functioning altogether. Less extravagant than Luther, Calvin was a quiet academic with simple, rather austere, tastes. And his legacy was simple, austere services, suspicion of all ceremonial, and stark churches, with little colour, decoration or obvious symbolism.

He was also a very systematic man, who thought that Geneva could become a model of the ideal Christian city. To this very day no one is allowed to lie in on a Sunday morning. At 9 a.m. I was rudely awakened from my slumbers by all the bells ringing out in unison, summoning a now largely unheeding community to worship. Leisure had no place on Calvin's agenda. The other six days of the week were for hard work. The Reformers thought sloth a major sin, success a reward from God for work done well. And though, throughout the West, the bells no longer induce the majority to worship, they go on ringing a doleful reminder in our heads that life is labour, leisure an indulgence. So that like Anne Townsend we fall into the workaholic's trap of thinking that every second must be usefully and seriously employed. Until every fibre of our being is stressed beyond endurance by slavish obedience to the tyranny of our own timetables, and we snap.

Driving ourselves, stifling the body's cry for renewal and recreation, denying it a wealth of revitalising sensations, is hardly "life in all its fullness", the potential Jesus intended for every human being. I have known very few workaholic Jews, though there must be some. But it is difficult to sustain an addiction compulsorily interrupted every Friday at sundown for at least twenty-four hours, and a great deal more in the winter. It is well nigh impossible to deny the body relaxation, when countless festivals disrupt the working routine, some for several days at a time, with good food and wine, and other, distinctly sensual, pleasures. Small wonder that the daughter of a friend of mine came home one Friday after school and announced her intention of becoming a Jew.

"But you know nothing about Judaism," said the mother.

"Neither do my Jewish school friends," replied the daughter, "but they do go home at 2.30."

The Jewish calendar creates an unavoidable rhythm of work and leisure. Just as well for people like my brother, who no longer enjoy that elusive quality which used to be known as job satisfaction. It really is very unkind of me, when the poor lad is bored half out of his mind, to tell him to take heart, because, after all, accountants seem to be the only ones making money out of an economic recession. And for producing precisely nothing – except reams of paper. He represents the millions who are fortunate enough to have work, hate it, and are no longer able to change direction. For the millions who do not have work at all, his boredom is a luxury. Which must radically alter our understanding of usefulness, and the importance of leisure. The spectre of unemployment highlights the need to find hope, joy and fulfilment at home, in the community, in the Church. "Life in all its abundance" can no longer mean professional achievement and the fulfilment of ambition. It is about finding God in the mundane, the ordinary, and the unexpected.

Every one of the temptations confronting Jesus at the beginning of his ministry offered him the extraordinary. But he opted instead for a simple lifestyle tramping the countryside, and everything that he saw, heard and touched, in true Jewish fashion, became a symbol, the opportunity for a story, a joke or a warning. He denied convention and remained unmarried, yet no human being was ever so whole, so fully alive, so aware of every sensation: the touch of Mary Magdalene massaging his feet with oil, the smell of fish baking on an open fire, the taste of bread and wine, the sound of the wind rustling the branches of a fig tree, the sight of a shepherd cradling one little lost lamb. After he had gone the disciples would never again have any similar experiences without remembering him, without discovering a new lightness in their step and joy in their marrow.

When Anne Townsend acknowledged her senses, her dormant sexuality quietly and gently awakened. She bought jeans for the first time, watched the sort of television programmes she would have once switched off, in case she was caught watching them, and was tickled by delicious, new stirrings within, her own burgeoning femininity. To her amazement, God would suddenly surprise her with his presence, in a forest of giant trees, by a canal, watching barges negotiate the locks. And he came to her in a new, tangible way, putting his arms around her, holding her tightly in a warm and loving embrace. It almost seems as if Christ himself were the handsome prince, come to awaken Sleeping Beauty with a kiss, leading her by the hand out into a world which shines and sparkles, as if she were seeing it for the first time.

This is surely what the now hackneyed phrase, "being born again", really means. "Heaven above is brighter blue, earth around is richer green." How I identified with the hymn-writer when all fell into place for the first time, and I realised, reading that forbidden book at the back of the Bible, under the bedclothes by torchlight in case I was caught, that when Jesus said, "He who has seen me has seen the Father", that he was the Messiah I had been looking for. I remember sitting upstairs on a double decker bus, a few days later, looking down at the grimy, industrial North-east which was my home, thinking, "Well it really is rather beautiful after all." I felt like a kitten which had just opened my eyes. Every impression seemed more acute, every taste sharper, every colour more vivid. The world was a new, exciting place, a sort of ante-chamber to heaven, where all was silver and gold and crimson, emerald, azure and amethyst, just like the synagogue.

Then, over the next months and years, I was taught to mistrust my senses.

"Never rely on feelings," I was told, "they let us down. They lead us astray. Faith is what counts."

In some ways that was true. There were times, in those early years, of such confrontation with my family, that I felt little more than acute misery and pain. Faith had to take over, a faith based on everything the Bible said about God never failing or forsaking his children. But faith is not brain power. My brain registered what I read, but I also felt it in my guts. An instinct deeper than the intellect told me I was a child of God. So I went on living like one. Little did I know it at the time, but this was a very Jewish thing to do, for in Hebrew thought, faith is more than theory. It is action, not intellectual certainty, based on what we know to be true.

Whenever I could I went down to the sea and stood for hours, watching the waves, sometimes lap-lapping softly on the beach, sometimes crashing against the rocks. And as I inhaled the familiar fishy, salty smell, I felt small and secure with this unexplorable, untamed vastness. God seemed to me to be like the sea, gentle and soothing when I needed it, yet also magnificent and free, more immense than I dared to imagine. And I longed to take off my clothes and dive in. That, in Britain, would have been foolhardy. A certain means of catching pneumonia or a great deal worse. So I never dared do more than remove my tights and gingerly dip in a toe or two. If I was feeling really brave I managed a whole foot. And that sensation, once the numbness had worn off, rekindled vivid memories of holidays on the Continent, and I imagined what it would be like to plunge myself into the billows, take my feet off the ground, and let go completely, to feel my body totally engulfed in water, yet carried along effortlessly by the flow. Like Abraham, setting out into the unknown, sure that God would carry him. I know no better picture of faith.

It seems strange to me, when so many readily available sensations bring such a rich dimension to our spirituality, that in the Reformed tradition, church services have tended to rely on the mind. It seems unnatural to switch our senses off, like some sort of electronic device, at the church door. Besides, they have a way of breaking through, uninvited. As I went into church a few months ago I remember thinking, "Oh good, it's communion." And then I became aware that I had never consciously registered the fact that the table was laid out at the front. How had I known it was communion? I suddenly realised it was the smell of the wine, wafting through the building, and took a long, enjoyable sniff. The rich, heady bouquet recaptured for me countless happy Sabbath and Passover memories. More than that, the scent created an atmosphere, a sense of anticipation for what was to come.

If, as Judaism claims, every part of our humanity has spiritual potential, the senses cannot be ignored. Used appropriately they are an invaluable tool. The taste and smell of pungent, slightly acrid herbs like horseradish, which I sometimes serve in a sauce to accompany roast beef on Sundays, and I am back around my grandmother's table on the Passover, recalling the bitter pain and tears of my ancestors when they were slaves in Egypt, and their merciful deliverance. Apples, almonds and cinnamon, whenever I bake them in a pudding for the children, force me to reflect, quite subconsciously, on the land of promise, and the sweetness of God's provision. The burgundy glow of wine in a silver cup, twinkling candles, the smell of the freshly baked chollah, the silky feel of the satin of a prayer shawl or bread coverlet, sweet-smelling oils and spices, smooth, shiny pebbles, crisp, crunchy unleavened bread, the haunting rise and fall of human voices chanting, and the shrill blast of the ram's horn are the essence of Judaism. It is an accessible religion. It can be touched, felt, smelt, heard and tasted. It created a thousand subconscious impressions in my childhood mind, associations which have never left me and well up, unbidden, at the most surprising moments. Even a visit to the dentist can spark off a positive, pleasant memory. One whiff of the familiar smell of oil of cloves used to line our cavities before they're filled, and instead of lying in the chair with my mouth wide open like a dying goldfish, I am transported to some joyful Jewish festival. Better still, these days, happy Christmas feelings flood into my mind, because of the cloves I stick in the onion when I am making the bread sauce for the freezer, thinking about the friends and family who will soon be there to enjoy it. And the dentist wonders what he has done to bring such a silly smile to my face.

The Catholic Church has known the value of the senses for centuries, positively encouraging its followers to sublimate sexual feelings into religious ecstasy. All the time-honoured symbols, candles, incense, robes, rich fabrics, are there. The more non-conformist the Church becomes, the more ill-at-ease with sensuality of any kind. Out with the candles, with colour, with smells and bells, with all but absolutely unavoidable symbols. Both have moved a long way away from their Jewish roots. For the Jew a symbol is only a symbol. The horseradish used at the Passover has no magical qualities. We grow it in our back garden, near the dustbins. Only because it's never available in the shops on that once a year occasion when we need it. It's a tenacious weed. Fortunately we have always moved house before it takes over our garden, and begins to spread next door. Successive removals firms have found, amongst our precious belongings, one pot, with what looks like a large, mangy dock leaf sticking up from the soil. Heaven knows what they, or the ministers who succeed us, have made of our choice of garden foliage. In the service it represents the bitterness of the Jewish people in captivity. The leftovers can be eaten, thrown in the bin, or on the compost heap. No such irreverent treatment for any symbol in the Catholic Church. It is elevated out of everyday life and placed in a special building or receptacle. You may see and hear and smell. But only the initiated may touch or feel. On the other hand, the Low Church tradition is so afraid that the people might invest it with special powers, and worship it, that the poor symbol is thrown out of the window altogether.

St James' in Coventry, Peter's first church, built in the thirties, had a decidedly Calvinist look about it. Inside, despite an open-plan seating arrangement which lent itself to dance and drama, and other decidedly Old Testament, non-cerebral ways of worship, vast expanses of bare brick wall gave a rather cold, austere feel to the building. Peter was informed however that he would be expected to wear robes when he was leading services. It has always been a mystery to me why some people enjoy dressing up their minister more than their building. I have to admit that there was plenty of this particular human maypole to decorate, but there was a great deal more of the wall. The first little number he was given to wear was some young woman's converted wedding dress. It wasn't the idea, it was the row of pin marks where the darts in the bust had been, which really bothered him. It was eventually, to his relief, replaced with a new cloak, and a set of lovingly embroidered scarves in colours matching the dazzling array of altar fronts, coverlets and banners, made by a small group to reflect the seasons in the Church's year. It became a delight to walk into the building on festivals, and see a mass of purple at Advent and Lent, crimson at Pentecost, white and gold at Easter, and feel a gentle whirring within, reminding me that today was not like any other day. "Why is this night different from all other nights?" asks the youngest child at the Passover table, which is laden with all kind of delicacies and ornaments which appear only once a year. Every festival is special. Every festival is unique.

The Rabbis see symbolic meaning in everything, which is difficult to our rational Western minds, for whom a spade is a spade and no nonsense. Who would have ever thought a boiled egg could inspire meditation? The beauty of symbol is that it bypasses consciousness. It is experienced rather than analysed, and can have as many meanings as there are people. Peter once came back from a retreat in Wales with a gnarled branch he had found when he was out walking. He stuck it on the dresser in the dining-room amongst the china ornaments.

"Take that filthy thing out of my dining-room," I shouted in true Jewish Mama fashion. Another walking-stick he had collected, the way men do, when they graduate from stamps and stones and toy soldiers. He always dumps his finds halfway between the front door and their final resting place: usually the cellar.

"But I like it there," he said. "It spoke to me."

I looked at it with new eyes. My husband isn't given to conversing with inanimate objects.

"What did it say?" I asked him carefully.

"Well, it speaks to me of the beauty of the natural order. I like carving wood, creating something out of raw material. This piece doesn't need carving. It's already beautiful, as if God had worked on it himself."

"And it wouldn't be telling you, by any chance, that it would rather go out in the garden, where it belongs?"

He looked hurt, so I left it where it was, planning to do a little rearranging after a few days. But the branch grew on me. I began to love its knobbly old shape too, and to appreciate it as the work of a master craftsman. And besides it does make a wonderful stand for angels at Christmas, and an even better one for chickens at Easter.

As an experiment he took it into church for the Lent course he was leading, and asked the group whether it said anything to them. Everyone sat and stared at it for some time. Some obviously loved it. With Easter at hand, it reminded them of the cross, of the immensity of the sacrifice necessary on their behalf. Others were fairly hostile. They didn't like it at all. It communicated barrenness and deadness. They wanted to see new shoots, new life.

We need a variety of symbols, we constantly need new symbols, for reactions to them vary enormously, depending on background, experience, and our point of pilgrimage. I know many people who find it helpful to have an icon in front of them when they pray. I do not.

As a Jewish child I was culturally conditioned to loathe any representation of God whatsoever. For the Jew, that is a deliberate infringement of the first commandment not to make a graven image, and distinguishes them from every other religion. Madonnas, statues of Christ, stained-glass-window saints are all an abhorrence to the Jew, all potential idols. God in his immensity cannot be encapsulated in the handiwork of humankind. So why tempt his creatures to worship a manmade, inferior version? I still struggle to find any aesthetic pleasure whatsoever in religious art. So I tend to look out for more commonplace stimuli to worship.

Some Messianic Jewish congregations in Israel have no place for the cross. After years of anti-Semitism it has become a symbol of pain, persecution and oppression, rather than freedom and forgiveness. The Roman Catholic Church has found it hard to understand why Jews are so hostile to having a religious community at Auschwitz, their huge cross dominating the skyline. For the Christian the large cross over what was a concentration camp says that goodness and hope have triumphed over the despair and destruction of a horrendous episode in world history. For the Jew it says that Hitler is still in cohorts with a Church which has never accepted them for what they are, but only in terms of their potential for conversion. For them the cross almost seems like a grotesque parody.

Michel Quoist, the French priest, whose books of unusual prayers were very popular when I was a slip of a girl, used to say that all of life was a blackboard. The extraordinary thing is that we each of us has our own individual, entirely unique, lesson written large, if we choose to see it. It is quite an enlightening exercise to invite any group to walk around the room, touching, listening, sniffing everything they see, then ask them to describe their sensations. We tried it one evening at a seminar in our present church building. The most innocuous objects suddenly take on spiritual significance. People enjoyed the smooth shape and polish of the wood. That, they said, was how God worked on our lives, lovingly over the years. They noticed the way the flowers wilted without water. Several were fascinated by the organ pipes, which reminded them that to create a beautiful sound, all of the pipes, even the smallest, had to operate in harmony. With time and space for reflection, God can speak to us through everything he has made, in the country, and equally in the squalid city centre, in the office or at home.

Nowhere is this quite so obvious as at the Passover. The last supper was Jesus' opportunity to transform the most loved and familiar symbolism of all into a series of audio-visual aids, so that when the disciples repeated it year after year, the whole of the history of God's plan for human beings would slot into place, and they would understand what Easter was all about.

17

A Festival of Freedom

"Easter," says my five-year-old nephew, who, to his parents' chagrin, managed to remain unnoticed in a religious education lesson in school, "is about someone dying on a cross. But ssshhhhhh, we don't say who."

I always felt it was a bit of a damp squib. Until we moved to Coventry. St James' had a prototype for the occasion, imbibed from various historic, para-Catholic influences, and honed to a fine art. Some sort of Lent teaching series led up to meditations day and night during Holy Week, until, by Easter weekend, the entire congregation was in the mood to celebrate. They had mastered the art of the slow build-up.

One favourite tradition was the daily breakfast, served after the early morning Holy Week meditations, when everyone stayed to eat together in what was known as the "narthex", one of those strange old churchy words which turn up in crossword puzzles and refers to the no-man's land between the church and the front door. It must have befuddled the neighbourhood to open their curtains early in the morning and see, through the glass doors, about two dozen people sitting round a table in the church porch, tucking into their cornflakes.

I couldn't understand the great attraction for my children. Why did they leap out of bed, in what I can only describe as the middle of the night, for quiet meditation? Neither had ever shown quite such piety before. I asked them whether they were enjoying the prolonged time of prayer. I was naïve.

"Prayer?" said Joel, "We don't go for that, do we, Abby? We arrive in time for breakfast."

"But it's still very early for breakfast, when you could have it here," I said to him.

"Ah yes," said his little sister, "but you won't let us have white toast or cornflakes, because they're not wholemeal, and not good for us."

But I couldn't really object to this sacrifice of roughage for a week, when they were made so welcome, and obviously enjoyed being part of a wider family.

The St James' Easter package was so effective that it was only with the greatest trepidation we dared suggest any additions. After all, each church has its own traditions, and they can be harder to change, oy, than the traditions of the Jews. Creatures of habit that we are, we find any change profoundly disturbing, and would rather miss out on potential benefits, than risk an adventure. But for me Easter would be incomplete without celebrating the Passover. We try, at home, to keep two sets of festivals, Jewish and Christian, but it's very hard work having fun. And wonderful when the two dovetail, as they so often do, for in the Old Testament the embryo of the New is hidden. Seed and flower, tree and fruit, and nowhere is that more evident than in the relationship between the Passover and Easter. At the last supper Jesus unashamedly took the rich Passover symbolism, and applied it to himself, so that the disciples would be in no doubt that he was the Passover lamb, spilling his blood, to deliver his people, once and for all, from the Angel of death. In years to come, long after he had gone, they would never be able to experience the Passover without remembering him and making the connection.

So we suggested having a "Seder night", as the Jews call the Passover meal, on Maundy Thursday, instead of the traditional communion service.

"That sounds great," said the enthusiasts.

"It might be interesting," said the careful.

"It's a dreadful idea," declared a small minority. "A party! On one of the holiest days in the Church's calendar? When we should be having a Eucharist, befitting the occasion!"

It was customary, after the Eucharist, to "strip the altar", an old tradition which involved removing every decoration from the front of the church, flowers, tapestries, banners, any gold or silver ornaments, until all that remained, for the night-long vigil into Good Friday, was a solitary wooden cross. It was an important tradition, but we felt that it only told half the story. If Jesus had been expecting the Last Supper to be a lugubrious, morbid sort of affair, why did he tell the disciples he was really looking forward to it? That didn't make sense. Most people, knowing their death was imminent, would want their last moments with loved ones to be memorable, even happy, so that they weren't left feeling unutterably depressed.

So we worked out a compromise.

We held a Passover on Maundy Thursday in the "upper room". St James' was a truly monstrous building, whose ceiling was so high that, many years earlier, a floor had been hung halfway up, creating a spacious hall above the body of the church, where we could enjoy all kinds of communal events. The association with the Last Supper was a bonus. And the room looked absolutely marvellous. The preparation had taken all afternoon. While I was chopping apples and walnuts and wine, concocting a mixture known as haroseth, symbolising the mortar the Israelites had to use to build walls in Egypt when they were slaves of Pharaoh, some contemporary slaves, their forced labour imposed by the minister, were humping trestle tables up six flights of stairs, groaning loudly as men do when they're enjoying themselves. Each table was covered with a white cloth, and decorated with a posy of flowers and a "seder dish", of unleavened bread, bitter herbs and "mortar". Enough space was left between them for the hardy to get up and do a quick hora in and out when the mood took them.

I had always loved the preparation, the sense of antici-pation rippling gently through the intestines. My mother never knew what to do with her children for those few, excited hours before we went to my grandmother's. We were so noisy and fidgety we made the house seem untidy. Fortunately, being Easter week, the BBC usually obliged with a Hollywood movie. One year *The Prisoner of Zenda* was reaching a tearjerking crisis when a low, deep ex-plosion thudded in our ears. Mother and I raced into the kitchen and found my father standing by the cooker, blinking, his eyebrows and eyelashes singed clean off, a blackened match in his hand.

"I smelt gas," he said.

I followed Mama's gaze from the match, slowly up-wards, to see the entire contents of the oven's pipes splattered across the ceiling. She had just finished her meticulous, regulatory Passover spring cleaning. Just sat down, for the first time in weeks. To this day the denoue-ment in Zenda remains a mystery to me.

When I arrived at the upper room early in the evening, children and adults had changed into their party gear, and the atmosphere was charged. The churchwardens, armed with corkscrews, decided the time had come to attack the crateful of red wine, and opened the bottles, ready for everyone to have their statutory four glasses. A series of low, full-throttled plopping sounds, and the scent of wine mingled with the already intoxicating, oriental smell of cinnamon and horseradish hanging in the air. I laid out my grandmother's best silver on the top table, the candlesticks, lit on every important occasion, the bowl of salt water, symbolising the Red Sea, or the tears shed by my ancestors in their captivity, the jug to be used in the ritual hand-washing ceremony, probably the moment in the evening when Jesus insisted on washing Peter's feet. Silver and satin, dozens of expectant faces, the entire room glowed in the soft light shining down from dozens of tiny spots, hidden under the heavy wooden arches.

We explained that apart from on a Kibbutz in Israel, the Seder, or Service, Night was usually celebrated at home. It was a bit like Christmas, in that several families would be together, but better than Christmas, because there was so much more than a meal. The service is contained in a book called the Haggadah, "the recital" or "narration", which recounts, in full, the escape of the children of Israel out of Egypt, through the Red Sea, into the desert. They do not, as far as the Haggadah is concerned, ever make it to the Promised Land, but then the service already takes almost as long as the first year in the wilderness. Thirty-nine more might have made the narration a little excessive.

My Haggadah, when I was a child, was illustrated. It contained graphic pictures of the effects of the plagues. Some could be altered by pulling a tab, so that I could watch the Egyptians drowning in the Red Sea. Now you see them, pull on the tab, and whoosh, now you don't. The archaic, Jewish version of a Sylvester Stallone movie. Except that there is no hero of this story. Moses is never mentioned. God alone takes the glory for saving his people.

"Tonight," said my husband, "abandon any preconceived ideas you may have about 'holding a service'. Forget reverent silence. The atmosphere will be the same as in a Jewish home. No distinction between story-telling, singing, praying, eating or chatting. If you want to hold a conversation with your neighbour, make a joke, go to the toilet, or doze off, as Michele's grandfather used to do, while he was leading the service, that's entirely up to you. I'll try not to nod off, and I certainly won't be waiting for you. If you miss something, tough! There'll be no repeat. This is the great freedom festival, celebrating the liberation of the Jewish people from the tyranny of Pharaoh, the liberation of God's people from the tyranny of evil. How you choose to celebrate that freedom is your affair."

I had organised a re-enactment of the scene in a Jewish home the night before, when the Papa, followed by the children, makes a tour of the house, torch in hand, searching for any remaining crumbs of bread or cake, anything with yeast in it. As every Jewish family knows, no self-respecting speck would have the gall to defy the mistress of the house, or her cleaning lady, so she leaves a small pile of something for them to find. "A little bit of yeast makes the whole batch rise," says the Apostle Paul to the Corinthian Church. He had seen it every year, played his part in this annual treasure hunt, examined every nook and cranny, every dark corner of his home, looking for crumbs, whooped with joy, as children do, when they discover Mama's oversight – however deliberate. "You must eradicate the old yeast of sin if you want to be pure," search it out with dogged determination, like a child on the eve of the Passover. I bet his torch batteries didn't run out at the crucial moment, as my father's always did. My mother didn't like the idea of leaving deliberate crumbs anyway. "Christ, our Passover lamb has been sacrificed for us, so let's celebrate, not with the bread of sin, but with the unleavened bread of purity and truth."

I lit the candles, and celebrate we did. With such gusto that there were times when the precariously hung floor began to sway and I feared we might all end up in the church below. It never ceases to amaze me how easily church congregations enter into the spirit of the occasion. I might have been a child at my grandmother's table.

"Who's asking the four questions this year?"

"I am."

I had been practising my Hebrew all day. "*Manish tanah ha'lilah ha'zeh*." "Why is this night different from all other nights?"

"You can't ask the questions. You're not the youngest child, and you're a girl."

So my younger brother always took over.

"Why do we eat matzah rather than bread? Why do we eat bitter herbs? Why do we dip twice? Why do we lean tonight?"

"And why do you ask the same questions every year, when you always get the same answers?"

It was my uncle's favourite joke. Each family develops its own Passover repartee. Every year, as we listed, in unison, the plagues sent upon Egypt to make them release their slaves, spilling our wine into our saucers to signify Jewish sorrow at the shedding of blood, my father added his own: his children, his mother-in-law, his patients.

The entire service contained in the Haggadah is in fact one rather verbose answer to the children's questions. We eat "the bread of affliction" and bitter herbs to remind us of all our ancestors suffered. We lean on cushions, because they were ready to leave Egypt at a moment's notice. In fact the entire Passover experience should transport every Jew through the centuries, until they feel as if they were actually there in Egypt themselves. Small wonder my grandfather used to groan in his slumbers at regular intervals and say, "Oy, I remember it well. But then, being in business is just as bad. Nothing much changes in this life."

My mother, who suffers from chronic constipation every year, when she indulges her love of matzah to the full, is sure that she has discovered another origin for the term, "bread of affliction".

The tradition of "dipping twice" is a little more culturally obscure. Presumably, as today, dunking biscuits into a mug of liquid was considered bad manners. Unless you did it only once. The first "dipping" in the service is the parsley in salt water, supposed to be the hyssop dipped in blood, which daubed the doorposts of the Israelites so that the Angel of Death passed over their homes. This is the origin of the word "Passover". God saw the blood and spared his people. The second "dipping" is a tiny stick of horseradish in haroseth. In ancient times this tasty morsel was regarded as a delicacy, the first bite reserved for any special guest. At the Last Supper Jesus handed it to Judas. It was a token of his special love.

For the church, the whole evening was a series of new sensations. Alternate groans and murmurs of appreciation reached us at the top table. The children coughed, spluttered and screwed up their faces as they took their first sip of wine. When it came to the parsley and horseradish it was the adults' turn. On some tables bowls of haroseth were left untouched. Other tables scavenged for second helpings. Some people scrunched their way through entire boxes of matzah. Others thought it tasted like sawdust. They really wondered what I was doing to them when we produced sliced hard-boiled eggs in salt water for them to eat as an *hors d'oeuvre*, and I told them the sliced egg was supposed to represent the eyes of the Israelites, the salt water their tears. The poor egg, traditionally enjoyed in every home at tea-time, lightly boiled with toast fingers, suddenly found itself blackballed. It's all a matter of association.

No one's appetite suffered in any long-term noticeable way, I have to say. A massive buffet to which we all contributed disappeared as if the plague of locusts had just occurred. While the adults were drinking their coffee the children scrambled under tables, into corners, up the walls, hunting for the afikomen. It is the middle of three matzot, represents the Passover lamb, and is broken in half and hidden during the meal. We actually hid about thirty, wrapped in serviettes. It means a great deal of cleaning up later, because matzah will disintegrate, but the alternative was two dozen disappointed children, a far greater ordeal. Peter ransomed all the pieces back with a small Easter egg. The egg is a symbol of mourning for the Jew, and of new life for the Christian. The whole game is a wonderful picture of the Passover lamb hidden for three days, and brought back to life.

Then, as the Jews do, immediately after the meal, Peter broke the pieces of afikomen and distributed them.

"Jesus, on the night He was betrayed, took unleavened bread, gave thanks to God and broke it, saying, 'This is my body which is for you.'"

Sharing the afikomen is followed by the third cup of wine, traditionally known as the Cup of Blessing, and accompanied by prayers blessing God for his unending kindness and mercy.

"After supper He took the cup and said, 'This cup is God's new covenant, sealed with my blood. When you drink it, remember me.'"

We used only two or three cups on this occasion, and sang quietly as the cup was passed from person to person, from child to adult. "It is cup of blessing which we now drink," said the Apostle Paul, not the cup of God's anger. For the fourth and final cup, known as the Cup of Wrath, accompanying prayers that God will pour out his wrath on the nations that do not fear him, was drunk in full on our behalf.

Every year it strikes me afresh that Jesus, knowing he was at the end of his life, that this was one of the last things he would leave behind, never said, "I want you to hold a special service in church once a week called Communion." He simply said, "Whenever you eat bread and drink wine, as you do in your own home at least once a week, from now on, remember what I'm going to do for you, and spare me a very special thought or two."

The clock ticked on. Outside the huge arched window behind the top table, darkness fell. We sang our way through dozens of psalms, and danced. We poured a cup of wine for Elijah, opened the door and waited, with baited breath, for him to announce the coming of the Messiah. He never arrived. Nor, thankfully, did any of our gentlemen of the road, looking for a shelter for the night, or we might have thought we had had a visitation. There were, however, plenty of volunteers to drink his cup of wine in his absence.

Then came the moment of compromise with Christian tradition. Just as Jesus had gone out from that great

feast of joy into Gethsemane, we were asked to leave the
upper room in silence, walk down several flights of stairs
in single file into a darkened church, where a solitary,
rough-hewn cross was illuminated by a single candle.
It was one of the most moving experiences of my life.
The contrast was immense. Bleary-eyed children, who,
a moment earlier, lay slouched with sleeping-sickness in
their chairs, walked up to the cross and instinctively knelt,
wide eyed, as if they were seeing it for the first time. Adults
sat motionless in the pews. The intense, profound silence,
after so much noise and celebration, drove home, as
nothing ever had before, the overwhelming desolation of
Jesus in the garden, having said goodbye to his loved ones,
now facing the unbearable, alone. No one wanted to leave
the building. Never was any Maundy Thursday vigil so
compelling. "You've danced and sang and laughed with
me, now won't you stay with me a while in my sorrow?"

It was the small hours of the morning, and even then
with reluctance, that the last few people trickled home and
Peter managed to lock up the church and go to bed.

I learned more that Easter than the starkness of contrast
Jesus must have experienced that terrible night. When two
great traditions appear to clash, it doesn't necessarily
mean one is right and the other wrong. Each may have
an insight the other lacks. Put the two together, and a
far richer picture is painted. What began as compromise
became revelation.

However tired they had been the night before, there was
little evidence of it the next morning, when the children
arrived, lunch-boxes in hand, for a Good Friday work-
shop. While they made unleavened bread, their parents
had a three-hour meditation, culminating at 3 p.m. precisely, when everyone was gathered in the church for
the snuffing-out of the candle.

"Ooooh," gasped one child in wonder, "is he dead
then?"

Mother nodded, resolutely refusing to break the silence,
a silence which hung over the church for the rest of the

day, and the whole of Saturday, waiting for an explosion of praise on Easter Sunday morning.

It was in Coventry I first started collecting Easter decorations, determined the festival should be every bit as good as Christmas, if not better. After all, there was so much to celebrate. I shall never forget the year of the Gulf War. We kept a candle burning in the church throughout the conflict, which shone out through the glass doors into the neighbourhood. Parents of lads who were out there would come and go, and sit for a while in the quiet. Sometimes I sat with them. It was one of the privileges of living two metres away from the church. Most of the time I was presenting a current affairs programme on local radio, living, breathing, sleeping the misery, fear and hatred of it all, worried out of mind, as many Jews were, that Saddam Hussein would use nuclear power on Israel, yet forced to keep a cool, clear, journalistic perspective on the situation. I remember driving into work one morning thinking, "Oh God, let this be over by Easter. Let it be over for the season of hope, joy and resurrection." And it was. That year it seemed as if life was beginning all over again.

We do now as a family have an Easter ritual. Friends join us for the weekend. They arrive late on Good Friday, just in time for tea and hot cross buns. On Easter Saturday, after the children are in bed, which gets later every year, we fill the house with streamers, miniature chickens, rabbits, chocolate eggs, twigs, branches and armfuls of flowers. Everyone wakens to the Hallelujah Chorus, blasted through the house from the hi-fi system, and comes down to a transformation, a magical, scented world, full of treats and surprises. After a lunch of roast lamb, and chocolate Easter-egg trifle, we hold our traditional bunny hunt, when the children, watched with some confusion by Sweep, our real live bunny-rabbit, have to find dozens of chocolate rabbits, hidden in the garden. One year the hamster died on Easter Sunday, which seemed terribly appropriate. She had a wonderful funeral. Joel, only eleven

at the time, preached a meaningful sermon full of hope in
the resurrection of the body to a glorious after-life.

Easter is undoubtedly my favourite Christian festival,
the culmination of all the promises God ever made to the
human beings he had created and loved so much. Each
event in Biblical history contributed to the spiral, circling
towards the fulfilment of his eternal plan. Adam and Eve,
by their disobedience, unleashed death into the world.
Sacrifice was the only ordained way of escape. Standing
on Mount Moriah, knife in hand, Abraham the patriarch
said to his son, Isaac, "God himself will provide the
lamb for the sacrifice." Then the children of Israel were
delivered from death by the blood on the doorposts and
physical slavery, when they crossed the Red Sea, a picture
of the spiritual redemption to come. The prophets, in particular Isaiah, saw one "led like a lamb to the slaughter".
"Because of our sins he was wounded. We are healed by
the punishment he suffered."

Ultimately, the Messiah came. Not just for the Jews.
All the nations, through Abraham, were to drink the cup
of blessing and mercy, not anger and judgement, because
the Passover lamb had been sacrificed once and for all.

We hear it so often that there is an enormous danger
of becoming almost immune to it. So many times during
the year I try and force myself to understand it, feel it,
grasp it, enter into the wonder of it all. But when Easter
and the Passover are integrated, the effort drains away.
I am there, two thousand years ago, in the upper room,
in Gethsemane, at the foot of the cross, and finally, at
the empty tomb. Then he appears, and I am face to face
with my destiny, my true freedom, my immortality.

Instructions for a 'Do-it-yourself Passover' can be found
on p. 317.

SUMMER

"Summertime and the living is easy." Or so it should be, when the exam season is over and dozens of parents no longer face the vicarious suffering inflicted by their children's nervous state. And while we adults recuperate from the stress and strain, they, unaffected by their recent trauma, with bright, smiling faces, lounge and play and gambol in the sun.

Every year, as the warmth of the sun begins to penetrate my body, and my poor old husband reaches for the antihistamine, I tell myself that I will take life easy. I will stop to laze occasionally. I will sit in the garden and read a good book. I will make the time to lean over the fence and chat with the neighbours. I will have picnics and bike rides with the children. I will take the time to enjoy the moment which is unique and will never come again.

Apart from Shevuoth, the summer harvest and equivalent of Pentecost, which is very early in the season, and Tishah B'Av, the ninth of the month of Av, a day of mourning for the destruction of the Temple, there are no major Jewish festivals in the height of summer. It is a time simply to be. The inner clock must tell us so, for we need no compulsory interruption of the normal run of our busy lives. No doubt the Jews of the Antipodean branch of the diaspora adjust their yearly schedule accordingly. Little could their ancestors, who first inherited the pattern of festivals, as they wandered around the desert in search of a promised land, have guessed how far those wanderings would take some of their descendants!

For many years summer for me included a four-week stay on the sun-drenched, Balearic island of Ibiza, where my parents-in-law lived in their lovely, whitewashed, wood and tile retirement home, built into a steep hillside, high up over San Antonio Bay, commanding some of the most magnificent views on the island. In the early days, before we tourists invaded and ruined it, Ibiza truly was a golden paradise, a large mass of volcanic rock and pine forest perched on the azure-blue immensity of the Mediterranean. "My launching pad to heaven", my father-in-law would say, as he stood outside his rooftop study, like the lord of the manor, scanning the miles of coastland, which curved and dipped into countless rocky inlets and bays, way beyond the pine forests which swept down to the sea. And so it was, one day.

I understood only too well why he could never leave his island paradise again, though I, unlike him, had my whole life before me. Standing on one of the terraces overlooking the vast expanse of sun-tipped waves sparkling like marquesite, with their mass of tiny white sails, bob-bobbing merrily towards the horizon, inhaling the pure scent of the pines, listening to the gracious swishing of their branches, stirred by the occasional breeze, feeling its gentle caress on my naked skin, I used to wonder if I leapt over the railings, down into the depths of the forest, might I, like some disembodied sylph, be allowed to wander and play in this magical fairyland for ever? Never have to go back to face rush, harassment, hurt or pain. But we cannot take hold of heaven that easily.

My parents-in-law were like children with a surprise present, continually going back to touch it and make sure it was real. They never took the view for granted, but oohed and aahed every time they stopped to look at it, as if seeing it for the first time. There were such variations every day. Of temperature, of light, of sky and sea colour. In the morning they would always stop to comment on the nuances of change. They read the clock by the position of the boats and the shadows on the water. English tea was always taken, in china cups of course, on the middle terrace at four thirty, on the dot. In the evening, as we ate our meal and the fishermen chug-chugged their way home, it was time to raise the blinds, to let in the last rays of a crimson sunset. The established routine with its unhurried pace was a vital part of their life. It removed the need for wasting brain power on the nitty gritty.

My father-in-law was writing a book on the involvement of Christians over the centuries in the creation of the State of Israel. It was the culmination of a lifetime's work and study, dedicated to encouraging Christians and Jews to understand their joint hope and destiny. Jews were awaiting the coming of the Messiah. Christians were waiting for him to come back. Meanwhile both, having experienced what a relationship with God could be like, had been given the responsibility of communicating its joys to a hostile world. Israel, refusing to proselytise since the fourth century, had, like Jonah, run away from its calling. Christianity had appropriated sole rights. Now both must come to see how much they have and do need the other, so that all of Biblical prophecy, from God's promise to Abraham to bless all nations through him, to the two olive trees which stand side by side in paradise in the book of Revelation, could be fulfilled.

He talked of little else.

"It was always Jews for breakfast, tea and dinner when I was a boy," Peter had warned me before I met his father. Little did I guess how much of an abiding passion the subject could be.

"Dad," I said to him, over dinner one day, in utter exasperation. "You could turn me into an anti-Semite."

"You can't hold back Niagara," interjected my mother-in-law, who never stopped trying.

But my father-in-law dreamed big dreams. Son of Henry Grattan Guinness, friend of Spurgeon and Moody and Hudson Taylor, and one of the greatest preachers and visionaries of the nineteenth century, born when his father was seventy-two, only two when his father died, he felt he must pick up his father's cloak. From his study of Biblical prophecy Grattan Guinness, who died in 1910, wrote in several of his books that as far as he could assess, 1917 and 1948 were the key years of Jewish restoration to Israel. The Balfour Declaration of 1917 gave the Jewish people free access to the Land of Promise. In 1948 the new State of Israel was born, and the vision fulfilled. These events, said Grattan Guinness, were crucial signs that history was winding up to its great and ultimate climax.

But as the century rolled by Grattan Guinness' voice was forgotten. Israel became a political entity, rather than a sign to the Church. My father-in-law dreamed of awakening Israel to its spiritual duty, and the Church to their joint inheritance in a new era.

With one foot in each culture, fighting for a way to integrate the two, I must have seemed a visible symbol of everything for which he strived and hoped. He certainly believed Peter would carry on the family tradition one day.

The Ibiza house too was a dream in concrete form. A warm, tranquil, invigorating haven, where he could write uninterrupted but for the twitter of the birds and the buzz of bees. There were times when it almost seemed too good to be true, God's paying his debts, the way he often seems to do. For as an army chaplain my father-in-law had spent four years as a prisoner of war, and giving away what tiny rations had been his, to those whose need seemed greater than his, succumbed to a slow wasting disease of the nervous system, induced by vitamin starvation. With large hands and feet which refused to do as they were told, he now needed the heat to stir his benumbed, aching limbs into any kind of action. My mother-in-law did all she could to make him as comfortable as possible, but it wasn't easy.

"Close the windows," he would call out in the evening, as we sat in sweltering temperatures, the perspiration pouring from pores we never knew we had. "The draught is unbearable."

And we would go out on to the terrace to finish our game of Scrabble, where we could enjoy "the draught" to its full.

Theirs had not been an easy lifetime of ministry. Years of overwork, disappointment, and false accusations had led to illness and breakdown. Years of scrimping and scrounging, for the pay was never substantial, made the dream of retirement abroad seem the deluded ravings of a madman. But in the end, at that time, it was cheaper to build in Spain than almost anywhere else. And for some reason their particular site had been overlooked and underpriced. A small Swiss pension in acknowledgement of several working years there removed any worries about daily survival. And the idyll became a reality.

For seventeen wonderful summers it was a gift to us too. We felt embarrassed at first telling our friends that we went to the Mediterranean for four weeks every year. It seemed more than just a little extravagant. But since our air fare was paid for, and we had no overhead expenses, it seemed silly not to take advantage of the situation. The four weeks were all the annual holiday we needed. The first week was spent throwing off the strains of our hectic lives at home. In the second week we began to unwind. In the third we really rested. By the fourth week I was writing books and Peter had begun to make all kinds of creative plans for a new year in the Church's life.

I am no longer ashamed of the idea of a four-week sabbatical in the summer. I am an extrovert. Unless I am made to stop, I don't. Unless I am made to take stock, I won't. Once a year I am truly reflective. God has me to himself for a while. Peter is an introvert. Making a spectacle of himself every Sunday exhausts him. So does being bombarded with every human and domestic crisis. He needs space and stillness. Mending faulty wiring, chopping wood for winter fires, overhauling the boiler, marching up the hillside through the pine forest with dog and children in tow, he discovered new inner resources, became truly human again.

Later on the gentle silence was disrupted by the raucous sound of barking dogs, revving motor bikes, and stereo rock, ricochetted across the rocky hillside, all the mindless blare of a humanity which cannot bear to confront itself in the silence, for fear of the emptiness it might find. No, this was not heaven, for humans blasted their way in by force and imposed their rule. We too abused it, drank and washed from its ever-decreasing artesian wells, converted its balmy, sea-salt air into choking, black, hired-car fumes.

We were among the privileged few wealthy enough to be there at all.

This was not heaven. Yet it gave us a tiny glimpse of what heaven could and might be. Just enough to keep us going and cheer us on our way on our journey towards that ultimate goal.

18

Even Pentecost is Jewish

I don't ever remember celebrating Shevuoth, the Feast of Weeks or spring harvest. Probably because my mother thought one harvest festival was quite enough for hardy city dwellers. Either that, or she couldn't remember what Shevuoth was all about. When we came back from Hebrew classes my brother and I would often test her out.

"What festival is it this week?"

"What am I, a walking Jewish Almanac?"

"It's Purim. What does Purim commemorate?"

"Esther."

When she got it right we all but fell off our chairs with surprise. Usually, when we asked her what a festival was about she would say, "How should I know? It all happened long before my time," and rely on my grandmother to make a meal and organise an occasion.

Yet she vividly recalled "Counting the Omer" with her own grandmother when she was a child. An omer is actually half a gallon of barley. Thankfully it isn't the barley which has to be counted, or there would be no time for any other festivals in the entire year. It is the number of days between the barley harvest and the wheat harvest. "You shall bring the first fruits of your barley harvest on the day after the Sabbath after the Passover . . . Then you shall count seven full weeks, and on the fiftieth day present to the Lord another new offering, this time of wheat."

The barley harvest began on the Sunday after the Passover, Resurrection Day. So when Paul told the church in Corinth that Christ "has been raised from the dead, the first fruits of a resurrection for all who were condemned to eternal sleep", it wasn't simply a neat little turn of phrase. Paul was not a studious intellectual, chewing the end of his pen, plucking original and rather clever concepts out of the air. As a Jew he simply made the obvious connection. The creative, original thinking was God's alone. The resurrection took place on exactly the right day to show the Jewish people that it wasn't simply a one-off, but the beginning of a brand new process, an eternal harvest.

When the risen Jesus appeared to his cowering, terrified disciples he told them to go out into the world as his witnesses. Small wonder, when he looked at them, that he told them they had better wait for power from above. But they would have been "waiting" anyway. It was time for the big count-down. Probably, like many Jews, they had a huge calendar on the wall, so that they could pencil off the days to the wheat harvest. Like children with an advent calendar, it must have filled them with a wonderful sense of anticipation and build-up. Something exciting was going to happen. Jesus had said as much at Tabernacles, the first pilgrim festival of the year, when the Temple was packed with visitors. Something about rivers of living water. Then he died at Passover, the second pilgrim festival. Who knew what he might not do on the third? And if he rose on the barley harvest, he almost certainly had something in store for Shevuoth.

And the wheat harvest was always worth waiting for. Of all the pilgrim holidays it was the most popular. The cloudless skies of the Promised Land were generally blue and benign, the weather caressingly warm, unmarred by the scorching desert wind whipping up the dust in the hotter summer months. Visitors from far and wide congregated the day before, just outside the city gates, and spent the night in the open. The combination of the festive atmosphere, good company and new kosher wine must have been a fairly lethal cocktail. But when dawn streaked the sky, tinting the rooftops crimson, a voice cried out, "Arise, let's go up to Zion." And the raucous noise died down, the visitors hoisted baskets of ripe figs, dates, grapes, pomegranates and honey on to their shoulders, formed themselves into as orderly a procession as Jews can manage, and marched into Jerusalem, singing to a flute accompaniment, "I rejoiced when they said to me, let us go to the house of the Lord."

As the procession moved on it grew and grew, so that the governors and leaders of the Temple, waiting at the city gate, could hear it coming. "Our feet are standing in your gates, O Jerusalem. This is where the tribes go up to praise the name of the Lord." As they marched into the city the craftsmen stood up to greet them. "Shalom aleichem," they shouted, calling out the name of each town which was represented. The singing rose to a crescendo as the procession entered the Temple. "Let everything that has breath praise the Lord." And the choir of Levites in the outer court responded, "I will praise you, O Lord, for You have not let my enemy triumph over me."

It must have been an extraordinary experience, with just the right combination of ceremonial and festival, dignity and spontaneity, which can be so hard to find. The nearest I ever came to such an occasion was the fiftieth anniversary commemoration of the blitz of Coventry. In 1942 the city had all but been rased to the ground by the Nazis. Thousands of ordinary civilians were killed. No one knew why this city, of all cities, should have been selected for such devastation. Fifty years on we had to keep reminding ourselves that this was a commemoration and not a celebration. But perhaps we were celebrating the resilience of the human spirit which rises above immense despair and destruction to create a new life.

"The day after the blitz," my friend Dorothy told me, "I tried to cross the city to collect my sister from hospital. Even that had been bombed, and there could be no more treatment. I set off, picking my way through the rubble, then began to feel frightened. I had to get to the hospital, but hadn't a clue where I was. All the familiar landmarks had gone. There was a feeling of total disorientation. At last I found the cathedral, or what was left of it. I'll never forget that sense of utter desolation when I first saw what had happened to it . . . the place I loved to worship in every week! But amongst the debris, the Provost found two charred beams. He formed them into a cross, and we met around it, as usual, the following Sunday, in one of the crypts. And perhaps our worship meant more to us that morning than it had ever done before, as we sat, stripped of all manmade trimmings, back to basics, thankful for the very gift of existence."

The ruins were left where they were. It is a rather wild and desolate place. The wind whips around the stark, jagged pieces of stonework which remain, and in one corner stands the charred cross with the words, "Father, forgive." The modern cathedral, adjacent to it, is in itself a visible symbol of resurrection, the new rising like a phoenix out of the ashes. The commemoration service, attended by a gracious Queen Mother, who had come to the city in the wake of the disaster to comfort and encourage the people, was a moving tribute to the many who lost their lives in what the Nazis had dubbed "Operation Moonlight". As a grand piano sadly picked out the haunting chords of Beethoven's Moonlight Sonata, one thousand one hundred leaves, representing each person who had died, swished from the ceiling to the floor, like the sound of a gentle waterfall. Some cried who had never been able to cry before.

"How could we?" asked Dorothy. "Everyone had lost someone. About half of a class of children I taught were killed. So was my fiancé, later, in active service. But why should I be entitled to my grief? We all had to be strong for each other."

In the evening, as the crowds filled the city for the great procession, the atmosphere changed and became a little more like a carnival. Sitting on the BBC Radio float, waiting to move off, I found it hard to make the adjustment. That afternoon I went, tape recorder slung over my shoulder, to interview one of the many special visitors to the city, a Czechoslovakian woman who had been forced to watch the Nazis round up and kill every man and boy in her town. "We were left," she said in a soft, lilting voice, "a town of grieving women. But we survived." There was no bitterness in her gentle face. With a fond, proud smile, she introduced me to her companion, a gracious man in his mid forties, the first male child born in Lidice after the war.

So much for the hard-nosed journalist, I cried all the way through the city centre back to the radio studio, clutching my precious tape. I wept for Lidice, for a world which still hadn't learnt its lesson from their tragedy, and for my own shallowness in the face of such grace and courage.

Sitting on a float, taking part in a procession, seemed a very superficial thing to be doing. But then, quite suddenly, the voice of Dame Vera Lynn, singing "When the lights go on again all over the world", broke into the darkness from every loudspeaker. She switched on the illuminations and I was transported in time into the heart of a world I had only dimly understood through the mass of unconnected recollections of my parents-in-law.

"When he rang me for the first time after four years in a prisoner-of-war camp, it was like a resurrection. He told me he would ring again later and hung up. He knew I wouldn't be able to cope. That I would need time to compose myself. And then, there he was, at the station, pale and bloated, too weak to lift his empty suitcase. But he was home."

It was a story I made her tell me over and over again, and she never tired of telling it. How it all ended. For him, the starvation, the isolation, the humiliation. For her, the separation, dodging bombs in London and torpedoes in the Atlantic, protecting her babies and bringing them up alone. They survived, their love for each other and their faith intact, stronger than ever, a source of challenge to their children. The procession was a fitting tribute. It convinced me of the importance of Whit walks, pageants, church fête days, carnivals, all manner of public and communal celebration.

In fact, for the Jewish people over the years, Shevuoth has come to be associated more with the giving of the Torah, the ten commandments, on Mount Sinai, than with the first fruits in the Temple. This is not as accidental as it may at first appear. The first Passover had just taken place. The Red Sea had been crossed. The people were free. But free for what? To do as they darn well pleased? God was only too well aware that humans tend to abuse each other with their individual freedom. Like a river, it needs banks to prevent it from becoming an unleashed, destructive force. Torah means "direction", rather than law.

My driving is a little erratic, especially at certain, rather more stressful times of the month. Fortunately, thus far, I tend to argue with walls rather than other vehicles. But as my dear husband keeps telling me, if I would only abide by certain basic rules of manoeuvring a motor car, I would not only be a better, more controlled driver, I would save us both a great deal of money.

The ten commandments were intended to protect the people God loved from a great deal of unnecessary hurt. Israel was "chosen" that day on Mount Sinai, to demonstrate the special relationship which could exist between God and human beings. Such would be their quality of lifestyle that the whole world would want to know their secret. It was the birthday of Judaism.

But the party, except for Cecil B. De Mille and Hollywood, was soon over. As he came down the mountain, Moses found the people dancing round a golden calf. Human behavioural systems are never enough. That was

the problem with Pharisaism, the first-century Jewish
equivalent of charismatic renewal. The Pharisees wanted
dynamic spiritual life. But a system of rules and regulations couldn't ensure that. "I will write my law on your
hearts, and not just on tablets of stone." Jesus had to
remind one of their great teachers, Nicodemus, that
there was more. And that it could not be reproduced
artificially. But what did being "born of the Spirit"
mean, Nicodemus wanted to know? If we cannot define physical life, Jesus explained, that moment when a
mass of cells becomes a living being, no more can we
understand the spiritual life. The "ruach", the breath
of God, cannot be forced into a filing system. Though
many Christians have tried to do so over the years.

So the disciples waited, and counted. Tradition has it
that when the great day finally dawned they were still
holed up in the same, small upstairs room where Jesus
had first appeared to them. Seven weeks is a long time
for 120 human beings to stay cooped up together like
battery hens. And how could thousands of people have
seen the amazing events which were about to take place
if they happened in private? Only if they were all carrying
binoculars or portable telescopes! And where would 120
good Jews be on the morning of Shevuoth? In the Temple,
of course. As they always were for every festival. The
drama took place in "the house", but the Hebrew word
for house also means Temple, as in, "Unless the Lord
builds the house", and "the glory of the latter house".
Once the geography of the event is right, it changes
the whole perspective of things.

There they all were, in a fever of expectation, surrounded by the noisy hub-bub of thousands of out-of-town
visitors and cousins. At nine o'clock silence falls
for the traditional early morning readings. First from
Deuteronomy, an account of the giving of the Torah,
God descending in fire, Mount Sinai wrapped in smoke
and quaking, while the trumpet blast grows louder and
louder. Then from the first chapters of the book of the

prophet Ezekiel. "High above on the throne was the figure like that of a man. I saw from what appeared to be his waist up he looked like glowing metal, full of fire, and that from there down he looked like fire." Suddenly, to the congregation's utter amazement, tongues of fire appear, and hover over the heads of Jesus' followers. The priest, hoping he's hallucinating, tells the reader to continue as if nothing has happened. "Then the Spirit lifted me up, and I heard behind me a loud rumbling sound . . ." At which point a sudden loud whooshing sound fills the building. Prayer shawls flap with its force, head coverings are lifted and debris scattered. And then the disciples begin to shout things in foreign languages, and roll around on the floor as if drunk. It's total pandemonium for a while, and the priest, knowing when he's beaten, sits down.

Peter takes control of the situation. He knows exactly what is happening. He has had seven weeks to work it out. God, in one blow, is fulfilling all the promises he has ever made to his people. And the Holy Spirit is the downpayment. Peter himself knew, more than anyone, how much he needed the power he had received. A trembling, lily-livered coward had become the preacher of the day. Three thousand were converted, the first fruits of a human harvest, and were baptised in the mikvot, the Temple ritual baths, which just happened to be handy and could process three thousand immersions in fifteen minutes. It was the birthday of the Church.

The first charismatics were Jews. There is an exact parallel between the Passover and Easter, Shevuoth and Pentecost. Each is a mirror image of the other. Each defines and completes the other. The giving of the law was accompanied by noise, smoke, fire and heavy drama. So was the coming of the Spirit. Shevuoth was a festival of first fruits. Pentecost is the guarantee of lots of good things to come. Which is why I long to make more of this lovely season, so easily taken for granted. How can we let it pass us by, when it marks the true beginnings of the Christian faith?

Some Jews fill their homes with greenery, reminiscent of Sinai, an oasis in the desert. I would love to decorate the church too, with twigs and branches, held together in clusters with red bows, just as the Jews used to mark the first fruits of their harvest by tying a red thread around them. Red is the official colour for Pentecost. It speaks of fire and power and glory.

There is also a tradition for eating dairy foods, supposedly because the Promised Land was flowing in milk and honey, probably because the Jews wanted an annual excuse to indulge their love of cheese blintzes. They eat two, to remind them of what else but the two tablets of stone.

The chollah bread, eaten each Sabbath, and made with egg and sugar, also appears at Shevuoth, in a new disguise. Instead of being braided, a ladder design is carved on the top, referring to the rabbinic tradition that Moses climbed a ladder to get to the top of Mount Sinai. A pity Hillary didn't think of that. It might have made the conquest of Everest so much easier.

And while poor Moses was up there, was Israel worried about him? Were they grateful that he was putting himself out for them? Legend has it that they slept soundly in their beds, and now, to make amends, must stay up all night, studying. They read again that rustic, romantic idyll, the Book of Ruth. Now that was a woman, spunky and determined, defying convention, following her heart, earning a special place in Jewish and Christian history, the only non-Jew in Jesus' family tree. The moral of the tale is to love the stranger, for who knows when we might not be sharing a meal with the nearest thing to an angel. I've lost count of the number of times I have huffed and puffed and complained about having yet another visiting speaker or missionary foisted upon me, just because I'm married to the minister. And then, to my shame, what began as an unwanted guest becomes an indispensable friend, enriching my life in ways I could never have anticipated, a gift in disguise from above, a bonus.

Which brings me to those other, dubiously wonderful little packages of potential from heaven: children.

TO CELEBRATE PENTECOST IN CHURCH OR AT HOME

The festival lends itself to countless opportunities for decorating our surroundings with baskets of fruit and flowers, processions, dramatisations (perhaps of the story of Ruth), story-telling and a feast. The traditional synagogue readings are:

Day One
Exodus 19:v.1–20:v.17
Numbers 28:v.26–31
Deuteronomy 5:v.19–20, 9:v.9–19, 10:v.1–5,10
Ezekiel 1:v.1–28, 3:v.12

Day Two
Deuteronomy 15:v.19–16:v.17
Habbakuk 2:v.20–3:v.19
Ruth

SOME CHARISMATIC RECIPES!

A Pentecost meal may consist of all your favourite, fur-lining, artery-warming dairy goodies. Or you can be boringly good and substitute the cream with low-fat alternatives, as suggested here. I'm always being asked why the Jews never mix meat and dairy produce. It is an interpretation of the commandment in the book of Exodus (in the same passages, incidentally, where Israel is told to offer the first fruits of the crop at Pentecost) not to boil a kid in its mother's milk. Many Jews will have meat crockery and milk crockery, meat cutlery and milk cutlery, separate tea towels, washing-up bowls, and, if they're really well off, separate dishwashers. The latter may well be a rather excessive way of obeying what was essentially a command not to get embroiled in the seasonal, pagan custom of worshipping a pastoral god.

DIPS

Served with crudities, or a selection of potato crisps.

500g low fat cream cheese
250g low fat fromage frais or 150ml yogurt
salt, pepper

Mix together until smooth, then add one of either ground garlic, chopped chives, drained, crushed pineapple, a little curry powder, or a little chilli powder.

CHEESE BLINTZES

The glory of the Jewish kitchen, a blintze is a paper-thin pancake, fried on one side only, filled, and fried again on its unbrowned side. Use your traditional pancake batter. Fry the pancake until the top side is dry, remove from the pan and place, bottom or brown-side up on a board. Cover with a tablespoonful of the filling (250g cream or curd or blended cottage cheese, mixed with 1 tbsp. sugar, and a little cinnamon if desired), spread thinly, then turn in the sides and roll up like a sausage. The blintzes can be refrigerated overnight now if desired.

Heat 2 tbsp. butter and 2 tbsp. oil in a frying pan, and when the butter ceases to foam, place in the pancake, joint-side up. Cook until golden, then cook the other side. Serve hot with soured cream. Serves 4.

MY GRANDMA'S TRADITIONAL BAKED CHEESECAKE

The Jews probably began making cheesecakes in the second century BC, when the Greeks occupied Palestine and brought the recipe with them. It has been a traditional Pentecost speciality since before the time of Christ, for the whiteness of the cheese was supposed to symbolise the purity of the law.

For the pastry crust:
100g self-raising flour (or plain flour with 1 tsp. baking
  powder)
65g butter or margarine
40g icing (confectioner's) sugar
1 egg yolk
several drops of vanilla extract

For the filling:
200g curd, or sieved cottage cheese
25g ground almonds
15g soft margarine
grated rind and juice of a lemon
50g caster sugar
2 tbsp. currants, plumped for 5 minutes in boiling water,
  then drained
2 eggs separated, and the extra white, left from the pastry

Mix all the ingredients for the pastry crust together and
press into a loose-bottomed cake tin about 8 or 9 in
(20 or 23 cm) in diameter. Blend all the ingredients
except the egg whites. Whisk until thick, then fold into
mixture. Spoon into the cake tin, then bake at gas mark
3, 325°F, 170°C for 60 minutes until golden and firm.
The top may crack a little. Serve cold, sprinkled with
icing sugar, with pouring cream.

19

Children in the Way?

When Israel stood on Mount Sinai ready to receive the Law, so the old Jewish legend goes, God said to them, "I don't know whether to give you the Torah or not. First, bring me some sort of guarantee that you will keep it."

"King of the Universe," they said, "our ancestors are our guarantee."

But God said, "I find fault with your ancestors. You'd better bring me a better guarantee than that."

"Our prophets will be our guarantee then," they replied.

"I find fault with your prophets," God said. "Can't you do better than that?"

Eventually Israel said, "Our children will be our guarantee."

And God said, "You're right. They are the best guarantee. For your children's sake, I will give you the Law."

Because of its emphasis on individual responsibility, because we have so little sense of history, there is a tendency in Christianity not to see beyond our own three score years and ten to the potential of our children. "God has no grandchildren," said the Dutch preacher, Corrie Ten Boom, who spent years in Ravensbruck for hiding Jews during the Second World War. She was right, in that unlike Judaism, faith and redemption are matters of individual choice, not birth. But if the Talmud sees children as a divine trust, how much more should those of us who believe that their salvation is by no means guaranteed by their parenting?

Neither Peter nor I will ever forget that extraordinary moment when we held our first baby in our arms. He was all of about five minutes old, a little old man, with wrinkled walnut skin, and fine, fluffy hair, but he was ours, and we thought he was beautiful. In the face of such an extraordinary miracle there seemed little else to do but hand him back, there and then, to his creator. It sounds glib when I think of it now, for, mercifully, that offering, despite enough visits to the local casualty department to entitle us to shares in the hospital, has never really been put to the test. I know from friends who have been where Abraham stood with his beloved Isaac, that it is the most desolate place in the whole world. Nothing is so terrible, so sad, as losing a child. When my uncle died at twenty-seven my grandmother lost her only son, the child she had awaited for seventeen years after the birth of my mother. In that long coffin, which stood for twenty-four hours in her hall, covered in a velvet cloth, with her Sabbath candles on top, lay all her hopes, her dreams, her future. The family line had been cut off, and all the years of mothering and worrying seemed a futile waste of time.

Only now, after almost two years of working as a press officer for a children's hospice appeal, do I fully appreciate how precious a life is. Some of the children I have met are severely handicapped, brain damaged by the progressive ravages of their disease, but no smile has the ability to give me the pleasure that theirs does. The very fact that a child has a life-shortening illness makes me stop and listen to them, treasure each moment with them in a way I tend not to do with my own children. And because I give a more intense quality of attention, I become aware of all kinds of responses I never normally notice, a deep throaty chuckle, a twinkle of merriment in the eyes, a moment of pensive wistfulness. That innate wisdom which is the birthright of every child, but we fail to encourage, because we're too busy, too distracted, or simply too deaf, is finely honed when every second counts.

"I want to die in the hospice, and not at home," said one little boy. "My Mum is on her own. And she would be so sad. I want someone to be there to look after her when it happens."

They have no fear of death. Only concern for those they leave behind. What I receive from these children far outweighs anything I might ever be able to give. In their short lives they make their mark on the world more than many adults. Ultimately, since our lives are over faster than a blink, whether we have seven years or seventy will be irrelevant in eternity.

The Talmud says a father must teach his children the precepts of religion, a trade, and how to swim, in that order. Presumably the latter harks back to a certain misfortune at the Red Sea. No lesson of history, however long ago, is lost on the Jew. Which is why parents are also strictly warned against showing favouritism to any of their children. Remember Jacob. What a series of confused, contorted events was initiated by the patriarch's preference for Joseph, his next to youngest son. To the delight of Andrew Lloyd Webber and children everywhere, it seems.

Bringing up children must be the hardest task any of us have to face. And are they grateful for all our hard work, sweat and enforced labour?

"Mum, why are there no decent yogurts in the fridge?"

"Mum, why isn't my football shirt washed?"

"Do we have to have sausages for tea again today?"

I look at my two sometimes, particularly first thing in the morning over the top of the sheets, when I have just been assaulted by a volley of complaints and wonder whether they were a good idea after all. Don't they realise that their father and I decided to have them, that without us they would never have existed? What makes them think they are entitled to a mind of their own? How did that beautiful little bundle nestling in our arms become this six-foot, answering-back, opinionated adolescent? Who, I have to say, is just as enjoyable as he was sixteen years ago. Probably more so, now that he doesn't bring most of his food back.

I am no expert at child-rearing. My children will tell you that, and only time will tell whether the accumulated wisdom I have offered them will find any place in their lives. But when it comes to passing on spiritual values I have tried to apply a Jewish approach. The key is this: that children learn with their hearts, as well as their heads. Judaism, being tactile, sensual, accessible, because it happens primarily at home, enables a child to experience, and not simply hear about, the spiritual life. The Church has tended to offer a more intellectual diet. It may well be unfair to make comparisons, for what the Jews offer their children is an indefinable feel for "the Jewish way of life", rather than a religion, and since what matters is how you behave, not what you believe, they may in fact be handing on culture rather than faith. On the other hand, if Christian children had more of an emotional feel for a "Christian way of life", it might, as in the case of many Jews, help them along the road to finding faith.

Precocious child that I was, I began to question the meaning of life when I was barely out of nappies. My mother tells me that whenever she had visitors she couldn't get rid of me.

"Go and play," she would say.

And I would reply, "I'd much rather stay and chat with the grown-ups."

By the time I reached my early teens even grown-up conversation failed to help me in my search for significance. There had to be more in life than working my way through the schools' examination system, so that I could go to college, get a job, work to eat and eat to work. A careers advisor confirmed my worst fears. Ahead of me, for a girl, there was teaching, nursing, or the Army.

"Mama, tell me the meaning of life," I said to her one day, as she straightened her Sabbath candlesticks on the sideboard. How did she know their exact places, to a quarter of a millimetre, without a tape measure?

"What am I, Freud?"

It really wasn't fair to distract her. She would have to start all over again.

"What have I got to look forward to?"

She never looked up, but I knew the process had recommenced at stage one.

"You meet a nice Jewish boy, get married, have a beautiful home, two beautiful children . . ."

"And then?"

"Then?"

"When you have all that, what then?"

There were no answers and the silence terrified me. I could end up a candlestick-straightener too.

Materialism drove me in search of greater good. I loved the rituals of my childhood. No child wants to be different. But they made it fun to be different. They were special ceremonies my school friends didn't understand. Ceremonies which brought the whole family together, made me feel safe, part of a people with a special destiny, whose history spanned countless generations. Ceremonies I shared in, though still a child, mixing the food, setting out the table, and lighting the candles with my mother. But important as they have always been for me, in the end they were not enough. As I grew older I needed some philosophical satisfaction too.

Apart from my Jewish heritage, the greatest influence on my attitude to children died over fifty years ago. She was Catherine Booth-Clibborn, the eldest child of the founders of the Salvation Army. Taking on hordes of hecklers, loud with lewd innuendo, unperturbed by the threats of abuse, "La Marechale", or "The Major", as she was known, established the work of the Army in Paris, single-handed, at a time when women preachers were something of a joke. She also managed to find the time to have ten children, all of whom grew up to play a leading part in the life of the Church. Here was no traditional, stay-at-home mother. A succession of nannies supervised the domestic front. But she passionately believed that children ought not be sheltered from the harsh realities of life. They needed to see immense poverty to appreciate how rich they were. They needed to see despair to understand what, by the grace of God, they had been saved from. Nor were they the Church of tomorrow. They were the Church here and now, from the moment they were born, when they could barely walk or talk. So she took them wherever she went, and they handed out food and clothing, helped her clean up filthy accommodation, washed brand new babies, played their musical instruments, sang, read a Bible story, prayed, preached. She practised the Jewish idea of encouraging her children to learn by doing, sharing her work with her, so that they knew, from experience, what being a Christian meant. And when they grew up it was perfectly natural to go on doing what they had always done.

I am thankful that my children's earliest memories are of a grimy mining town, sooty and strike-bound, where life was raw and tough. When I saw, for the first time, the play area just outside the house we were to live in, littered with rubbish and debris, covered in broken glass and mounds of stinking dog mess, I held my babies close and said, "Oh God, you can't want me to bring up my children here." And he said yes, he did, and, as ever, it was the best idea he could think of. And I remembered the words of my ancestors who had moaned at God that their children were going to die in the wilderness. And how he told them that their children would see the Promised Land, though they, for their complaining, would not. And that little town became our Promised Land, a land flowing in the milk and honey of human love and kindness. The children learnt there that relationships are a far greater treasure than possessions, education, or success, that nuggets of gold are to be found in the blackest, bleakest soil. "Wherever you go," they said to the children when we left, "you'll have friends. But always remember you have family here."

The problem for adults is that we tend to see children as those we do something to, not as those who have something to give to us. We fail to respect their integrity and wisdom. One of the saddest aspects of our humanity is that we forget so quickly what it feels like to be a child.

"You get patted on the head, then ignored," said one child, on the way back from Communion.

Patronised, that is how it seems to them.

After years of having Kiddush in our home on Friday nights, my son bitterly resented being unable to take Communion.

"Why can't I have bread and wine?" he asked. He was only six at the time.

"The official argument is that you're not old enough to appreciate what it means."

"Are you?" he asked.

A reply escaped me.

They can so easily feel as if they are only part of the Church under sufferance. We hush and shush them, make them sit still, stop fidgeting, make them self-, not God-, conscious. Then heave a sigh of relief when they are banished to "their own classes". Small wonder they feel as if they are in the way. If we don't lose them when they discover that adults don't close their eyes or fold their hands when they pray, we lose them when they reach their early teens, and realise that only adults are allowed any real respect or responsibility.

Whatever the state of his body, whatever his degree of maturity, a Jewish boy becomes a man at thirteen, when he has his barmitzvah (the Blessing of a Son). In the old days the poor young man used to be the ungrateful recipient of five suitcases, six sports hold-alls, ten alarm clocks, and twenty fountain pens, all laid out on display, so that the guests could see that Aunty Sadie had sent an inferior version of Aunty Sophie's clock. But a "barmitzvah list", like a wedding list, now eradicates the problem of multiple, unwanted gifts, making the whole occasion less of an ordeal. After all, it is stressful enough having to stand up in the synagogue on the Sabbath before your entire family from near and far, and the local community, sing several portions of the Torah solo, your parents willing you to get it absolutely right, without having to appear grateful afterwards for a set of disappointing presents.

The whole day focuses on the child. There are now equivalent ceremonies for daughters, though sadly they tend to process the girls in groups, rather than individually. None the less, nothing can detract from the importance of this ritual transition from puberty to adulthood. Once they simply swallowed everything their parents told them. Now they are deemed old enough to make up their own minds, to know the difference between right and wrong. From this moment they must exercise self-control, and are accountable for their own behaviour. They are full members of the community, and can be called upon to read the Torah, lead prayers, or be elected to the synagogue council. And the Church has no real equivalent.

Some denominations have confirmation. Some have adult baptism. Neither is a "coming-of-age" ceremony, in the true sense, for they do not necessarily confer eligibility for what are regarded as strictly adult roles. I have heard few early teenage confirmation candidates reading a lesson or saying a prayer at their own service, let alone making up their minds to become part of the decision-making process of the Church.

Proportionately few Jewish youngsters ever end up in the penal system. But how we complain about the young of today having no Christian values or standards. Many children still walk through the Church's door at some point in their lives. If all we do is tell them to sit down and shut up, if all we offer is a cerebral exercise, and if, and this is probably the greatest sin of all, we bore them half to death, we can hardly be surprised when they want none of us, and none of our God.

I'm not advocating pandemonium. But children are only obstreperous when they are bored. If they are caught up in the whole experience, if they have a part to play, they are far less likely to end up swinging from the beams. And must there be silence when the Christian community comes together? People gather to meet each other, to communicate with each other. There are organised retreats for those with a taste in communal silence. At St James' in Coventry the children would often sit together in an open space at the front of the church. Occasionally one or two of them would climb on to Peter's lap, or play at his feet, while he was leading the service. Some liked to be in his arms at the very end, so that they could help him with the final blessing. Others, when the mood took them, and it often did, would get up, spontaneously, and dance. Visitors always commented on it. Nothing is as potentially liberating as the example of children at home in their church, enjoying worship.

There are times, inevitably, when children simply haven't the concentration power, but the alternatives should be equally creative and imaginative. There was a couple in Coventry particularly gifted in youth work. For several years they ran an open club for local kids in the upper room, and it was hard grind. I always knew it was Thursday night when the church bell sounded. We only had one. It only had one cord. And the kids always went out of their way to find it. It was one of those ventures whose value will remain a mystery, until the day when all is made clear. Ian and Andrea, who deserved a medal for faithful service in the face of the impossible, came to Peter one day and said they needed a change. They had been thinking for some time that they would like to try out some form of experimental worship with the children of church families. Based on the home group model, the children would meet every week in a leader's house, instead of in the church, and be given opportunity to read, discuss, watch a video, pray for each other, sing, try out role plays and drama games.

"In other words," Ian said, "they would be calling the tune."

"And at what point would they come back into church?" Peter asked.

Ian and Andrea looked at each other.

"They wouldn't," they said in unison. "It would spoil what we want to do."

"I don't know," Peter said doubtfully.

"It may work. It may not," Ian said, "but you'll never know unless you take the risk. The point is, do you trust us?"

Three out of four Sundays a month, while I was at church, my children ran gleefully round the corner to their home group. And they developed a spiritual wisdom I barely imagined possible for children their age. Their faith was boundless, often making me feel totally inadequate. Joel on one occasion came home from school with severe nausea.

"Pray for me quick," he shouted as he rushed through the front door.

"I'll bring a bowl instead," I said, full of faith, as ever.

"No, a bowl won't make the nausea go away," he shouted down the stairs.

So I did what he told me to do, as he was lying on his bed.

"Thank goodness for that," he said, as I finished, and fell fast asleep. When he woke up the nausea had gone.

On the fourth Sunday, when the whole church family was together, it was this little group of youngsters, aged between eleven and fourteen, who often led the prayers, performed a drama, and taught us new songs.

Abby comes with me to church in the evenings, but the service is a bit long for her, so when she has had enough, she slips out and sits chatting with her friends in an upstairs lounge. Watching her appear and disappear, like the Cheshire cat in Alice in Wonderland, reminds me of how I used to dip in and out of services at the synagogue when I was a child. In for a song or two, out for long prayers, in for a dramatic moment, out for the sermon. Three hours was a trifle exaggerated. And running up and down from my father to my grandmother and great-aunts in the gallery provided a little light relief. No one ever told us to sit still. In fact, many of the adults, looking for light relief themselves, would stop us for a chat as we rushed past. "My, you look pretty! Is that a new dress? How's Mummy? How's school? Any boyfriends?" I always felt noticed, a valued part of the community.

There were never any religious occasions in my childhood which were adult only. All worship, at home and in the synagogue, threw all the ages together. I often wish our mid-week home groups didn't mean one of the couple staying behind to baby-sit, so that a small group of grown-ups can exercise their grey cells. From time to time, couldn't they meet earlier in the evening for a slap-up meal with the children? Then, as the night draws in, this large, extended family would recount again the history of our people, the legends of the saints, the great tales of redemption, handed on from one generation to the next. Lest our children forget.

20

Who'd be a Woman?

"Next time I'm coming back as a man!"

It was Mama's constant refrain, the ultimate vilification hurled at my father, as she bounced his meal on the table in front of him. Roughly translated it meant, "See the heavy burden of sacrifice and suffering I am forced to bear in this life – because of you." She had no actual belief in reincarnation. And even if she had, I don't suppose she would have ever really opted to be a man, any more than the rest of the female population, who almost certainly, at some point in our lives, have said something similar.

For the Jewish women of my mother's generation it was part of an elaborate game they played with their men. They pretended their gender was the ultimate snub. The Almighty had created woman as an afterthought, an efficient way of using up leftover clay. And upon this slightly inferior model he had conferred the dregs of the physiological processes at his disposal: periods, pregnancy, childbirth and the dreaded menopause. But tucked away in Mama's mind, carefully hidden from my father, was the truth adhered to by many a Jewish woman, that the male of the species, created first, weak and malleable, manifestly a trial run, was the inferior model. Apart from one, sadly necessary, biological function, he was, in fact, utterly dispensable. The aim of the game is that he must never find out. He must go on believing that he is the master and centre of the universe. The slightest suspicion of the truth could dramatically affect the fundamental balance of nature, bringing an abrupt end to matriarchal civilisation as they knew it.

My father had an entirely typical view of his role, expectations inculcated by the society in which he was raised, and reinforced by his Jewish upbringing. His parents, like most Jewish parents, had longed for a son to carry on the family name. For many years they managed to produce only a daughter. When he was born, he became the hub of their very existence, and grew up believing that since his mother and sister revolved around his masculine needs, so would the entire female race. He never realised there was a price to pay, until it was too late.

"Oy, to have a doctor in the family!" It was the dream of every Jewish family in the nineteen thirties and forties. It meant security, status, acceptance, and the chance to play a useful part in society. If you couldn't make one out of a son, you could always ensnare one with a daughter. My paternal grandparents managed both. Uneducated as they were, it was no small feat, and my grandmother was not unduly proud of her achievements.

In the long-forgotten days just after the war, any young professional aspiring to the lifestyle of that most intolerant and unforgiving of breeds, the British middle classes, needed the status symbol of a wife in the drawing-room. Not in the kitchen of course. There were staff to perform the more menial duties, armies of Mrs Walkers and Mrs Smiths who "did" for the country and saved it from a slow descent into certain filth and squalor. The ladies who employed them did not "work". A man was not a gentleman who could not keep his wife floating around the house in sheer stockings and elegant clothes, her nails beautifully manicured, her hair fixed into its weekly set. She had coffee mornings with her friends, performed charitable works, played an occasional game of bridge, dead-headed the roses and made sure that life ran as smoothly as melted chocolate for the man in her life.

The lot of the Jewish man was never quite so sweet. Not if his marriage was kosher. Many, like my father, sowed their wild oats in non-kosher fields, but knew, in the end, that they could only bring a nice Jewish girl home to Mama. And while that conferred a rather cosseted lifestyle, with plenty of chopped liver and chicken soup just like his Mama used to make it, it cost him dear. He had to abide by the rules of "the game". He could play the dictator at work, but the moment he crossed the threshold of his home, be it Orthodox or lax in religious practice, he was a subordinate in woman's kingdom. At home the authority of a Jewish woman is sacrosanct, her power inviolable. Those who blame Judaism for what they call its oppressive attitude to women, have never had close contact with a real Jewish Mama.

"Why don't you put your foot down?" mine said to me, after I had been married for several years, when Peter and I were discussing the decor of one of our many new vicarages. Moving is a professional hazard.

"What about?" I asked her.

"About the way he interferes in what is your prerogative. The colour of the carpets and curtains are none of his business. Since when has a man good taste? Tell him to stick to his responsibilities. And you stick to yours."

This was just one of many areas where, according to Mama, my husband was a trespasser. Either he didn't know the rules. Or he played foul deliberately. Being non-Jewish as he was, and a clergyman as he became, she gave him the benefit of the doubt, and opted for the former. It was evident to her that taking on a Gentile, untrained, unfettered, out-of-control as he evidently was, was quite an undertaking. It would take a very firm hand to force him into any kind of reasonable shape.

"And in whose name is the house?" she asked when we first launched into property.

"His," I said sheepishly.

"His? His? You must be mad. And if he goes bankrupt? Has an affair with a dolly bird? Throws you out, so that he can install her? Don't come running to me if you have no roof over your head!"

In the area of women's rights, Judaism has been centuries ahead of most of the "Christian" cultures in which its people lived. When a woman brought property into a marriage, it remained hers. Her husband could not touch her capital. He was entitled to a share in any profit it might make, only if he had promised in the ketubah, the marriage contract, to be responsible for her maintenance. If she had decided to support herself, he was not eligible for any of the profit, since he was doing nothing to deserve it. In the event of a divorce, she took back everything she had brought into the marriage. If she had no property, she could claim the sum of money he had been forced to put in her name when they married.

Jewish parents have learned through bitter experience the waywardness of human nature. A daughter must be protected from that potential little heap of wanton destructiveness she is marrying. She must have security. She must have property. The home must be in her name alone. In the event of bankruptcy no one can take it from her. In the event of his unfaithfulness, he could come home to find his belongings stacked in the garden. Jewish men think very hard before they commit an infidelity. It could be a costly business.

"And you must have your own bank account too," Mama told me, "a little something put away that he can't lay his hands on. You have one, don't you?"

I hadn't.

"So you know what he'll do if anything happens to you? Don't think a man can survive on his own. He'll marry again faster than he can clear your clothes out of the wardrobe. All that you've earned all these years, the money you've sweated and sacrificed for, the money you were putting away for your children . . . her children will get the lot."

"Oh no, Mam," I said, "Peter would never do a thing like that."

She shook her head in despair. Was I naïve or was I naïve?

"A man obsessed," she confided all-knowingly, "is not a normal man. There's no knowing what nonsense he won't get up to. Mark my words."

I have lost count of the times I have been forced to admit, possibly with regret, that my mother's outlook on life, with thousands of years of Jewish experience to back it, has proved to be the voice of wisdom. Some years ago I made a documentary for Central Television called *Great Expectations*, on the strains and stresses facing the family in the manse. I met several ministers' wives who, when their marriage broke up, often because of their husband's adultery, found themselves destitute. Most had enjoyed being a minister's wife, had entered into the role, given their best for the Church, had no career to fall back on. Since the house did not belong to them, there was no home to split. While he got himself a new job, with a house, she was left homeless, penniless, disenfranchised. On the whole Jewish women have been spared that kind of trauma.

That was why I never resented being a girl. Though I knew my father, like many men, had really wanted his firstborn to be a boy. Girls wore nice clothes. Girls had weddings. And babies. Most important of all, girls were mistresses of their own kingdoms. A man's responsibility ceased when he walked through his front door. My father interrupted his house calls every day to come home for his lunch, and expected to see his meal on the table. When my mother complained about a broken tumble drier, a leak in the loo, problems with the staff, he would say, exasperated, "Can't you see I'm having a very busy day, dear? Sort it out yourself."

Men were such feeble creatures. They couldn't cope the way women coped, with more than one crisis at a time. At the all-girls' Christian school I attended, we six Jewish girls were sent into an empty classroom every morning, while Assembly was taking place, and instructed to "say our prayers". We all found it an acutely embarrassing experience. In the Orthodox tradition, women never normally pray together. Formalised prayer is not necessary for women, who, say the Rabbis, have far more important duties to attend to. In the end we read the morning portion, thanking God we were neither Gentiles, nor women. And I wondered who in their right mind would want to be a man? He may well have religious duties to perform, and apparently, he is thanking God for such opportunity. But that was all he had. And man cannot live by prayer alone.

A man's stomach has always been putty in a Jewish Mama's hands. I often wondered, in my childhood days, what havoc would have been unleashed if one Jewish man had taught himself to cook.

Woman's power in Judaism rests not only in the financial arrangements of the marriage, nor solely on her ability to control man's stomach, but also in the respect her role commands. Though male and female roles have been rigorously separated, they are seen as being equally important. In fact, since the home is the centre of religious life, the woman takes the lead in the superiority stakes. Particularly since the race and religion are handed on through the mother's line. This is why there are two different genealogies for Jesus in the Gospels, one showing his priestly descent through Joseph's line. The other, through Mary, proves beyond doubt that he was a genuine Jewish boy.

Mistress of her world, never have the words "I'm just a housewife" crossed her lips. She has never been "just" anything. Historians have been convinced that the very survival of the Jewish people, against all the odds, was entirely due to the Jewish Mama. The historian Moritz Lazarus wrote:

In the days of horror of the later Roman Empire, throughout the time of the migration of nations, it was not war alone that destroyed and annihilated all those peoples of which, despite their former world-dominating greatness, nothing remains but their name. It was rather the ensuing demoralisation of home life. This is proved by the Jews; for they suffered more severely than any other nation; but, among them, the inmost living germ of morality – strict discipline and family devotion – was at all times preserved. This wonderful and mysterious preservation of the Jewish people is due to the Jewish woman. This is her glory, not alone in the history of her own people, but in the history of the world.

Evidence from excavated inscriptions now suggests that at the time of Christ and for some time after, women served as council members, and even as leaders, of local synagogues, where they would have taken part in the services. When Paul told the Corinthian Church that the women should keep silent, he was in fact demoting them. Some years would pass before synagogue decorum demanded the separation of men and women. But even today, banished to the gallery, unable to take part in the services of Orthodox jewry, her apparent exclusion from religious life is illusory. The reason that man, and not woman, is required to say daily prayers, explained one eminent Jewish scholar, is that woman, by very dint of her menstrual cycle, has a kind of in-built clock which helps her to appreciate the sanctity of every moment. Man, on the other hand, has no natural apparatus to teach him self-discipline. Feeble and weak-willed, he needs the discipline of regular prayer, the visual aids of phylacteries and prayer shawl.

Adam, Abraham, Jacob, Jewish men have always listened to their wives. "Women persuade men to good as well as evil, but they always persuade," says the old Jewish saying. Women have shaped the destiny of their people. Miriam, the sister of Moses, was a prophetess in her own right. Deborah was a wise and much loved leader. Huldah the prophetess was consulted on matters of state. Esther,

Ruth, Hannah, Abigail, all had major roles to play.

My niece, at twelve, celebrated her "bat chayil", or "Blessing of the Daughter", with ten of her friends. It was not, the Rabbi was at pains to explain, the female equivalent of a barmitzvah. Reform Jewry may well have submitted to that particular social pressure. But not the Orthodox. This was a graduation from Hebrew classes. Each of the girls read out a piece she had prepared about her favourite Jewish heroine. Some were Biblical, some medieval, some contemporary. Each had changed the world in which she lived. The girls sat down and the Rabbi got up to give his address. His students were, he claimed, looking proudly at their parents, well prepared by their female teachers, to fulfil that high calling of every Jewish woman, to be a wife and mother.

Sitting along the row from me was my cousin whose only son had been killed recently in a car crash. What did the Rabbi's words make her feel, I wondered? What sort of a mockery was made of her life if what she had just buried was her only reason for existence. The women whose lives the girls had just described were women in their own right, valued for who they were, not in relation to anyone else, not for what their bodies produced.

Women have been Hasidic Rabbis. There was Perele of Kozienice, Malkele the Triskerin, and Hannah Rachel, the Maid of Ludomir. But on the whole, being the Rabbi's wife was power enough. And their husbands had the sense to treat them with great respect, deferring to their wisdom. "He who has no wife," said one eminent Rabbi, "lives without good or help or joy or blessing or atonement." The Yiddish writer Isaac Bashevis Singer tells the story of the sage who was about to perform an exorcism on a dead chicken, which kept sighing loudly every time its purchaser put it on the table to prepare it for the Sabbath lunch. In came his wife, who promptly removed its oesophagus, and the problem was solved.

This portrayal of woman, whose earthed and practical wisdom has often been the salvation of her people, is a far cry from the portrait painted by the early Church Fathers. For them the only respect she deserved was the respect due to hell itself. "A sack of manure", one of them called her. So demeaning and debilitating was all contact with her that abstinence from sexual contact of any kind was the only route to spiritual purity. She simply had no real contribution to make to religious life. And never in the Christian West, has she really managed to regain the status in her own home which belongs to her Jewish neighbours.

"I'm just a housewife!" I used to say it myself before the children went to school, and my horizons only stretched as far as I could push a buggy. It was what I thought I had always wanted.

"You won't want to work, will you?" he said to me, before we were even engaged, sitting at the corner table of a cosy little café.

"Of course not," I said, the lovelight shining in my eyes.

"You will cook for me and clean for me, darn my socks and iron my shirts?"

"Of course, I will."

I couldn't imagine any experience nearer heaven than caring for this man for whose proposal I had waited four long years. Despite an academic education, rated very highly for Jewish daughters, to provide them with security, independent minds, the ability to be better Mamas, my work had been a job, a "filling-in time", until my prince rode up on his charger, and swept me off into the distant sunset. Perched on a rainbow, I would set up a perfect home, potter, tinker, cook and clean, change nappies and witter merrily at my babies. I thought it my Christian, as well as my Jewish, duty. And was very content. At first. Hardly aware of the slow, subtle diminishment of my negotiating powers. How I shun confrontation, tremble if a shopkeeper's shirty. I'm a walkover at the doctor's. A doormat when a workman does a lousy job. And please don't ask me to make a decision. Ask my husband. He knows the answer to everything. I am simply his "other half". I have no other name, identity or independent existence.

Somewhere, between the arrival of the firstborn and the departure of his little sister to nursery school, I have been deskilled. Then one day, unsought and unexpected, a new world beyond my front door begins to beckon, but it terrifies me half to death. I only know baby talk, how to make dungarees, butterfly cakes, flour paste and sandcastles. That hard-won confidence, for which my parents made so many sacrifices, has been eroded by the continual drip-drip of depreciation.

Sad, when running a home and raising children requires such skill, such creative ingenuity, that it is so demeaned. Few educational establishments extol its career virtues along with nursing, teaching or engineering. But nor do women want to be put on a pedestal, to be treated like some fragile, plaster of Paris statue of the Virgin. Jewish women are immensely strong. It is expected of the matriarch. Everyone relies on her in a crisis. And an event, for the Jew, is a crisis. Such are the expectations she faces, that only the fittest survive. It is no coincidence that Judaism produced a Freud, and other leaders in the field of psychiatry. The subject was very close to home. "The allergies may well come from your side of the family," I say to my husband, as we gaze fondly at our offspring, "but the neuroses are from mine!"

Eventually I made that quantum leap across the gorge of my feelings of inadequacy into the career stakes, and discovered that after running a home, a job was as good as a rest. The problem is that I now have to juggle work, a home, a husband, children, the rabbit, the hamster, the Church, and my own inner life. And, what is more, fulfil all my callings perfectly. I am a prime example of that paragon: "The New Christian Woman", she who really has it all, because she has God too. She rises at six forty-five, showers, exercises and prays, then sets the breakfast table for her family. With curling tongs

in one hand and mascara wand in the other, she pre-
pares the evening meal, pops it in the oven or slow
cooker and sets the timer so that it will be ready when
everyone arrives home in the evening. She makes the
sandwiches, hunts for her husband's car keys, "What,
lost again, dear?" remembering to put bread out for
the birds before she leaves the kitchen. She collects her
papers together and puts them into her briefcase, along
with the shopping list, so that in her lunch-hour she can
just nip into the supermarket for those few rich-in-fibre
commodities the family should eat fresh every day. To
keep them all regular in their habits.

By eight forty-five she has braved the rush hour traffic,
dropped the kids off at school, and arrived at the office
just in time to pre-empt the boss, organise his schedule,
brief her colleagues, and make everyone their first cup of
coffee of the day.

After several hours of answering the telephone, sorting
through filing systems, writing those urgent letters the
boss was supposed to reply to last week and completely
reorganising his schedule because of that dental appointment he forgot to put in the diary, she realises it is
twelve forty-five, collects her bags and heads for the
nearest supermarket. But is intercepted by a colleague
whose wife doesn't understand him. An opportunity to
"minister" to a soul in need. He talks at her for an hour.
She nods sympathetically, wondering whether her teenage
son has gone out in the socks she forgot to darn last
night. Then completes the shopping in twenty minutes,
a record, manoeuvring her way through the check-out
with the dexterity of a circus acrobat.

She is back in the office by two, reorganises the filing
system again, resolves a potentially lethal argument between two of the clerks, clinches a couple of deals for
the boss who's too unwell to do it himself after his
dental treatment, rushes out to get him a couple of as-
pirin, finishes off a few more letters and memos, and
arrives home just as the oven dings and the child minder

is about to leave in a huff and never come back because little Jimmy has poked holes in her book of scripture readings with her hat pin.

Her evening is divided between the work she brought home from the office, helping the children with their homework, ironing the husband's shirts, organising a local Neighbourhood Watch, and making a pizza or a quiche or both for the faith supper at church. At eleven she finally heads for bed, to sink into a well-earned stupor? Not a bit of it. She knows the temptations facing mankind and, being "the New Christian Woman", acknowledges the importance of keeping her marriage on the boil.

Parody this may well be, but not so far removed from the good wife of the Proverbs, who manages to run a home, a family and a business, and whose virtues are sung every Sabbath by appreciative Jewish men everywhere. But when she excels at work as well as at home, has "the New Christian Woman" finally earned the respect and equality she covets? Probably not. Slumped in utter exhaustion in her seat in church on Sunday, she may well be doomed to be "just a housewife", or her husband's "back-up" for a while longer. A state of affairs which has sad repercussions for the many single women, who, while entrusted with great responsibility and authority at work, can be undervalued by a church for whom woman has tended to become the moon, reflecting another's light, and not the sun, shining in her own right.

In New York, a group of Liberal Jewish women have begun looking at rituals which restore the dignity to woman she can so easily lose, even from birth. They have written prayers of thanksgiving for the birth of a girl baby, so that her existence is affirmed in the same way as a baby boy at his circumcision. There are short ceremonies for women who have been sexually abused, and for women who have been raped; treasured prayers for woman to use when shock and pain rob her of her own, prayers

expressing communal horror, sympathy and grief, to wrap
round her, like a blanket, until the worst of the trauma is
past and she feels safe and strong and well again. Here
is a group of women who have refused to play political
games, but instead, in the best tradition of Judaism,
have perceived the obvious, practical need confronting
them, and are attempting to integrate a painful, messy
reality with the tenets of their religion. It is a way of
saying publicly, you are the victim, not the perpetrator.
God sees, God knows, God understands. God will judge
one day. Meanwhile, he wants nothing more than your
full restoration to health, wholeness and dignity, the
dignity he gave to Leah, despised by her husband, yet
blessed over and over again by God, a real Mother in
Israel.

In the end, no one wants the abuse of being treated as
a drudge, or taken for granted or passed over because
we no longer fulfil society's criteria of attractiveness.
Nor are we someone's wife, mother or daughter. We
are ourselves. We covet the dignity Jesus gave to all
women, to a prostitute, a woman caught in a tabloid's
dream of a seamy scene, a woman rejected because her
body was in a permanent state of menstruation, to his
mother and even to a little girl.

"We knew, your father and I, that one day the worm
would turn," Mama said smugly, when I started my first
full-time job as a researcher and presenter for an independent television company, and began to show signs of
an energy and confidence I never knew I had. "We didn't
educate you for nothing." Discovering that I could create
television programmes, and ultimately win a national
award for one of them, was one of the most exciting,
affirming experiences of my life. When I left, they gave
me one of the most magnificent bouquets of flowers I
have ever seen. I struggled through the busy city centre
with it and on to the train home, revelling in the admiring
looks. I kept it on my knee, occasionally stroking the
cellulose paper or lifting it slightly to prevent a petal

from crushing. My flowers weren't going on any luggage rack. An elderly woman in a headsquare with a papier maché face and work-worn hands eventually leant across the carriage and said to me longingly, "They must be for someone special."

"Yes," I said, "they are."

21

Unto your Grey Hairs

I was looking in a shop window, when I suddenly noticed the face staring back at me. It was one I vaguely recognised. Yet not quite. It almost seemed a caricature of the face I knew. The lines were more deeply set. The bags under the eyes more pronounced. The nose more prominent. To my horror, I realised it was me. How had I come to this? When had it happened and why had I never really noticed it before?

Ageing creeps up on us, and suddenly takes us by surprise. I wish I could welcome it with open arms, as it deserves, considering its inevitability, considering it moves us nearer by the moment to our ultimate triumph over human decay and failure. But it is hard to grow old in a society which has so little respect for the elderly.

Jewish Mamas do not age. They simply become more powerful. Their sphere of potential influence widens. Not only children, there are now children's children to look up to them, listen to them, and hang on to their words of wisdom. Any physical alteration over the years, and I refuse to say deterioration, is purely accidental. Like "The Golden Girls" they still have more than their fair share of living, loving and laughing to do. No one seems to have told them that the fashion industry has finished with them, that good looks, glamour, and even sexual passion, are reserved for the young. There is a rather risqué Jewish joke about an elderly widow, who, deciding the time has come to find herself a new man, is fixed up with a date by a Jewish dating agency.

"Not him!" says her friend, as they discuss the prospective date over coffee and strudel.

It turns out the agency had fixed her up with the same date the week before.

"What was he like?" asks the widow.

"A madman!" says her friend. "First he snapped off my designer gold jewellery. Next he tore off my brand new Gucci two-piece. Then he ripped my Janet Reger underwear. And finally, he had his way with me."

"So I'd better not go out with him?"

"I didn't say that," her friend replies, "but if I were you, I would wear your shmatters."

My fight to stave off the ageing process is brutal, and bloody. "Why do I do it?" I ask myself, as my poor old limbs creak and groan their way through my aerobics class every Monday evening. "Why do I submit to this torture, this agony? What am I? A sado-masochist?"

Mama is convinced I've taken leave of my senses. At my age, she says, I should be taking care of myself. I am, I told her. That's why I joined an aerobics class. To exercise the heart and lungs. To stave off the hereditary coronary heart disease for another few years. To put a halt to the wearing down of all my bodily processes, to live longer, stay healthier, and, let's face it, allowing myself a little female vanity, to repair some of the ravages of time and use. Because, at forty-something, you do notice that gravity is taking over. And whether it really works or whether it's simply the power of persuasion, it makes me feel so much better to hear the teacher shout, "Come on, girls, clench those buttocks. Let's get those bottoms back into tight trousers!"

A girl has to have something to hope for in the "Mid-Life Crisis"! So do men, or so I gather. In fact, if reaching forty-something is difficult for women, it's even harder for the male of the species. I have been fortunate. As that eighties phenomenon, "the woman returner", I started my career as a journalist late, once the children were beginning to grow up, so I have new challenges to face. And though some may still fête nubile, leggy beauty, we more mature ladies are now being told by the media that we acquire a certain "interest" as life's rich experience draws its picture on our faces. But men, said a women's magazine recently, reach an age when they're forced to face the fact they're not going to be the MD of the company, they're never going to become a world professional footballer, and they're certainly not married to Raquel Welch. My husband, so I tell him, is one of the fortunate few. He never wanted to be a world-class sportsman, he is a kind of MD of the company, and he is married to a Raquel Welch lookalike.

But it is all too easy, as the years roll by, to allow disappointment rather than hope to dominate our lives. Perhaps that's because we put our hope in the wrong place. I tend to succumb to the pressure of investing it in my physical, rather than my spiritual, shape. Then a hard lesson brought me face to face with my own foolishness.

I found a lump in my breast one day. It's the moment every woman dreads. Blind panic says it can only mean one thing: surgery, amputation, chemotherapy. In that second she writes the scenario of her own demise. I don't know if men have an equivalent experience, a condition which acts as a catalyst to watching your whole life pass before you. "What if I die now? What will I leave behind? What have I achieved?" Sitting alone in the little room at the top of the house which is now my pad, a study, sewing-room, quiet room, whatever I want it to be, confronting the possibility of my own mortality, which is at least realistic, I suddenly realised that the only regret I would have was not seeing my children grow up and marry. And yet, if I was to die, I had given them all the love I could, the wisdom of their Jewish ancestors, the hope and joy I had found in my Christian faith. They would have a foundation upon which to build. And if we were separated, it would simply be the matter of a sneeze before they, and their children, joined me in a glorious eternity. Wasn't that what Christianity was all about? If there was no resurrection of the body, said Paul, the Apostle, why bother with a faith at all? The Jew, of course, would say for the benefits it brings here and now. But when the here and now is under threat, forever becomes a major consideration. It would not be easy to be parted from my family. But knowing it would be temporary gave me a great deal of peace. As I sat in the doctor's waiting-room, the possibility of losing a familiar and cherished part of my anatomy seemed much harder to bear.

And that, in the end, was exactly what was needed. But the piece under threat was not the piece I was expecting. The breast lump was nothing to worry about, the doctor said cheerfully. Lying on the couch, my stomach lurched with relief. But did I realise I needed a hysterectomy, she went on, her tone softening as she noticed the look of shock on my face. Reason told me that if I had to lose some part of my body, the non-visible variety was certainly preferable. But my emotions could not catch up. I was a long way off the menopause, far too young for a hysterectomy. I liked my periods. I wasn't one of these women who found them messy or a nuisance, or who went on complaining about them, until the doctor was browbeaten into sending them to have their extraneous bits removed. As a Jewish woman I appreciated the way they gave me a sense of the rhythm of life, reminding me of my ongoing potential to bear children. I realised how, subconsciously, I had always used the slight weariness of the first day to slow down a little, and be a little more reflective. I had planned to hang on to them for as long as I could. When my mother finished with hers, well into her fifties, she arrived at our house with a car boot full of sanitary protection, and held an almost ceremonial handover from mother to daughter in the middle of the street. I was desperately sad that mine would cease, before my daughter had even started hers.

"Cheer up, Mum," she said, comfortingly. "I'm nearly twelve. By the time you have the operation, I may have started."

Coming to terms with what felt like a loss of womanhood, a loss of youth, was a surprisingly slow and agonising process. "Will you still find me attractive," I said to Peter, "when I'm uterusless?"

"I go through an inventory every morning when I look at you," he said. "And I always think, 'what a beautiful uterus. Now I remember what it was I fell in love with.'"

"Consorting with uncircumcised men, that's what does it," Mama said to me in her usual comforting way. "There's no cervical cancer amongst Jewish women."

"I haven't got cervical cancer," I said to her. "And I only 'consort' with one man."

Having a friend the same age who was expecting her first baby, left me feeling extremely wistful. I dreamed I was pregnant over and over again, and woke up deliriously happy, until I realised it wasn't true. Realistically, I would have been horrified to have had another baby. My subconscious mind was simply trying to recapture some of those magical years of young motherhood which had vanished, almost before I had had the time to savour and appreciate them. Memory, as it does, wiped out the frustrations and the fatigue. When I thought about the caesarian I had had so long ago, I remembered the deadly feeling at 2 a.m. when a nurse woke me and told me to go and feed my baby. I crawled along the corridor, stiff from sleeping very, very still, sore without the help of painkillers, to the little nursery, and putting a pillow over my wound, let her feed. How I wished that on this occasion there would be someone to wake me in the small hours of the morning, so that I could experience again the joyous, tender moments of having a precious little bundle, the positive results of the surgery, nuzzling against me.

It was an old, familiar verse from a psalm which finally managed to penetrate the gloom, the way the psalms so often do, identifying with us in our pool of despair, then hauling us out by our hair roots. "Be still and know that I am God." Why had I never noticed before that the Hebrew for "be still" also meant "stop fighting"? I'm a born fighter. It makes me a survivor. But there is a time to fight, and a time to admit defeat. A time to wrestle and a time to rest. There's an old Jewish proverb which says, "If a man breaks a leg, he thanks God it wasn't two. If he breaks two, he thanks God it wasn't his neck."

Hysterectomy was not the worst occurrence which could befall me. Nor was I the first woman to lose her spare parts. I needed to mourn them, to have a good old Jewish lament the way the psalmist did, but then comes the moment to go with the flow, to wonder, with a touch of excitement, why I was being forced to take a little time out, as it were. I might even have the chance to catch up on some reading. To make me still for longer than five seconds has always required a major crisis.

The Jewish women's group in New York which has been creating new rituals and writing new prayers for women, has introduced a post-hysterectomy ceremony. As the woman drinks from a cup of wine, her friends gather around her and pray that this new stage of her life may be as fruitful as her child-bearing years. It is an acknowledgement that we need some kind of ritual, like bar- or batmitzvah, to help us cope, not only with trauma, but with major transitions in our lives, so that we can leave the past behind and press on into a future, continually rich in potential.

A friend of mine, struggling to come to terms with the menopause, told me how, when she was out walking one day, she saw a tree which looked as withered and dead as she felt. Only when she examined it closely did she notice the lush new shoots pushing their way towards daylight. The tree became a vivid symbol for her of the new life in death which is every Christian's heritage.

This is what puts the withering of our physical beings into proportion. My poor old husband may not have to cope with "women's problems", as men like to call them, but his struggle to come to terms with his hair loss has been equally interesting. If the hairs on our head are counted, he hopes God is as good at subtraction as he is at addition. Vanity of vanities! The Hebrew word for vanity is the same as for a soap bubble.

"I am your God and I'll take care of you until you're old and your hair is grey. I've made you, and I'll care for you right to the very end of your days."

However our society, with its inherent ageism, may see us, however much our faces crease, our brains malfunction, our vital organs sag, decay, or even disappear, God sees past it all to the inner me which he made, the part of me which never ages or decays. This is what he values, now and for ever. And it certainly puts a different complexion on the wasted efforts, the disappointed dreams and all the other baggage we human beings carry around with us. And try and offload into strenuous workouts, low-fat diets, healthy living and punitive exercise! And all our other efforts to hold back time, the way King Canute tried to halt the tide.

One of the most disappointed people I ever met was my paternal grandmother. She was tiny and frail, with spiky, straight white hair and a bird-like nose, very like a typical, rather sour old granny, and not at all like my maternal grandparents and their sisters, who were all rather smart and glamorous. She and her family emigrated from Latvia when she was a young girl. In much of Eastern Europe the professions had been closed to the Jews. Some had become landowners, money-lenders and businessmen, incurring wholesale Latvian resentment and dislike. Others remained poor and became the scapegoat of the long-suffering peasant folk there. Many heard of a better life for Jews on a certain little island in the middle of the North Sea and decided to take their chance. Nothing could be worse than the life they had.

My grandmother's four brothers found work quickly. But her parents couldn't settle and went back to Latvia, leaving their two daughters to clean and keep house for their four elder brothers. Back in Eastern Europe, well into middle-age, the parents had two more daughters who grew up hearing all about the six elder brothers and sisters in Britain they had never met. But life was still hard in Latvia. Poverty and persecution continued unabated and the old couple decided to emigrate again, to die in peace in the real land of promise, the United States. They chose to sail on a ship which docked en route in Southampton, so that the two younger girls could meet their six brothers and sisters for the first time, so that they could see their beloved children again, possibly one last time.

My grandmother and her brothers were beside themselves with excitement at the thought of seeing their parents again and meeting their two younger sisters. For weeks they spoke and thought of nothing else, as they saved up the precious pennies and planned the great adventure.

At last the great day came and the six of them sat on Southampton quay in a fever of expectation. A dot appeared on the horizon and materialised slowly into a ship, coming ever closer. Suddenly it stopped and weighed anchor. They waited and watched, but it didn't move. Frantic, they hunted round for someone to ask and were informed that due to unfavourable tides, the boat would not now be docking after all.

For several hours they continued to sit on the quay, straining their eyes to catch the tiniest glimpse of someone vaguely resembling a person. They didn't even have a pair of binoculars. And they were still watching when, at last, the ship pulled away and disappeared into the distance.

Disappointment on such a scale is hard to imagine. And that was simply one amongst many for my grandmother, who became a living example of the proverb, "Crushed hope makes the heart sick." She never really recovered from the death of her husband, and though she managed to eke out her existence for a further twenty years, finally ended her own life.

As winter succeeds winter, as the ageing process continues unabated, and adolescent dreams and aspirations fade into the distance and vanish like that ship, I think I can identify with her feelings a little more than when I was young. "But . . ." the proverb continues, "a dream come true is a tree of life." I've always believed that God plants his dreams in our hearts so that he can make them come true. Even though I may have to wait until I'm in my bathchair to see their fulfilment. That's why the disappointments must be left behind, and the present lived to the full, for who knows what the future holds? Even now, it carries the seeds of promise.

One day, not many years after my grandmother's death, we received a letter from my Great-aunt Regina in Philadelphia. She was seventy years young and the time had come to make that trip across the Atlantic to meet up with her family at last. We were all terribly excited. The family congregated at my cousin's house in Manchester to await the arrival of the dear little old lady, imagining, I suppose, a hillbilly granny with a bun and brogues. Nothing prepared us for the vision who walked in through the front door. Aunt Regina was a wizened, rather wild-looking woman with waist-length blonde hair, in leather boots and a leather skirt which barely covered her bottom. My father choked on his brandy, then managed to pull himself together enough to go and give his aunt a kiss. I couldn't reconcile the woman standing before me now, with bright, bead-like eyes and a huge smile, and my poor, slow, depressed little grandmother. Aunt Regina came and left in a whirl which left everyone breathless. But the abiding impression was of someone full of life and laughter, who was immense fun and eternally young.

I have finally come to terms with the fact that the wolf whistles which once accompanied me past any building site, are now increasingly rare. Some inner feminist voice tells me I should never have enjoyed them anyway. But a minister's wife does need to be reminded occasionally that she is, after all, a woman. Despite the promises of my aerobics teacher, I have made a very necessary trip to the local charity shop and said goodbye to some of my tighter pairs of jeans.

This does not mean that I am prepared to submit to ageist pressure. One friend of mine, who went out for a walk, slipped and sprained her ankle jumping over a stream. The general consensus was, that she deserved it. "At your age," people said to her, and she wasn't yet fifty, "you should know better than to go leaping over streams."

God preserve me from becoming sedate, cautious, fearful or dull at any stage of however many years may be mine. Let me grow old with grace, like my mother-in-law, who read books and newspapers, commented on world affairs the week before she died, listened and loved, was wise, interested and interesting to the very end. And is now dearly and sadly missed. But let me also grow old with all the colour, drama and splash God puts into his world. And if I am occasionally "mutton dressed as lamb", like Aunt Regina, better that than looking and acting ninety at fifty-five. And how much better to give the younger generation a positive, joyful, life-enhancing impression of later life, than a miserable picture of a disappointed, drab and dreary old age.

A PRAYER IN LATER LIFE

Thank you O Lord for the gift of life,
For protecting me from all the dangers and difficulties
    which crossed my pathway,
For bringing me in safety to the coveted goal of old
    age.
Now, as I look back over the years which have gone,
my whole past shines out before me, revealing my inner-
    most self.
I humbly confess the sins and errors which cast their
    shadow over my life,
the wilfulness of childhood,

the waywardness of youth,
the vanity and selfishness of later years,
the frailties of today.
How often I fell from the pure motives and noble ideals
you had for me.
How often I failed to make use of the gifts you gave
me.
All my sins and failures now loom up before me like
spectres.
Forgive them all, I pray.

Grant me clarity of vision to see life from youth to age
as a whole,
to know in faith that the best is yet to be.
In moments of doubt and despondency, remind me of the
blessings maturity and ripeness of experience alone can
give.
Grant me the joy of those who serve others with
their counsel and guidance, gained in the school of
experience.
And let me, at whatever age I am, hold on to the spirit
of youth,
so that I may never lose my sense of wonder in the
presence of Your creation.
As my bodily powers weaken, let me not be afraid.
Instead, grant me the kind of communion with You which
restores my soul,
And may the imperishable worth of life uphold me in the
deathless hope of the life to come.

22

And Finally . . .

Even while summer is at its height, autumn beckons
with a long, bony finger. Year succeeds year, and the
babies flutter their wings and prepare to fly from the nest.
Children of a Jewish–Christian conglomerate, will mine
integrate the sacred and secular in their lives even better
than their parents? Only time will tell.

Joel must have been no more than nine or ten when he
asked me the inevitable question. He was sitting in front
of the television watching a programme about the Nazi
invasion of Europe. He turned to me quite suddenly and
said, "What would have happened to me if I had been
living in Germany or Poland or Holland in the nineteen
forties?"

It was the moment I had waited, and dreaded, never
anticipating it would come so soon. The moment of
realisation of what it means to be a Jew. The moment
when you have to try and explain to your child that for
many people he would have been of less value than horse
manure. You try and make it easy. If not acceptable, then
comprehensible. But you look into the face of innocence and
see, "Why me? What did I do to deserve that?" and know
that there is not, and cannot ever be, any explanation.

I once asked Joel, now a teenager, whether he was made
to suffer at school for being a minister's son.

"No, not for that," he said.

"Then for what?" I asked him.

"For being a Jew."

I was shaken rigid. Memories of being splashed with muddy water from playground puddles stabbed their way back into my mind. "You killed Christ." "Go home, Yid." I had thought those days were over.

"Everything is always all right," he said, "until the teacher begins to talk about the holocaust. And then they laugh. The whole class laughs. I try and explain, but they laugh more. Why, why, why?"

It is hard for a child to understand that laughter may be the only possible response to horror on such a scale. Kill six hundred Jews, Goebbels is supposed to have said to Hitler, and that will go down in history as a tragedy. Kill six million and they will be a mere statistic. For fifty years Jews have been fighting the statistic. This is me, my flesh and blood, my holocaust. Such wholesale destruction of everything I am demands a response. But instead of the reassurance that would give me, there is nothing but a deafening silence.

St James' in Coventry was twinned with a church in Germany. It was part of a policy to build bridges and bring reconciliation between the two cities after the war. There were several exchange trips, and on one occasion we invited all thirty of our German visitors into our home for a Friday evening supper. It seemed both natural, and necessary, for me to light my Sabbath candles, and for us to share in the Kiddush of bread and wine together. I found it immensely moving, and sensed that they did too. Though what we felt remained politely unsaid. I had no means of knowing whether their intent expressions reflected sadness for past history or interest in a now unfamiliar culture. I didn't want their guilt. It is too hard a burden for any country, or any individual, to bear for any length of time. But an acknowledgement would have helped. For Joel, for his school friends, for a world for whom it now seems history. And surely, together, Christians must be able to confront the past and lay it to rest.

At a buffet supper attended by several professional Christian counsellors, engaged in chit chat over the canapés and coleslaw, I had said I was Jewish and a Christian, and was incensed, a few moments later, to hear one saying to another that he had never yet met the Jew who didn't need some form of severance from the misery of their people's past. He may well have been right. I have yet to meet the Jew who is not haunted even in his dreams by the hurt and rage and despair of centuries of persecution. But before I am prepared to get in touch with such immense pain, I need the Christian brother or sister who will acknowledge the Church's centuries-old complicity in allowing anti-Semitism to ease its way into the human heart.

For Jew-hatred runs like a blood-red thread through the history of the Church, in the otherwise spiritual writings of the favourite medieval mystics like Julian of Norwich, in the words of the reformers like Luther who said their synagogues should be burnt to the ground, in the decrees of the Vatican laying responsibility for the crucifixion firmly at the Jew's door.

It was the deeply, fervently Christian states of Latvia and Lithuania which drove out my great-grandparents, before they could kill them. My reaction to their liberation from Communist rule has been mixed. Warsaw once housed the second largest Jewish community in the world after New York. Until the Second World War, when they handed over the Jews they hadn't managed to drive out, to Hitler. Now, as the liberated millions attend Mass, they relate to the only Jew they will probably ever meet. For they successfully eradicated every other Jewish component from their midst.

Today's Jews have inherited the Pharisaic tradition. But Pharisee is often used as a term of contempt. Despite the fact that Jesus was a Pharisee, in sympathy with the religious renewal movement of his day, aggravated when its followers adhered to the letter rather than the spirit of its precepts, which is a trap waiting for any who genuinely thirst for renewal, who start with bubbling exuberance and end in rules and regulations.

Anti-Semitism, destroying the Jew and discrediting the Church with one and the same stroke, is a fiendishly, devilishly clever trick. A master plan, one might even be tempted to say, designed by someone determined to prevent the triumphant conclusion of world history, as the Bible foresees it. For the destiny of Jew and Christian have been inextricably bound together since the time of Abraham. And that, says Paul the Apostle in his letter to the Church in Rome, is that. "The calling of God is irrevocable." It does not depend on good behaviour. If it did, there would be no church at all. There would certainly be no hope for someone as wilful as I am. To say, as some churches do, "God has finished with the Jew. We are the new Israel," is to take up the banner of generations of crusaders, who snatched the Old Testament promises for themselves and left the curses for the Jew, feeding anti-Semitism, making the New Testament virtually incomprehensible, ultimately turning God into a liar.

Believing in a shared future for the Jewish people and the Church does not mean condoning Israel's political policies. Harassment of the Palestinian Arabs grieves me more than I can say. But if at times I would like to dissociate myself from Israel's government, how much more do I feel ashamed of my own, when unjust policies are introduced which discriminate against the poor? Perhaps the old parable of splinters and logs in the eye is as relevant here as anywhere. Are we just enough to sit in judgement?

"When you criticise Israel, you are being anti-Semitic," says the Jew, with emotion.

"No, we're not," says the Church, with the voice of reason, "It isn't the same thing at all."

"Ah, but we don't believe you any more," says the Jew. "Do you think, after twenty centuries of unjustified criticism, that we would listen to a genuine complaint, if you had one?"

The Church must earn the right to speak. Israel must stop bleeding. Each censure seems like a barb, reopening wounds which have never properly healed, forcing the nation further and further into entrenched defensiveness. Israel is a country which, in its racial memory, has only known scorn, humiliation and oppression. The millions went to the gas chambers subdued and defeated. Never, says the rebellious spirit, will we be cowed into submission again. We will fight and conquer before anyone dares so much as lift a finger against us. Without effective, consistent, loving therapy the battered child becomes the abusing parent.

Healing could begin when the Church acknowledges that instinctive feeling that something, at grass roots level, has been missing for years. And the Jewish people admit, like their philosopher Martin Buber, that for centuries they have been listening to a symphony without a climax. For Latvian and Lithuanian Christians it would take a miracle to eradicate the horror of realising that they have been grafted into a Jewish vine. But entering the totally Jewish world of the Bible requires an emotional response, and not merely an academic one. I need to feel, and not simply think, my way in. "Which are you first, Christian or Jew?" Joel was asked at one church. It was like asking whether he was flesh or blood. Hopefully the day will dawn when the question is irrelevant.

"Christianity isn't a religion," I was told, years ago. "It's a way of life." I'm not so sure. Judaism, affecting how you eat, how you wash, how you breathe, is a way of life. The real test is whether faith seems a normal, natural state of things to a child.

"How did Jesus go up into heaven?"

Answer, from Lucy, aged five, at our Sunday School: "He fell out of an aeroplane."

"Why did Zacchaeus climb the tree?"

Answer, from Lucy again: "To pick an apple."

"That child thinks laterally," one of her teachers said to me.

But actually, Lucy was giving the straightforward answer. It's we, with our other-worldly way of thinking, who ask lateral questions. But when the other-worldly is integrated in the normal, everyday occurrences of home and church, then they become reasonable, acceptable. In Hebrew thought being spiritual is being fully, gladly, freely, joyfully human, not bionic woman or superman, detached from the reality of this earth, floating around in some strange, supernatural limbo, neither truly human nor divine. When God made us human beings, limited in this existence by time and space, by our minds and bodies, presumably he knew what he was doing. Earthed as we are, we can use the daily experiences, the pattern of the fabric of our lives, to nourish our spirits.

"Without our traditions we lose our sense of balance," says Tevye, the milkman, in *Fiddler on the Roof*. For generations the rituals and routines of their faith have given Jewish children a sense of mystery, security, and warmth, so that when they grow up and are far from home, their Jewishness is associated with their happiest memories, something so much a part of them that they continue to practise it, automatically, without effort or thought. It has preserved the entirely separate identity of the Jewish people throughout their long, tortuous, precarious history.

Enforced for its own sake, tradition is a rigid, implacable master. Used well and wisely, it is an invaluable servant, transforming the cerebral exercise of faith into colourful, natural, normal fun. Within the Church there is plenty of fun, waiting to be had, as roots and shoots become one, old traditions are renewed and the best of Jewish and Christian celebration brought into play. Some of the minor festivals like Mothering Sunday, All Saints' Day, Shrove Tuesday and Ash Wednesday seem a little jaded, and need to be rethought. Some of the major festivals like Pentecost and Easter could do with the sparkle which an injection of Jewish life would give them. I missed the Seder night at our church this year. I was in hospital, in a post-operative, morphine-induced state of semiconsciousness. The night before, sitting in the bath in the clinical, stainless-steel hospital bathroom, awaiting surgery, I was tempted to howl with disappointment. And then a thought occurred. Perhaps it was important that I was here, while they would be there, celebrating the Passover, to prove that enjoying Jewish celebration did not require my presence. Within the long history of the Church, both Jewish and Gentile, there is a whole world of story-telling, drama, dressing up, food, procession, study, debate and pageant to draw from. The potential is there for every Christian to make their faith a way of life.

So why fear or fight the gathering dusk of our autumn? In Hebrew thought, life is not a race towards death, desperately seeking to avoid the clutches of time. Nor is history boringly, monotonously circular in motion, tied to the cycles of nature. It is linear, progressive. Halakah, the application of the law, means, "the way", "walking" or "progression". The law, drawn up by God himself, is a rich and colourful map. With Egypt and slavery behind us, like the children of Israel, we can only go forward. Even if it means straight through the Red Sea. That is the way of faith, the grand adventure. In Christian terms it is for each one of us to use the map, and plot out our pilgrimage. We are, each of us, with our ancestors who went before us, our community who walks with us, and our children who will follow us, history in motion, en route to its glorious, inevitable climax at the end of the age, when the Messiah will reign for ever.

APPENDIX

Instructions for a Shortened
Do-it-yourself Passover

FOR USE AT HOME
OR IN A CHURCH HALL

For use at home, follow these instructions but make the "top table" your only table, and of course use your own cutlery and best crockery etc.

For the hand washing (somewhere accessible from the top table):
jug of water
hand towel
bowl

On the top table:
Three-tier matzah holder. You can buy one or make one. It is often simply a flat cloth bag, decorated with embroidery, into which three matzahs (unleavened bread "slices") are placed, one on top of the other
Cup for Elijah. A small glass left ready for a guest who never arrives!
Communion chalices (one cup only for home use)
Two candlesticks and candles and matches
Serviettes in which to wrap the Afikomen
Prize(s) to redeem the Afikomen
A cushion to lean on
Seder dish (a large ordinary, or decorative, plate or platter will do) on which is placed:
    Haroseth (recipe below)
    Baked egg (a token of grief for the destruction of the

Temple, and a symbol of resurrection)
Parsley or watercress (representing the hyssop)
Shankbone of a lamb (to represent the lamb sacrificed at
Passover when there was a Temple. It is best for
someone to buy a leg of lamb some weeks before and
keep a part of the bone in the freezer until you need it)
horseradish (the bitter herbs – symbolic of the suffering
in Egypt)

So that the team who are arranging the event know everything that is required, we usually give them the following
instruction sheets. They look a bit daunting, but in fact
it is hardly more complicated than a harvest supper, or
church fellowship meal. If helpers know the ethos of the
event, they are more likely to prepare the room appropriately and have the items required out and ready.

From experience, we have found that congregations
tend not to know what to expect, and therefore in the
advertising we always quote the first paragraph of the
team instructions given below, to encourage families,
single people, the elderly and the very young to come.

A microphone and simple amplifier is essential for the
leader of the evening, because he or she will need to be
heard above the general noise, and speak while others are
talking. As at most family occasions, the family does not
always listen in awed silence to the head of the household
each time he opens his mouth! In our experience, when
the meaningful moments come, such as remembering what
Jesus did at the Last Supper, a profound silence descends
upon even the smallest children. The music group will add
to the atmosphere with worship songs, while everyone
shares in the Communion. If of course you are celebrating
at home in a smaller group of say twelve people, then it
is all much simpler. You can do without microphones
and music groups and sing unaccompanied. But you
will none the less need to read the liturgy out loud
when other members of the family group may be chattering, youngsters asking questions or causing a distraction.

INSTRUCTIONS FOR THE ORGANISING TEAM

The Aim & Objective of the event you are organising

People are coming to an event which lasts about three hours, but passes very quickly.

The Passover is essentially an extended family celebration at home. So we are keen for it to seem a family occasion with young and old present. Singing, worshipping, chatting and enjoying a good meal are all interwoven. A snack is not appropriate. Each person or group is to bring enough food for a reasonable evening meal (first course and dessert) to share with others from a buffet. The meal is very much part of the occasion.

Arrangement of the room

Have one "top table" for the service leader(s) and a group with them. Then have tables of eight to ten people so that groups of eight to ten can "copy" what is being done at the top table. The leader(s) will be using microphones and amplification, so everyone will hear instructions, teaching and liturgy. The head table needs to be big enough for candlesticks and a few other items.

Food and equipment to buy

1. Plastic *transparent* "glasses" for each person (for wine). Small, low ones are best.

2. Cutlery and crockery (as in summary list below).

3. Tablecloths. Paper catering rolls are quite acceptable.

4. Paper napkins for each person (essential). Colourful too.

5. Red wine – 70cl bottles are best, because you can spread these around the room, so groups of people

can help themselves. Buy one bottle per four or five adults plus three extra. (You can sell off excess bottles.) The top table needs some extra wine for Communion.

6. Orange juice for youngsters. Why not spoil them with real stuff, rather than squash; it is a special occasion.

7. Some non-alcoholic wine for teetotallers.

8. Water in jugs, for drinking.

9. Coffee and tea, for after the meal.

10. Eggs; to be hard-boiled, then peeled and sliced. These will be eaten by everyone just before the meal begins. Prepare one egg per three persons. (One egg per person is more correct, but many find this a bit daunting as an appetiser!)

11. Unleavened bread – Matzah. Buy as soon as you can get it from supermarkets; it keeps. You will need one box per ten people (at least one box per table). Buy a few extra boxes. The boxes, made by *Rakussens*, are blue or red (they do not need to be "kosher for Passover"). They keep for ages, if dry. On the day, open the box, tear off the lid and slit both inner packets along the top with a sharp knife. Leave the Matzah in the boxes on each table. People will help themselves. The boxes usually have some Hebrew on them, it adds to the occasion.

12. Buy fresh parsley from the grocer's. Order it beforehand because they won't be expecting such a quantity. One small sprig is needed per person. (Failing that, buy watercress instead.)

13. Buy salt. Provide a bowl of salt water for roughly every ten persons. They will need it to dip parsley and for the hard-boiled egg.

14. Try to obtain horseradish root. In some areas of the country it is hard to find a supplier of horseradish root. You need one root about ¾ in diameter and 6 in long for a hundred people. This must be cut up into small pieces to look like half-length matchsticks. This item creates a lot of interest, and some tears if it is strong! If you really cannot get the root, then you will have to use horseradish sauce, but it is not the same visually. You could ask a friend living in an area of the country where there are Jewish delicatessens to post you a root or two the week before. (Roots are the size of a reasonably large carrot.)

15. Make Haroseth.
Recipe: serves approx eight, but for a large group of up to 150, four times this quantity is ample, because you can use a dessertspoonful per group, which will suffice.

100g chopped walnuts
½ large cooking apple
2 tsp. sugar
2 tsp. cinnamon
Red wine to moisten

Blend all the dry ingredients in an electric mixer, then moisten with the wine to the consistency of mortar.

16. Chalices for Communion will be required immediately after the meal, distributed from the top table.

17. Word sheet for the parts of the liturgy in which everyone shares and words for the songs.

18. Do anything to help make the meal special. The only thing *not* to bring is leavened bread (i.e. ordinary bread). Some floral table decorations are nice. You would make Christmas dinner special – Passover is in the same league.

Summary list of requirements

Each person needs in front of them before the start:
1 transparent plastic "glass" for wine/drink
1 side plate (could be paper one) for egg and other things during the event
1 spoon for dessert
knife and fork
1 napkin

Each group of between five or ten needs, before the start:
1 plate/bowl with hard-boiled egg ready sliced from which to serve, and a spoon to serve it
1 medium-sized plate with parsley on it, and a dessert-spoonful of Haroseth, and two slivers of horseradish per person
1 bottle of wine per five persons; opened!
1 jug of water for drinking
1 small bowl with salt water in it, and a teaspoon
1 box of Matzah (unleavened bread), ready opened and inner wrapper slit open. Matzah stays in the box (one box will do per ten persons)
a table decoration e.g. small posy of flowers

During the meal each person will get up and serve themselves from the buffet. After coffee or tea to end the meal, the service continues. Some clearing can be done during the coffee time, but full clearing will need to wait until the very end.

TIMINGS (FROM EXPERIENCE)

6.30 p.m. start. Delays usually mean 6.45 p.m.
First part of service
7.30 p.m. eat
8.30 p.m. tea/coffee
Second part of service
9.30 p.m. finish

LAYOUT OF ROOM

Make space for dancing conga-style around the room. Buffet lay-out should have access all around for speed.

MUSIC

A strong lead from a music group makes a big difference. The choice of songs and hymns needs to be familiar, though there is opportunity to learn some folk melodies very easily. Some of the songs we have used from time to time are inspired by the Psalms used in the actual Passover service liturgy. See the notes in the service itself. Most modern hymn and chorus music books have the words and music and copyright can be paid for through Christian Copyright Licensing Ltd, 26 Gildredge Road, Eastbourne, BN21 4SA, tel. 0323 417711. Obviously you can choose hymns like "Glory be to Jesus, who in bitter pain" and "When I survey the wondrous cross", for the time when the chalice is being passed round. But livelier ones at other times. Jewish folk songs are sung at the Passover. Choose your own to give the event that special Hebraic flavour. Examples are, "Hinei Ma Tov Umanaim, Chevet Achim Gam Yahad" and "Hevenu Shalom Aleichem". There are a number of new songs by Messianic Jews, notably "Great and wonderful, are thy wondrous deeds" and "You shall go out with joy and be led forth in peace" by Stuart Dauermann. Some songs used in churches now make it almost impossible not to dance. Encourage a few people to start a slow grapevine dance around the tables and others will eventually join in, like a long conga, but holding hands.

A Passover Service

ORDER OF SERVICE

An introduction to the Jewish Passover.

Lighting the candles for a festival.

Kiddush (blessing of the festival). Drinking of the first cup, eating of herbs in salt water, breaking of the middle Matzah – the Afikomen.

Haggadah (The "narration" or "telling"). The four questions, the reply, the ten plagues in Egypt, Da-yainu, the Seder dish, singing of Psalms (the Little Hallel), drinking of the second cup, the men wash hands, and eating Matzah, Maror and Haroseth.

The meal. After the meal children search for the Afikomen. Sharing out the Afikomen.

Grace and thanksgivings after the meal. Singing of Psalms, grace after the meal, blessings, the drinking of the third cup (the cup of blessing), Elijah's cup, singing of Psalms, concluding blessings, the fourth cup, ending.

AN INTRODUCTION TO THE PASSOVER

The Jewish festival is called Pesach, from which we get the word "Paschal", from the Hebrew verb, "to pass over" or "to spare". Pesach is celebrated for seven days, and nothing with yeast in it may be eaten. Only unleavened bread is permitted. Hence it is also known as "the Feast of Unleavened Bread". On the first evening of Passover the Seder – the Service or Order – is read and chanted in Jewish homes. The father of the household leads, and the mother in particular has been preparing the home and the festival meal and special unleavened cakes and recipes for many days. It is the night when Jews remember that they escaped to freedom from the tyrant in Egypt and the night when the angel of death passed over their homes which had the blood of a lamb daubed on the doorposts. The Torah (the Old Testament Law, the books of Moses) instructs that the festival must be fulfilled with groups of friends and relatives. No one should be left on their own. It commands that this festival should be kept annually even after the Messiah has come. The account of the first Passover is to be found in Exodus chapters 12–15.

The service liturgy is in a book called the Haggadah. Copies are often beautifully illustrated for children and adults. The service is in Hebrew and Aramaic, which means that for most Jews it is not in their everyday language, so children and many adults will not understand fully what they are saying. It is only fairly recently that Israeli Jews have a service in what is their common language. The Haggadah that is given here is much abridged, and in English. It has been paraphrased using the English translations from three Haggadahs, given in the bibliography. Jewish groups have written their own adaptations. Most are for home use, but there are many for communal use, especially in kibbutzim in Israel where the whole community takes part. In some ancient communities the Rabbi would lead the Seder. The first part of the Haggadah is very old. Copies from the tenth century prove its antiquity, but hints about issues from the Second Temple period make it evident that parts predate the time of Jesus. The general form and the wording used for the first part and the blessings after the meal are very likely the same as would have been in use during the time

of Jesus. Scholars believe the early parts are much older.
Various Rabbis are mentioned in the Haggadah: Rabbi
Hillel, an old man when Jesus was young, and a very influential and respected Pharisee; Rabbi Gamaliel, doctor
of the law and a member of the Sanhedrin, and teacher of
the Apostle Paul; and Rabbi Akiba, born around AD 40
and martyred in AD 137. The latter supported the revolt by
Bar Kochba against the Romans. The theme of freedom
and liberation from tyrants is used over and over, and
has inspired persecuted Jews in different ages, including
this century. Christians could well benefit from a realisation that they rejoice in a freedom obtained on that
particular Passover around AD 29, but that they still wait
with longing for the full freedom when they celebrate this
feast in the kingdom of heaven.

The Gospel writers all assume we know about Passover.
Jesus' parents went every year to Jerusalem for the
Passover, and when Jesus was twelve he got into trouble
for not going home with them. On the fourteenth day of
the month of Nisan at mid-day the slaughter of the lambs
took place in the Temple precincts. In Jesus' last week,
according to Matthew, Mark and Luke, this took place on
the Thursday afternoon until sunset. Fifteenth Nisan starts
at nightfall on the Thursday, the evening when they celebrated the Passover – just the twelve disciples and Jesus.
After the Seder (Jesus' Last Supper with his disciples) they
sang hymns (as we will do) and went out to Gethsemane,
having had a full meal, wine and a long service. In the
night Jesus was arrested, tried and by Friday mid-day the
Roman authorities had crucified him. He died at 3 p.m.
He therefore was crucified on the first day of Passover.
Friday nightfall is the start of the Sabbath, so Jesus' body
was hurriedly placed in simple grave clothes and laid in
a new tomb nearby. It is a little puzzling how so much
travelling from Gethsemane to Annas' house at night,
then on to Caiaphas, the High Priest's house, Pilate and
Herod, back to Pilate and then to ill treatment by the soldiers and crucifixion could all occur between midnight

Thursday and mid-day Friday on a festival day. Some even suggest Jesus had this early Passover meal on the Wednesday, so that there is enough time for the trial and the travelling. John, uniquely in his Gospel, keeps the same timing and sequence as the other Gospel writers, but has the proper Jewish Passover on the Friday night. He begins the account of the Last Supper with, "Now *before* the feast of the Passover" (John 13:1). In John's Gospel, Jesus celebrates a Passover meal on Thursday evening, one day earlier than everyone else. Judas Iscariot is able to go out and do his betrayal. The events take place during Thursday night and Friday morning. So that Jesus is himself killed between mid-day and 3 p.m. at the *same* time that the Passover lambs are being slaughtered in the Temple precincts. John ends his account with the need to get Jesus buried in a hurry because it was the day of Preparation. They did not want to leave the bodies on the cross for the Sabbath, "for that Sabbath was a high day" (John 19:31). It was the day of "Preparation for the Sabbath" and Passover. The main significance for John is that Jesus is the Passover Lamb. For St Paul the idea is paramount: "Christ our Passover has been sacrificed for us, so let us celebrate the feast, not with the old leaven of corruption and wickedness, but with the unleavened bread of sincerity and truth" (1 Corinthians 5:17). The chronology of the events is much discussed. Whichever view one takes, either John's or the Synoptic Gospel's view, it is evident that Jesus celebrated a Passover meal with his disciples during that week, died and was buried on Friday afternoon.

What was the possible arrangement of the guests that evening? Roman and Greek meals at the time were held at low tables, at which one lay down, leaning on one's elbow. A typical table is likely to have been in three sections, in the shape of a squared C. The disciples lying on their sides, Roman style, at right angles to the low table, would all have their feet pointing out to the walls of the room. The servant could supply food from inside the C shape, gaining access at the open end of the C. A servant could wash feet by going along the walls of the room, washing them one by one, whilst dinner was being eaten. One can conjecture that Peter is at the extreme end of one of the branches of the C shape. John is at the other end of the C across the gap. Jesus lies next to John, Judas next and the remaining disciples in turn round to Peter. At one point in the evening Peter cannot hear what Jesus has said, so he calls across to John to find out. John is lying at the end position on the other end of the C shape, "close to Jesus' breast" (John 13:23–6). John can then ask Jesus, "Who is it that will betray you?" Jesus replies that he will give a dipped morsel to that person. Judas must be within reach, possibly lying on the other side of Jesus from John, so that Jesus can supply him with this morsel. It is reckoned that this place is reserved for the honoured guest, right next to the host. If so, Jesus is giving Judas a sign of friendship.

The Passover rules required that four cups of wine be drunk, because it was a feast and great celebration was encouraged. Normal meals would not have wine.

The Jewish Passover is a time for laughter and plenty of jokes. Jews talk easily about the way many in the world have tried to destroy them – and laugh. It is essentially a festival of freedom, and therefore rejoicing. There are other times for fasting. The Passovers we have enjoyed with church groups of 60 to 150 have been wonderfully exciting, and celebratory, with children sensing the power of the occasion. Singing, laughing, dancing and plenty of noise. And yet it can move to a deep sense of reverence and awe.

Passover has great significance for the Christian. It is the source, inspiration and meaning within the Communion service. It is a celebration of the freedom from the bondage of sin, it is a Eucharist – a thanksgiving – for our deliverance from the sting of death, and looks to the joy of Easter.

In the following service (p.330):

Instructions are given in italics.

Bold text is for the liturgy that all participants should say. There are eight such sections in all, the first one, the blessing for the wine, is repeated a number of times, and therefore is to be typed only once. The leader then only has to announce the paragraph number (shown #1) for all to join in.

Small print is for information and background, and for New Testament texts which we have added and need to be read out.

A PASSOVER HAGGADAH
THE LIGHTING OF THE CANDLES

The mother lights the candles as she says:
Blessed are you, O Lord our God, King of the universe, who has made us holy through your word and has commanded us to kindle these lights in honour of the festival.

KIDDUSH AND FIRST CUP

All say together whilst each holding up the first glass of wine:

#1   **Blessed are you, O Lord our God, King of the universe, who created the fruit of the vine.**

(Baruch Ata Adonai, Elohenu Melech ha'olam b'ray p'ri hagafen.)

The leader continues:
Blessed are you O Lord our God, King of the universe who has chosen us from among all peoples and made us holy through Your word. For in Your love You have given us times for gladness, rejoicing and festivals; You have given us this feast of unleavened bread as a celebration of the freedom You give us and in memory of our departure from Egypt.

Blessed are you O Lord our God who has kept us alive and brought us safely to this day of rejoicing.

Now all drink (a sip will do) from the first cup, the Cup of Sanctification or Holiness.

THE FATHER WASHES HIS HANDS

The leader only washes his hands, a young person pours some water over his wrists, and hands, and then the leader dries them.

This practice originates from the ritual washing before offering sacrifices in the Temple.

PARSLEY DIPPED IN SALT WATER

This "first dipping" is to be passed round and then before it is eaten, the leader says:
Blessed are you, O Lord our God, King of the universe who brings forth fruit from the earth.

This is purely to arouse interest! The parsley reminds us that they used sprigs of hyssop to daub the doorposts with the blood of the lambs, so that the angel of death would see it and pass over.

THE BREAKING OF THE MIDDLE MATZAH

The middle of the three Matzot is taken out of the coverlet, and broken in half. One half is wrapped in a serviette and kept hidden by the father. This piece is called the Afikomen (the "dessert"). It will be the last thing to be eaten, and will represent the Passover lamb. The other half Matzah is returned to lie amongst the other two.

The three loaves under one coverlet are called a unity, for the Christian a picture of the Trinity. The wrapped Afikomen could be seen as a picture of the death and burial of Christ. On all Sabbaths and festivals, two Matzot are used because two portions of manna fell during the time of wandering in the wilderness when Moses took the people of Israel out of Egypt. The extra middle Matzah commemorates the Exodus, and is also known as the bread of poverty.

Raise the three Matzot and the Seder dish and say:

This is the bread of affliction which our fathers ate in the land of Egypt. Let all who are hungry come and eat. Let all who are in need come and celebrate the Passover.

Fill the second cup.

THE FOUR QUESTIONS

These are asked by four different children, who each in turn read from a card on which the questions have been copied:

1. Why is this night different from all other nights? Why can we eat leavened bread or unleavened bread on any other night, but tonight only unleavened bread?

2. Why can we eat all kinds of vegetables on any other night, but tonight only bitter herbs?

3. Why do we not normally dip our food, but tonight we dip it twice?

4. Why can we eat sitting or leaning on any other night, but tonight we are supposed to lean?

THE REPLY GIVEN BY THE FATHER

The leader says:

There was a time when we were slaves of Pharaoh in Egypt; but God brought us out from there with His mighty hand and an outstretched arm. It's a terrible thought, that if the Lord, blessed be His name, had not brought our forefathers out of that country of cruelty, we, our children and our children's children might still be slaves. The more one speaks about the escape from Egypt the better. We must mention it all the days of our lives, even after the Messiah has come.

We suggest that three persons be chosen to read out the comments made below by the wise son, the wicked son, and the stupid son. (They are best copied on a card and given out before the service begins.)

The Torah speaks of four kinds of son which the father must answer; a wise son, a wicked son, a stupid son, and one who never asks the right questions.

The wise son says, "What is the meaning of all the signs and rules which the Lord our God has commanded us?" (Deuteronomy 6:20)

The father's duty then is to explain all the laws of the Passover to him.

The wicked son says, "What does this service mean *to you*?" (Exodus 12:26)

Now because he says "to you" it shows that he has no interest in the service. This is a very serious thing, for it means that he is separating himself from the rest of the people of Israel. The father should therefore give him a sharp answer and say, "It is because of what the Lord did for me when I came out of Egypt." (Exodus 13:8) "For me," the father should point out and not for him; for if he had been in Egypt, God would not have thought him fit to become a free person.

The stupid son says, "What's this for?"

The father then explains quite simply, "This is to remind us of how God brought us out of Egypt and out of bondage by the power of His mighty hand." (Exodus 13:14)

Now since the fourth son cannot ask the right questions, the father has to answer what he hasn't been asked!

"Long, long ago, before the days of Abraham, our forefathers were worshippers of idols. But now, the Lord is our God and we serve only Him.

"Joshua told the people, 'The Lord God of Israel says, "I took Abraham your father out of the land east of the river Euphrates and led him into the land of Canaan. There I increased his family and gave him Isaac his son. Isaac had two sons, Jacob and Esau. To Esau I gave the country around Mount Seir, but Jacob went down into Egypt." ' (Joshua 24:2-4)

"Blessed be God, who keeps the promises He made to Israel. Blessed be He, for He calculated the exact number of years we should spend in slavery in Egypt so that He could fulfil what He had told to Abraham. He said, 'One day your children will be strangers in a land which isn't theirs. They will be slaves to the kings and peoples of that country and will live in misery for four hundred years. But I will punish that cruel nation and they will come out with great wealth.' " (Genesis 15:13-14)

Moses is not mentioned anywhere in the service. No one is to attract attention away from God. It is God himself who rescued the people.

Raise the second glass, but do not drink it.

This is the promise which we and our forefathers have clung to. Pharaoh is not the only tyrant who has tried to destroy us. There have been Pharaohs in every generation, but the Holy one, blessed be He, delivers us from their hands.

The six million who died in the Holocaust 1939-45 are remembered this night.

My father was a wandering Aramean. He went down into Egypt, because of a famine in Canaan, and took refuge there. We were few in number when we went, about seventy people, but we multiplied and became like the stars of heaven. We grew strong and great and powerful and the Egyptians became afraid. They mistreated us and made us suffer terribly. Then we cried to the Lord the God of our fathers and the Lord heard us and saw our sorrow, toil and oppression.

He brought us out of Egypt with a mighty hand and an outstretched arm, not by an angel or seraph or messenger, but the Holy One, blessed be He, did it Himself alone in the power of His might.

He said, "I will pass through the land of Egypt on that night and will strike down every firstborn in the land both man and cattle. I will destroy all the Egyptian gods, for I alone am the Lord."

And these are the ten signs which the Holy One, blessed be He, brought upon the Egyptians:

Spill a drop of wine from the cup as each plague is mentioned. This is done by dipping a finger in your own wine glass and then touching your plate. This is repeated with each plague. All say each plague slowly together:

#2		
Blood	**Dom**	
Frogs	**Tsfardeyah**	
Lice	**Kinim**	
Wild beasts	**Arov**	
Pestilence	**Dever**	
Boils	**Schechin**	
Hail	**Barah**	
Locusts	**Arbeh**	
Darkness	**Cheschech**	
Death of the firstborn	**Makas Bechodos**	

Participants often add to the list, "mother-in-law, kids . . . "! The wine is spilt to signify the spilling of blood. The Jews remember with sadness that their enemies had to endure these judgements.

Set down the second glass.
The raising and setting down of the second cup of wine without its being drunk, is humorously called "the false alarm".

DA-YAINU

The word "da-yainu" (#3) to be said or sung by all, in response to each phrase:

"Da-yainu" means, "It would have been enough for us", or "that would have been sufficient".

If He had only brought us from Egypt and not executed judgement on them. **Da-yainu.**

If He had only slain their firstborn and not given us their wealth. **Da-yainu.**

If He had only given us their wealth and not divided the sea for us. **Da-yainu.**

If he had only divided the sea for us and not caused us to pass through it on dry land. **Da-yainu.**

If He had only satisfied our needs in the wilderness and not fed us with manna. **Da-yainu.**

If He had only brought us to Sinai and not given us His law. **Da-yainu.**

If He had only brought us into the land of Israel and not built for us His temple. **Da-yainu.**

In building the Temple for us He gave us a place to atone for our sins. Therefore how much more must we go on thanking God for all His great mercies to us.

Rabbi Gamaliel used to say, "He who does not explain the following three things on Seder night has not done his duty."

The leader points to the item and says:
  1. The Paschal Lamb – "Pesach" (the shankbone).

Apart from the Afikomen (the half Matzah) this shankbone is the only reminder today of the lambs sacrificed in the temple. A shankbone – a forearm of a leg of lamb – is used because, "He brought us out of Egypt with an outstretched arm."

The leader points to the item and says:
  2. The unleavened bread - "Matzah".

This bread is strictly made so that it does not rise. As a precaution, it is pierced, to prevent any fermentation during baking. "He was pierced for our transgressions." (Isaiah 53)

The leader points to the item and says:
  3. The bitter herbs – "Maror".

The horseradish's bitter taste is to remind us of the harshness of the slavery in Egypt. The baked egg is a symbol of mourning in the Middle East. It is burnt to remember that the Temple was burnt and destroyed. Since then Jews cannot offer sacrifices without the Temple. This symbol, seen on the dish but not mentioned, is a reminder of this sadness.

The leader continues (different voices can be used, if you wish, for the questions and answers):

1. Why did our forefathers eat the Passover lamb when the Temple was standing?
   They ate it because the Holy One, blessed be He, passed over and spared the homes of the people of Israel on the night when He smote the Egyptians.
2. Why do we eat unleavened bread?
   We eat it because of the time when the supreme King of Kings, the Holy One, blessed be He, rescued our forefathers. They were in such a hurry that there was no time for their dough to rise.
3. And why do we eat bitter herbs?
   We eat them because the Egyptians embittered the lives of our fathers in Egypt.

   So you see, in every generation every Jew should feel as if he himself actually came out of Egypt.

All:

#4 Therefore it is our duty to thank, praise, glorify, exalt, honour, bless, extol, and adore him who performed all these miracles for us and for our forefathers.
He brought us from slavery to freedom, from anguish to rejoicing, from mourning to feasting, from darkness to light, from bondage to redemption.
Let us therefore sing a new song to him, Hallelujah!

At this point the "Little Hallel" (Psalms 113 and 114) are sung. There are various contemporary songs available, the best known currently available one is "From the rising of the sun" by Paul Deming. See the Scripture index in many song books. This is the only group of songs to be sung before the meal, and helps to warm up the atmosphere and prepare for worshipful singing after the meal. Traditional songs like "Hevenu Shalom Aleichem" and "Hinei matov uma na-im, shevet achim gam yahad" are quite suitable.

After singing the psalm(s), all lift the second cup and all say:

#5 **Blessed are you O Lord our God, King of the universe, who redeemed us and our forefathers and has kept us alive to eat Matzah and Maror tonight.**

Leader:

So, Lord our God, God of our fathers, grant us health and happiness so that we can enjoy many more anniversaries and festivals in the future. Blessed are you O Lord who has redeemed Israel.

All:

#1 **Blessed are you O Lord our God, King of the universe, who created the fruit of the vine.**

(Baruch Ata Adonai, Elohenu Melech ha'olam b'ray p'ri hagafen.)

Drink the second cup.

Then the leader says:

Blessed are you O Lord our God, King of the universe who commanded us to wash our hands.

The men wash their hands.

A small quantity of water is poured from a jug over the hands into a bowl. Provide a small towel to dry them. In ancient times, the servant would have washed the feet of the guests at the Passover meal as well. Read John 13:1–16 for background. We suggest someone reads out loud the following text, whilst the men wash:

"During supper Jesus ... rose from the table, laid aside his garments, and girded himself with a towel. Then he poured water into a basin and began to wash the disciples' feet, and to wipe them with a towel." (John 13:2–5)

EATING THE PASSOVER SYMBOLS

Each table should follow the example of the top table, wait for the "father" to say the blessing, then eat.

The father breaks off pieces of Matzah and hands them out to each person and says:

> Blessed are you O Lord our God, King of the universe who brings bread from the earth and has commanded us to eat Matzah.

The father dips Maror (a matchstick-size piece of horse-radish) into the Haroseth, gives a piece to each person and says:

> Blessed are you O Lord our God, King of the universe, who has commanded us to eat bitter herbs.

This is the second dipping. The use of cutlery is a later convention! It is a Middle-Eastern custom for the host to give his most honoured guest a morsel dipped in food. For background read John 13:21–30. Here it would be appropriate to read the following text out loud: "So when Jesus had dipped the morsel, he gave it to Judas, the son of Simon Iscariot." (John 13:26)

The "father" makes a small sandwich out of two small pieces of Matzah, filled with Haroseth in between and a stick of Maror pushed in, and says:

> We do this to remind us of what Hillel said when the Temple was still standing. He did it to fulfil the verse which says, "With unleavened bread and bitter herbs they shall eat it." (Numbers 9:11)

This is meant to remind them of the mud and straw bricks they had to make in Egypt.

THE MEAL

The meal is now served. The first thing to be eaten is a hard-boiled egg, with salt water poured over it. We suggest each person eats a few slices of this.

The egg is a sign of mourning, the salt water a reminder of the tears of those who were in captivity in Egypt.

During the meal, the "father" hides the Afikomen. In very large gatherings, we suggest several half pieces of Matzah be hidden, each wrapped in a serviette. (Use a different

*colour serviette than those being used by everyone else; or
expect forgeries!) These will be redeemed by the "father"
after the meal, by exchanging the Afikomen for a small
prize, such as a chocolate egg.*

*During coffee, the children search for the Afikomen. The
"father" redeems it.*

*After the meal the Afikomen is broken and shared with
everyone. Nothing more may now be eaten.*

The Afikomen (literally "dessert") represents the Passover lamb.

Someone says:

Christ our Passover lamb has been sacrificed for us. So let us
celebrate the feast, not with the old leaven of corruption and
wickedness, but with the unleavened bread of sincerity and truth.
(1 Corinthians 5:7)

Jesus, on the night when he was betrayed, took bread and when
he had given thanks he broke it, and said, "This is my body which
is broken for you. Do this in remembrance of me." (1 Corinthians
11:23–4)

THE GRACE AND THANKSGIVINGS
AFTER THE MEAL

*Fill the third cup. (At this point we use chalices, which can
be shared around by everyone, children included, when the
time comes to drink the third cup.)*

The third cup, the "Cup of Blessing", comes after a series of Psalms
and prayers giving thanks to God. To bless, in Hebrew, "Baruch",
means "to give thanks". In Greek the word is "Eucharisteo", from
which we get the title "Eucharist" for our Communion service,
remembering the giving thanks over the bread and wine.

Psalm 126 is sung.

"I will enter his gates with thanksgiving in my heart . . . He has
made me glad." Use several other songs. One or two can lead off
groups to dance a grapevine round the hall, holding hands.

Then all say:

#6 **Blessed are you O Lord our God, King of the universe, who in his goodness feeds the whole world. With grace, loving kindness and mercy he gives food to all flesh, for his mercy endures for ever. By his great goodness we have never been without food and never will be, because he does good to all and feeds the creatures he has created.**

Various blessings occur here, which are omitted except for:

Leader:

The all-merciful! He shall reign over us for ever and ever.

The all-merciful! He shall be blessed in heaven and on earth.

The all-merciful! He shall be praised through all generations. He shall be glorified among us and honoured for ever.

The all-merciful! He shall break the yoke off our neck and lead us to our land.

The all-merciful! He shall send abundant blessing on this house and table at which we have eaten.

The all-merciful! He shall send Elijah the prophet who will give us good tidings.

The all-merciful! He shall bless . . . (relations, friends, family etc. present).

The all-merciful! He shall make us worthy of the days of the Messiah and of the life of the world to come.

May the Lord, the maker of Shalom (peace), give Shalom to us and to the land of Israel.

All say:

#1 **Blessed are You O Lord our God, King of the universe who created the fruit of the vine.**

(Baruch Ata Adonai, Elohenu Melech ha'olam b'ray p'ri hagafen.)

The third cup, the Cup of Blessing, is passed round for everyone to drink. While this takes place several songs or hymns with Communion themes or the Passion of Christ are sung. Before these songs begin someone reads out loud from the earliest account in the New Testament of the Last Supper, and a commentary on the third cup, both written by St Paul.

"In the same way after supper he took the cup and when he had given thanks, he gave it to them saying, 'Drink this all of you; this is my blood of the new covenant, which is shed for you and for many for the forgiveness of sins. Do this in remembrance of me.'" (1 Corinthians 11:25-6)

"The cup of blessing which we bless, is it not a sharing in the blood of Christ? The bread which we break, is it not a sharing in the body of Christ?" (1 Corinthians 10:16)

THE FOURTH CUP

Fill the fourth cup and fill Elijah's cup. Revert to each person using their own glass.

Elijah's cup is a spare goblet that has been on the top table since the beginning. The Jews expect that Elijah will return before the Messiah comes. Jesus' disciples asked him, "Why do the scribes say that first Elijah must come?" Jesus replied, "Elijah does come, and he is to restore all things; but I tell you that Elijah has already come . . ." Then the disciples understood that he was speaking to them of John the Baptist. (Matthew 17:10-13)

The Scripture verses connected with this cup mean that it is called the Cup of Wrath. We remember that Jesus drank the cup of wrath, when on the cross He was forsaken by God for our sake.

The mother, followed by some of the children, goes to open the front door of the house and the father says:

Pour out your wrath on the nations that do not know You and the kingdoms which do not honour Your name, for they have devoured Jacob and laid waste his home. Pour out Your fury on them, pursue them in anger and destroy them from under Your heavens.

(Psalm 79:6-7; Psalm 69:25; Lamentations 6:66)

The remainder of the "Little Hallel" or Praise is sung here; Psalms 115-18 followed by the "Great Hallel", Psalm 136.

This is a great opportunity for lively songs of praise. "O give thanks to the Lord all you his people"; "You shall go out with joy and be led forth in peace"; "Jubilate, everybody"; "Great and wonderful, are thy wondrous deeds, O Lord God the Almighty", and many others. This is the second occasion after the meal when people will join in a grapevine dance around the hall.

Leader:

The soul of every living creature shall praise you O Lord, and the spirit of all flesh shall glorify your memory. From everlasting to everlasting you are God. We have no king, redeemer or saviour to deliver and rescue us except you. For the Lord never slumbers or sleeps.

The actual Passover service is much longer than this abridged version. Children and others will be somewhat sleepy by now!

He awakens the sleeper, rouses the slumberer, makes the dumb speak, frees the captive, supports the weak, and lifts the burdens from our shoulders.

Even if our mouths were filled with song like the sea, our tongues with joy like its mighty waves, our lips with praise like the breadth of the sky, if our eyes shone like the sun and the moon, and our hands were spread out like the eagles of heaven, if our feet were as swift as the hind, we should still be incapable of thanking You adequately for one thousandth part of all the love You have shown us.

All:

#7 **For You have redeemed us, freed us, fed us, delivered us, saved us and spared us. Therefore, our limbs which You have made, the spirit and soul which You have breathed into our nostrils, the tongues which You put into our mouths will thank, bless, praise, glorify, exalt, reverence, sanctify, and ascribe kingship to You, O Lord our King. For every mouth shall thank You, every tongue shall swear to You, every knee bow to You, and every being fall down before You. (Isaiah 45:23)**

Leader:

Praise be to Your name for ever, O our King. You Lord God of our fathers are worthy of song, adoration, hymn, psalm, might and dominion, eternity, greatness, strength, glory, holiness, kingship, blessings and thanksgivings, now and for all eternity.

All:

#8 **Blessed are You Almighty God and King, great in praises, God of thanksgivings, Lord of wonders, who enjoys our singing and our worship.**

Leader:

Next year in Jerusalem!
Blessed are You O Lord our God, King of the universe who created the fruit of the vine.

(Baruch Ata Adonai, Elohenu Melech ha'olam b'ray p'ri hagafen.)

Drink the fourth cup.

"Next year in Jerusalem" is the cry of hope for every Jew in the Diaspora.

Leader:

Our Seder is now complete according to the laws and customs of our people. As we have observed it here, so may we fulfil it in our lives in the days to come.

SOURCES

Scripture quotations from the Revised Standard Version 1946, 1952.
Jessop, Gordon. *Passover.* Olive Press 1980. Church's Ministry Among the Jews, 30c Clarence Rd, St Albans, AL1 4JJ, England.
Klein, Mordell, Ed. *Passover.* Popular Judaica Library. Keter Books, Jerusalem 1973.

Lehmann, J. *The Lehmann Haggadah,* 1969. Lehmann:20 Cambridge Terrace, Gateshead NE8 1RP.

Roth, Cecil. *The Haggadah with English Translation and Notes.* London Soncino Press 1959.

Silbermann, Dr. A.M., Ed. *Children's Haggadah.* Shapiro, Vallentine & Co. London 1954 (4th edition). Translation in prose and verse by Isidore Wartski and Arthur Saul Super.

Marshall, I. Howard. *Last Supper and Lord's Supper.* Paternoster 1980. Paternoster House, 3 Mount Radford Crescent, Exeter.

Maccoby, Hyam. *Judaism in the First Century.* Sheldon Press 1989. Holy Trinity Church, Marylebone Road, London.

Glossary

AFIKOMEN – the middle piece of the three main Passover pieces of unleavened bread. Symbolic of the Passover lamb, hidden and ransomed back by the children.

BARMITZVAH – the blessing of a son. Ceremony when a boy is thirteen to mark his initiation as an adult member of the community.

BATMITZVAH – the female equivalent of barmitzvah, when a girl is twelve. Unlike Reform Jews, the Orthodox do not count the ceremony as equal in importance with barmitzvah.

CHOLLAH – a slightly sweet loaf of white bread, made with milk and egg, plaited for the Sabbath, round at the New Year, and decorated with a ladder at Shevuoth.

GEMARA – "the Learning", a compilation of all the commentaries analysing and interpreting the Mishna. A compendium of three centuries of Rabbinic wisdom in response to community questions, written down AD 500, which, with the Mishna, forms the Talmud.

HAGGADAH – "the Narration", the order of service for the Passover.

HALAKAH – literally, "the Way", or "Walking", the application of the complex Rabbinic interpretation of the law, contained in the Talmud.

HALLEL – "Praise". The "Great Hallel" consists of Psalm 136, the "Little Hallel" of Psalms 113–18.

HANUKKAH – "Lights", the Feast of the Dedication of the Temple.

HASIDISM – the ultra-Orthodox wing of Judaism, characterised by the distinctive style of dress (black coats and ear locks), and by their joyful form of worship (song and dance).

JAHRZEIT – a day set apart to remember a loved one who has died.

KABBALAH – an ancient Jewish mystical tradition which evolved in the late Middle Ages. A very mixed bag of Biblically valid concepts, numerology, paganism and magic.

KADDISH – prayers in memory of your loved ones.

KETUBAH – the Jewish marriage contract.

KIDDUSH – the Sabbath eve service, including the sharing of wine and bread.

MENORAH – a seven- or nine- (used at Hanukkah) branched candelabra.

MISHNA – "the Repetition", four thousand legal decisions regulating every phase of Jewish life, the first interpretation of the Torah, written down in AD 200 by Jehudah Ha Nisi.

MISHPAHAH – relatives.

MITZVAH (pl. MITZVOT) – good deeds.

NACHUS – pleasures, blessings.

PURIM – "Lots", the Feast of Esther.

ROSH HASHANAH – the "Head of the Year", or Jewish New Year.

SCHUL – the synagogue.

SEDER – "Service" or "Order" – the first night of the Passover.

SHALOM – Hebrew for "peace", but it also means "wholeness", the integration and well-being of mind, body and spirit.

SHEMA – "Hear". The most important of all Jewish prayers, called after its first word, "Hear O Israel, the Lord our God, the Lord is One."

SHEMINI AZERET – the extra eighth day of Succoth, also known as Simchat Torah, "Rejoicing in the Law", as the occasion is marked by dancing around the scrolls.

SHEVUOTH – "Weeks", the Jewish spring harvest, commemorating the giving of the law on Mount Sinai.

SHMATTERS – (Yiddish) rags or tatters.

SHOFAR – "trumpet" or ram's horn.

SUKKAH – the booth or tent itself.

SUKKOT – "Booths" or "Tabernacles", the Jewish autumn harvest.

TALLIT – the prayer shawl. A long, rectangular white shawl, with fringes on its four corners. A blue thread runs through it, as a reminder of the holiness of the law. Some Jews will wrap their prayer shawls around their heads when they really want to concentrate!

TALMUD – "the teaching", a compilation of the Mishna and the Gemara, the complete body of the Jewish law, compiled in Babylon, the most populous Jewish city in the world at that time, and a centre of Jewish learning.

TISHAH B'AV – "the Ninth of Av", a day of mourning for the destruction of the Temple in AD 70. All ornaments are removed from the synagogue, a possible precursor for the ceremony of the "stripping of the altar", performed by some churches on Good Friday.

TORAH – the first five books of the Old Testament, the law as it was handed to Moses.

TSORUS – aggravation.

TZIZIT – "fringes", a kind of white vest with tassels on each of its four corners, with a blue thread running through it, worn by Orthodox Jews to remind them to keep the law. "You are to make tassels on the corners of your garments," Numbers 15:37–41. It has generally been replaced by the tallit.

YOM KIPPUR – "Day of Covering" or "Atonement".